# The Faerie Queens

# The Faerie Queens

A collection of essays exploring the myths, magic & mythology of the Faerie Queens

### Edited by
### Sorita d'Este & David Rankine

### With contributions by

*Aili Mirage, Ceri Norman, Cliff Seruntine, Dan Harms, David Rankine, Dorothy Abrams, Emily Carding, Felicity Fyr le Fay, Frances Billinghurst, Halo Quin, Helena Lundvik, Jack Wolf, Joanna Rowan Mullane, Katie Stewart, Pamela Norrie, Sorita d'Este, Thea Faye & Valerie Karlson*

Published by Avalonia
www.avaloniabooks.co.uk

*Published by Avalonia*

BM Avalonia
London
WC1N 3XX
England, UK

www.avaloniabooks.co.uk

The Faerie Queens

Copyright © 2012 Avalonia

Individual authors, artists and other contributors retain the copyright (c) to their work. All rights reserved.

First Edition, July 2013

ISBN 978-1-905297-64-1

Design by Satori, for Avalonia.

Cover Art *'Mélusine in the Bath'*, illustration to Thüring von Ringoltingen's *Mélusine*, 1477

British Library Cataloguing in Publication Data. A catalogue record for this book is available from the British Library.

All rights reserved. No part of this publication may be reproduced or utilized in any form or by any means, electronic or mechanical, including photocopying, microfilm, recording, or by any information storage and retrieval system, or used in another book, without written permission from the authors.

*Dedicated in Reverence and Admiration to
The Queens of Elphame – Past, Present & Future
... as well as their sons and daughters.*

*The Reconciliation of Oberon & Titania* by J. Noel Paton (1847)

# An Invocation

## By Philip Dayre
### (A.E. Waite)

By the Moon-Queen's mystic light,
By the hush of holy night,
By the woodland deep and green,
By the starlight's silver sheen,
By the zephyr's whisper'd spell,
Brooding Powers Invisible,
Faerie Court and Elfin Throng,
Unto whom the groves belong,
And by Laws of ancient date,
Found in Scrolls of Faerie Fate,
Stream and fount are dedicate,
Wheresoe'er your feet to-day,
Far from haunts of men may stray,
We adjure you, stay no more,
Exiles on an alien shore.
But with spells of magic birth
Once again make glad the earth!

# Acknowledgements

I would like to take this opportunity to thank all the contributors - Aili Mirage, Ceri Norman, Cliff Seruntine, Dan Harms, Dorothy Abrams, Emily Carding, David Rankine, Felicity Fyr le Fay, Frances Billinghurst, Halo Quin, Helena Lundvik, Jack Wolf, Joanna Rowan Mullane, Katie Stewart, Pamela Norrie, Thea Faye and Valerie Karlson; as well as Rose Spinne, Ana Jones and Laura Daligan. You have all been marvellously patient with the delays in production and completion of this project, and it is our sincere hope that you are pleased with the end result you now hold in your hands. Without your enthusiasm and wonderfully unique contributions this project would simply not have been possible!

Thank you to Andrea Salgado-Reyes and Lezley Cunningham-Wood for help with proofreading.

Likewise, thank you to all the friends who supported me with the process of overcoming "faerie-time" and finally getting this project completed, in particular Lokabandhu, Francis Aedo, Paul Harry Barron, Hannah and Peter Horne, Sophia Kirke, Katie Gerrard, Aleq Grai, Sue Render and Rose Berwhite. Thank you for your support.

Thank you to Jerry Buterbaugh and Josephine Fox for providing access to additional research materials and contributing to the expansion of the esoteric horizons through their dedication and love of knowledge.

David Rankine joined me as co-editor, in recognition of his significant contribution to this project. In addition to an invaluable article on the important character of Melusine which he researched and wrote especially for *The Faerie Queens* David also kindly provided his transcripts (with editorial notes) of previously unpublished texts from historical grimoire manuscripts. These texts provide a unique glimpse into the magical practices of yesteryear, and illustrating the importance of the Faerie Queen to the practitioners of magic. Thank you for your help and contribution David.

And finally, *to the reader* I hope that *The Faerie Queens* will shine light and reveal mysterious and enchanted corners of folklore, mythology and magic for you as it did for me. Maybe one day we will find each other on a hillside, in a valley, climbing a mountain or walking by the seashore exploring the marvellous pathways of this world of ours, eyes wide open at the possibilities of what we might glimpse in the hidden and liminal places.

*Sorita d'Este, June 2013, Glastonbury*

---

Editorial note regards the spelling of **Faerie**: I decided on the spelling of *'faerie'* rather than the numerous other ways the word is spelled based on my own personal preference. It is the spelling I have most often encountered in older magical texts and grimoires and is also of course the spelling used by Edmund Spencer in his famous work *The Faerie Queen*. Additionally, I took the decision to not standardise the spelling in the contributions I received for this project, but rather to leave the spelling favoured by the individual contributors. As a result you will find numerous spellings for *faerie* in this volume.

# Contents

**CONTRIBUTORS** ................................................................. 10

**TO SEE A GARLANDED LADY**
  Or 'How To Recognise a Faerie Queen when you meet her ...'
    by *Sorita d'Este & David Rankine* ........................................ 19
**DIGGING DEEPER**
  Faery Queens, Death and the Soul by *Emily Carding* ........................ 31
**SPIRITS AT THE TABLE**
  Faerie Queens in the Grimoires by *Dan Harms* .............................. 41
**WRITING FAERY**
  A Tale of Viviane by *Jack Wolf* ........................................... 59
**MAIDS OF ICE AND MEADOWS**
    by *Cliff Seruntine* ..................................................... *65*
**TRANSATLANTIC FAIRY QUEEN**
  Helen Adam's Fairy Inspiration, Masks and Veils by *Katie Stewart* ......... 75
**MELUSINE**
  Enduring Serpentine Queen by *David Rankine* ............................... 87
**HOLDA**
  Winter's Faerie Queen by *Ceri Norman* .................................... 101
**THE SKOGSRÅ**
  Queen of the Wild Woods of Sweden by *Helena Lundvik* ..................... 107
**THE VALKYRIES**
  Norse Fairie Queens? by *Valerie Karlson* ................................. 130
**MORVEREN**
  The Sea Queen by *Dorothy Abrams* ......................................... 137
**THE TRANSFORMING ILLUSION OF MORGAN LE FAY**
    by *Frances Billinghurst* ............................................... 150

**NIMUE**
   Ambiguous Enchantress by *Aili Mirage* ..................................................... 166
**CLIODHNA**
   Faerie Queen and Potent Banshee by *Pamela Norrie* ........................... 174
**RHIANNON**
   Faerie Queen, Mortal Throne, Divine Equine by *Halo Quin* ............. 179
**ÁINE**
   Celtic Faerie Queen of the Summer Solstice
   by *Joanna Rowan Mullane* .................................................................................. 190
**WHOSE QUEEN?**
   by *Thea Faye* ............................................................................................................ 196
**QUEEN OF THE UNDERWORLD**
   and the Fruit of Knowledge by *Felicity Fyr le Fay* .................................... 204


**THE PASTIME AND RECREATION OF THE QUEEN OF THE FAIRIES...**
   *by Margaret Cavendish The Duchess of Newcastle (1623-73)* .................. 218
**THE PASTIME OF THE QUEEN OF FAIRIES ...**
   *by Margaret Cavendish The Duchess of Newcastle (1623-73)* .................. 220
**ENTERTAINMENT OF THE QUEEN AND PRINCE AT ALTHORPE**
   *by Ben Jonson 1603* ............................................................................................. 222
**QUEEN MAB**
   *by Percy Bysshe Shelley 1813* ............................................................................. 223
**SONG OF THE TWILIGHT FAIRIES**
   *by Thomas Lake Harris* ..................................................................................... 224
**FAIRY REVELS**
   *by Anonymous* ........................................................................................................ 226
**FAIRY SONG**
   *by Felicia Hemans* ................................................................................................ 227
**AN A-Z OF EUROPEAN FAERIE QUEENS** ............................................. 228
**CONJURATIONS**
   From the Grimoires by *David Rankine* ........................................................ 239

**INDEX** ........................................................................................................................ 254

# CONTRIBUTORS

The essays in this volume represent the research, experience and passion that each of the contributors have for the myths, magic and mysteries of *The Faerie Queens*.

## Aili Mirage

Patrycja *Ailinon* Stańczyk is a professional graphic artist and an illustrator from Poland who turns into an amateur essayist by night and tries to spread her love for European mythologies and folklore. By embracing paganism and traditional witchcraft from the perspective of a naturalistic pantheist and an open-minded rationalist, she created her own, less esoteric and more practical approach to religion and tradition.

She has been a part of the Polish Pagan community since 2002 and runs the *Crossroads* forum (created in 2004). She loves dancing, cooking, all kinds of DIY crafts, travelling, adventure games, fantasy and sci-fi TV shows and all things Goth and purple. More info: http://grimoire.silverion.org and her art here: http://ailinon.deviantart.com

## Ceri Norman

Ceri Norman is a folklorist, historian and freelance writer. She has been fascinated by mythology, faerie tales and folktales ever since she can remember, and has made it her life's work to read, research and re-tell these magical tales in order to keep them alive for future generations.

Her first novel, *Celtic Maidens* (2010), was influenced by the landscapes, legends and lore of South Wales. Her second novel, *Serpent's Mound* (2012), was inspired by a supernatural urban myth about Sutton Hoo. Ceri's work has also featured in national and international magazines, she has written articles on a wide range of topics, from ancient history to modern fashion. A regular columnist for *FAE*, *Mermaids & Mythology* and *Avalon* Magazines, Ceri enjoys sharing her work with others in a variety of ways, through her writing, teaching workshops and online. She is currently working on a number of non-fiction projects all based around British and Scandinavian faerie lore. Currently Ceri lives with her husband by the sea. See www.cerinorman.com

## Cliff Seruntine

Cliff Seruntine is a devoted permaculturist, a practicing shaman, a writer and fiddler, and a psychotherapist with a busy private practice. He was born in New Orleans and grew up in the bayou country on his grandfather's farm among French speaking Acadians.

Cliff and his wife, Daphne live in the misty wooded glens of the Nova Scotia highlands, ancestral Canadian home of the Gaels. There they maintain organic gardens, raise dairy goats and keep alive old skills such as horse driving, brewing and woodscraft. They also teach classes on how to live green while living well. Cliff is the author of *Seasons of the Sacred Earth* (Llewellyn, 2013), *An Ogham Wood* (Avalonia, 2011) and *The Lore of the Bard* (Llewellyn, 2003). He has contributed to a number of books, including *The Faery Craft* (Llewellyn, 2013) and has been invited to write several times for Llewellyn's bestselling *Witches' Calendar*. Cliff has also been published in magazines on Celtic history, paranormal phenomena and written for webzines about ecology, sustainable living and earth-based spirituality.

## Daniel Harms

Daniel Harms is a writer and librarian living in upstate New York, who writes on a range of topics from Lovecraftian fiction to roleplaying games to the grimoire tradition. His books include *The Cthulhu Mythos Encyclopedia* (Elder Signs, 2008), *The Necronomicon Files* (Weiser, 2003), *The Long-Lost Friend* (Llewellyn, 2012), and the *Experimentum Potens Magna* (Caduceus, 2012). His piece on the *Green Butterfly* from the *Grimorium Verum* appeared in the Avalonia anthology *Both Sides of Heaven* (2009). At this time, he is working on a transcription of a medieval manuscript of spirit magic that mentions the Fairy King Oberion. You can find out more about him at his website, http://danharms.wordpress.com .

## David Rankine

David Rankine is an author, esoteric researcher and magician who has been making major contributions to the modern occult revival since the 1980s, through lectures, workshops, presentations, articles and books. His esoteric expertise covers a wide range of topics, including the Western Esoteric Traditions, especially Greco-Egyptian magic, the Qabalah, the Grimoire tradition and Ceremonial Magic, as well as British Folklore and European Mythology. David's esoteric knowledge and scholarship can be seen in the twenty-five books he has authored, his essays in various anthologies, and hundreds of articles for magazines, journals, international part-works and websites. His published works include *The Isles of the Many Gods* (2007), *The Guises of the Morrigan* (2005), *Visions of the Cailleach* (2009), *The Book of Treasure Spirits* (2009) and *The Grimoire of Arthur Gauntlet* (2011). To find out more visit www.ritualmagick.co.uk

## Dorothy Abrams

Dorothy Abrams practices Witchcraft, paganism, and shamanism in Central New York. Co-founder of the Web PATH Center, a pagan church and teaching centre, Dorothy has served as priestess and teacher since 1994. Her spirituality is inclusive and feminist. *Identity and the Quartered Circle*, her new nonfiction title compiled from her teaching materials, is set for release 28 June 2013. Dorothy's essays have been published in *Sage Woman* and *PagaNet News*. Her short story *"Ela of Salisbury"* appears in *HerStory* an anthology of flash fiction compiled for women's history month 2013 by editor Tata Chevrestt.

You can reach Dorothy through Dorothy L Abrams-Writer's Page on Facebook or through dorothyabramsonlife.blogspot.com


## Emily Carding

Emily Carding lives in Cornwall with her amazing husband, ethereal daughter, the glorious Albus Dumbledog, (who has created his own oracle deck), and the three cats known as the Supurrrnal Triad; Kether Kitty, Chokmah Cat and Binah Puss. Here she has created various offerings, such as the *Transparent Tarot*, the *Transparent Oracle*, and the *Tarot of the Sidhe* for Schiffer Books. She has also contributed book covers, articles and artwork for several works from Avalonia Books. To date these titles include *Towards the Wiccan Circle* (Cover), *Both Sides of Heaven* (Cover and article *"The Salvation of the Sidhe"*), *From a Drop of Water* (Article *"Nimue: The Archetypal Priestess"*), *Hekate Her Sacred Fires* (Cover, Article *"Painting Hekate"* and internal illustrations), and *Vs.* (Cover, Articles *"Sun and Moon"*, *"Painting Polarity"*) and of course, *The Faerie Queens*. Avalonia also published *Gods of the Vikings* which features cover art and numerous illustrations by Emily.

She is a regular columnist for *Mermaids & Mythology* magazine and her latest book *Faery Craft*, a new faery lifestyle and magical practice book, was published by Llewellyn in Autumn 2012. Emily is also an actress and is currently studying for an MFA in Staging Shakespeare at Exeter University whilst also developing her own magical theatre company, So Potent Arts.


## Felicity Fyr Le Fay

In a real life faerytale, Felicity Fyr Le Fay grew up in the rugged landscape of New Zealand, conversing with sprites and wood nymphs. This unusually charmed childhood gave her a special connection to nature and the elemental kingdom; and her life's purpose is now to share that magic with the world! Felicity's quest led her first to performance art; and she began hosting Faery parties for children, introducing them to caring for animals and the environment. The fantastical otherworld of the circus industry was her next calling and Felicity spent a number of years training in aerial silks, Spanish web and trapeze, before going on to tour with several circuses. She has since written and directed several shows with a large emphasis on using mythology to enhance ecological awareness.

Within the budding Faery arts, festival and life-style movement she has found her clan and become an integral part of the Faery events scene. She now runs her own performance company called 'Cirque Des Fees' (Sussex and Somerset) hosting parties for children and providing event entertainment that gives the audience a glittering glimpse through the veil into Faeryland. Felicity began her writing career in broadcasting; composing and voicing commercials and radio plays. Her number one love is working as a travel and features writer for *FAE* (Faeries and Enchantment) Magazine. Fore more see www.cirquedesfees.com


## Frances Billinghurst

For Frances, growing up in rural New Zealand, the Otherworldly realm seemed never far from her doorstep nor her imagination, and through her interest in mythology, it was only a matter of time before the Arthurian legend caught her attention. In the late 1980s, when she read *Mists of Avalon* by Marion Zimmer Bradley, she felt her calling – she wanted to be Morgan le Fay and experience the wonders of Avalon. In mid 1990s, this happened when she travelled around Britain on a *"Celtic Sacred Sites"* tour, which resulted in her spending time in Glastonbury, the famed Isle of Avalon.

Now residing in Australia Frances spends much of her spare time writing and journeying between the worlds. With the passing of her Celtic studies tutor in 2011, Frances dedicates this essay to Lynne Sinclair Wood, *"someone who parted the mists"* and introduced her to all things Celtic.


## Halo Quin

Between the ivory tower of academic philosophy and the emerald green forests of enchantment I have long pursued the Faery Queen in all her guises. The flick of a white tail led me through the darkness into her realm and I've lived here ever since I can recall. In the human realm I moved to Wales to study Philosophy six years ago and it has lead to down a path more magical than I can say; the tales of myth live within the bones of the land here and Rhiannon is queen of the land I dwell in still.

I have written two books; one on *The Faery Heart* within each of us and in another a collection of *Pixie Kisses* to re-enchant your world. As a postgraduate student of philosophy I am exploring the spirit of creativity and veering nearer to synthesising my two worlds each moment, especially since I am devoted to the Faery Queen Herself and work to bring the magic of the otherworlds closer to the land of mundanity through art, philosophy, stories and other magics. Enchantment through art and philosophy is my passion, under the guidance of my muse, The Faery Queen Herself. Find out more at www.haloquin.net

## Helena Lundvik

Helena Lundvik is a healer, teacher and priestess from the ancient lands outside Uppsala, Sweden. Helena has been studying various traditions over the years such as the Greek, Egyptian and Celtic but now focuses on her native Norse mythologies and Sagas as well as Seid craft and the runes.

As a 5-year old Helena discovered Greek mythology through a children's program. She has always loved Scandinavian folklore and the tales about faeries, trolls, witches, gnomes and other otherworldly beings. The deep, dark woods and unspoilt Swedish nature have always been a source of inspiration for her. After spending more than 12 years abroad, mainly in the UK, Helena has now returned to her native Sweden. In her work Helena focuses on helping her clients finding their Path through healing, meditation, shamanic journeys and a connection with nature. www.willowtherapy.com or www.willow.se

## Jack Wolf

Jack Wolf wanted to be a singer until his interests in faerie tales and in social history led to a writing career. He has spent most of his life in rural Somerset, and wrote most of his debut novel while living in a tumbledown eighteenth century cottage a few miles outside of Bath. He is currently studying for a PhD whilst working upon his second historical novel at Bath Spa University. He has a Cavalier Spaniel bitch and several ginger cats. He remains a friend and ally of the Fae.

*The Tale of Raw Head and Bloody Bones* was published by Chatto and Windus (UK) Penguin (US) and Belfond (France) in 2013. It received excellent critical reviews in the national press and in the blogosphere. What the faeries made of it remains to be seen, but he hopes that they enjoyed it.

## Joanna Rowan Mullane

For over eighteen years, Joanna Rowan Mullane has worked with and most importantly, learned from, the Faery Realm as a pathworker beyond the veil. Carrying a deep reverence for all of Nature, she studies the Herbal Arts and Celtic Folk Magic along with her yearly journeys to Ireland where she traverses the ancient sites that surround its sacred landscape. Joanna divides her time between her hometown of San Diego and Arizona to teach classes including numerous subjects to include working with the Fae. As an artist, she offers her artwork and paintings as a portal to her visions of Faery and her herbal blends as a way to tangibly work with and connect to them. She is the author of the book; *Betwixt & Between, A Faery's Herbal* and has recently opened a new distance school called The Sidhe Grove. You can find her art, hand crafted herbal blends and learn more about The Sidhe Grove at: www.hedgefaeryherbals.com

## Julia Helen Jeffrey

Julia Helen Jeffrey is a Scottish artist and illustrator. She studied painting at the famous, Charles Rennie Mackintosh designed, Glasgow School of Art.

Her faery and fantasy-themed work, of recent years, has attracted considerable acclaim and attention, with features in numerous fantasy journals. October 2008 saw the publication of her first book cover (and illustrations) for the young-adult fantasy novel *Lament* (by Maggie Stiefvater), followed in 2009 by more sinister supernatural fare for fellow Scot Daniel McGachey's *They That Dwell In Dark Places*. Her work features alongside celebrated artists and best-selling authors including Neil Gaiman, Holly Black and Charles De Lint, in the short story collection *Ravens In The Library*. She is currently working on her first tarot deck, *The Tarot of the Faery Realm*, for publication in 2013.

## Katie Stewart

Katie Stewart completed a PhD at the University of Glasgow in 2008, with her thesis titled *"'A Kind of Singing in Me": A Critical Account of Women Writers of the Beat Generation'*. It drew a map of an area of women's writing which lacked a definitive history, focussing on themes of patriarchal vs. matriarchal literary communities, the city, the body, motherhood and the road. Her research on Helen Adam is a development of this work, and comes as a result of a deepening interest in spiritual and esoteric subjects.

She lives in Glasgow and is a songwriter, music workshop facilitator and a student of healing arts. Contact her at mail@myladyofclouds.com

## Pamela Norrie

Pamela Norrie is a First Degree Gardnerian Witch and Priestess of Hekate and Apollo living in Dundee, Scotland. She lives with her familiar and good friend - the most mischievous cat, Osiris Loki (Ozzie). She enjoys creative writing and sinking her teeth into a good book, and she owns many good books which are slowly taking over her home. She has written articles for *Pagan Dawn* and *Witchcraft & Wicca* magazines. Her interests include mythology, divining, foraging for wild food, good company with good conversation and the endless, but rewarding, pursuit of knowledge and understanding. She is a self-confessed Sherlockian and like her literary hero she *"shares a love of all that is bizarre and outside the conventions and humdrum routine of everyday life."*

## Sorita d'Este

Sorita d'Este is an esoteric researcher, author and Priestess who manifests her knowledge and passion for the Mysteries through her work. Her research and writing pushes at the boundaries of Western Esoterica and beyond, often questioning and challenging the status quo and inspiring others towards experiential mysticism with firm foundations built on lessons learned from history, standing positively in today and looking with enthusiasm towards the future. She is the author of *Artemis Virgin Goddess of the Sun and Moon* (2005), and co-author of works such as *Hekate Liminal Rites* (2009), *Visions of the Cailleach* (2009) and *The Isles of the Many Gods* (2007). Sorita previously compiled and edited a number of anthologies, including *Hekate Her Sacred Fires* (2010), *Both Sides of Heaven* (2009) and *Horns of Power* (2008).

She passionately believes that it is possible to manifest creativity, positivity, love and enchantment through the creation of independent, freethinking and spiritual communities, with firm foundations in truth, natural balance and generosity. Find out more about her work at www.sorita.co.uk

## Thea Faye

A Modern History Oxford graduate, Thea Faye is an initiate of the Mysteries with both Craft and ceremonial lineage. She has long since had a fascination with the Wheel of the Year and penetrating the many layers of this deceptively simple cycle. She is the author of many articles which have appeared in numerous magazines, e-zines and anthologies, including *Horns of Power* (2008), *Talking About the Elephant* (2008) (where she discussed the difficulties of transporting the Wheel to New Zealand) and *Howlings* (2009). At the moment, she is working on a book focusing on ceremonial magick for women, but also writes fiction and is currently co-authoring a horror novel. Happily married for over ten years, Thea has five children, three of whom were born while she was living in New Zealand. Now based in South Wales (UK), Thea home educates and can frequently be found exploring the countryside and castles, looking for fairy rings with her children and faithful hound, Galahad.

## Valerie Karlson

With a lifelong passion for magic and mythology, Valerie lives a quiet life in a small English town where she spends her time exploring the many interesting facets of life with her twin cats Freya and Freyr. In addition to Norse Mythology her passions include Middle Eastern and Celtic history and magic.

With mixed Norse and Celtic heritage, Valerie is fascinated by the cross-fertilisation of ideas and material between the Celts and Vikings, an area of study she feels is highly neglected and in need of more attention. Her article on the Valkyries is her first attempt to try and explore this interface in print.

## Additional artwork by:

**Ana C. Jones** was born in Brazil and trained as a teacher and electrical engineer, in 1989 she moved to England with husband and their three children. Her interest in Traditional Astrology led her to complete C. Warnock's Renaissance Astrological magical course, plus two others of the same calibre. At the moment she is studying Alchemy from Adam McLean courses, Hermetic Magic with the OMS as well as Mithraism. She practices Traditional British Witchcraft and Stregoneria.

**Laura Daligan** has loved drawing and painting for longer than she can remember and has illustrated books on magic, poetry and romance. She creates personal commissions, oracle decks, animal portraits, logos, illustrations, landscapes and visions of Goddesses & Gods, her work has appeared in many magazines and she regularly exhibits throughout the UK.

See www.lauradaligan-art.com for more information.

**Rose Spinne** is an artist living in Roberts Creek, British Columbia, Canada. Her work builds visual gateways to hidden realms of Dream and Spirit. Rose has illustrated cards, posters, cd covers, and books and her work has been exhibited across Canada and sold internationally.

See www.wix.com/spiderdreaming/faerieforest for more information.

MORRIGHAN FEA, ROSE SPIDERLING

# TO SEE A GARLANDED LADY

## Or 'How To Recognise a Faerie Queen when you meet her ...'

### SORITA D'ESTE & DAVID RANKINE

*All hail, thou mighty Queen of Heaven!*
*For thy peer on earth I never did see.'*
*'O no, O no, Thomas,' she said,*
*That name does not belong to me;*
*I am but the queen of fair Elfland,*
*That am hither come to visit thee.'*

~ Thomas the Rhymer, Border Ballads, Walter Scott, 1888

On meeting the faerie queen, Thomas of Ercilbourne was struck by her beauty and otherworldly nature, and immediately assumed she was the Virgin Mary. With her dress of grass-green silk and *"fifty silver bells and nine"* woven in her milk-white horse's mane, the Faerie queen encountered by Thomas beneath the Eildon tree (said to be a hawthorn, the faerie tree) epitomises several of the characteristics commonly associated with faerie queens. Her physical beauty, ethereal presence, white horse and green dress all speak of the faerie sovereign, with the silver bells also emphasising her faerie nature, as silver is commonly seen as the faerie metal.

But why would Thomas have confused the faerie queen with the divine Virgin Mary? The answer may be found in the classical world, where we encounter a number of goddesses and historical figures who would later be celebrated, appeased or feared as faerie queens. These include the Roman goddesses Diana and Proserpina, the Roman Sibyls (Sibylia), the Jewish queen Herodias, the *'Greek'* goddess Hekate, and the maiden Kalé. In central Europe too we find numerous faerie queens based on Celtic figures from the Dark Ages and Medieval period, often with their origins in older Celtic goddesses, including Áine, the Cailleach, Cliodhna, the Morrigan, Nicneven, Rhiannon and others. Indeed, the Irish myths recount how the gods of the Tuatha de Danann, on being defeated by the Milesians, retreated into the mounds of Ireland and lived beneath the earth, becoming the Sidhe or faerie folk of Ireland.

The old gods and goddesses do not disappear, rather they assume forms accessible within the dominant religion of the time, or are *'assimilated'* into contemporary folklore. So it is that many of the old gods became viewed as saints, whereas others defined their own interaction with humans by remaining in the liminal wilderness places – like the faerie queens. To our ancestors, the inherent power of nature and her denizens was an accepted part of life, particularly in forests, on mountains and by water sources, favourite places of the faerie queens.

Writing on *The Old English Herbals*, Rohde observed that, *"To the early Saxons those unseen powers were an everyday reality. A supernatural terror brooded over the trackless heaths, the dark mere pools were inhabited by the water elves."* Certainly, a common theme in Anglo-Saxon herbals is protection from *'elf-shot'* and *'elf diseases'*, particularly in the *Leech Book of Bald* (900-950 CE) and the *Lacnunga* (C10th-11th CE). Where there are elves or faeries, so too we might expect to find their queens, and it can thus be suggested that the faerie queens were already present well before the Middle Ages. In her *The Visions of Isobel Gowdie: Magic, Witchcraft and Dark Shamanism in Seventeenth-Century Scotland*, Wilby supports this assumption with her comment that:

> *"Among contemporary scholars, the Scottish fairy queen and her train or host are generally agreed to represent a version of the 'European nocturnal goddess' commonly associated with these narratives. This link is also reflected by the fact that educated Scots linked the fairy queen with Diana, one of the deities identified with the female spirit-group leader as early as the first decade of the tenth century."*

The worship of some of the ancient goddesses like Diana did not disappear under the onslaught of the Christian church in its early growth pangs through the Dark Ages. This period seems to be the one where the goddesses assumed the role of faerie queens, when the elves, wights and nature spirits of the Celts, Saxons, Norse and other cultures became conflated with the dryads, fauns and nymphs of the Greco-Roman world, and all became demonised by the control-focused Church, in its efforts to control the lives, minds and beliefs of the populations under its sway across Europe. Baroja discusses this in his *World of the Witches* when he notes that:

> *"There seems to have been a flourishing cult of Diana among European country people in the fifth and sixth centuries ... occasionally she*

> *appeared in the company of certain spirits referred to as 'dianae' – according to texts such as that of St Martin of Braga which deals with beliefs of country folk in the north-western regions of the Iberian peninsula."*

By the Renaissance the evolution of the faerie from the ancient world was an accepted idea, proliferating through art, architecture and poetry, and also found in the writings of such major figures as Edmund Spenser (*The Faerie Queene*) and William Shakespeare (various works). In his translation of *The Aeneid* (1573), the English lawyer and author Thomas Phaer (1510-1560) emphasised the popular opinion of the link between the dryads and nymphs of the classical world, and the faerie queens of the Renaissance:

> *"The woods (quoth he) sometime both fauns and nymphs, and gods of ground, And Fairy-queen did keep, and under them a nation rough."*

Spenser's epic *Faerie Queene* has become one of the most significant influences on the literature associated with this theme. Published in two parts, in 1590 and 1596, it is an allegorical epic containing many levels of symbolism, and drawing on numerous earlier works for inspiration. One of the best known themes is the equation of Queen Elizabeth I to the figure of the faerie queen Gloriana in this work, though many modern authorities also argue that she is also represented by the characters of Belphoebe and Lucifera, bringing in the triplicity motif often associated with faerie queens. The work was well received by Queen Elizabeth I, containing such themes as the destruction of the evil of Catholicism (which was well received in a Protestant England that had recently undergone a period of Catholic rule under Queen Mary), and theological aspirations through the embodiment of virtues such as truth, faith, hope and charity. Royal approval resulted in a handsome pension of £50 a year and the *Faerie Queene* became the defining work of Spenser's career.

Spenser drew heavily on earlier epics, such as Virgil's *Aeneid*, and the Italian works *Orlando Furioso* (Ludivico Ariosto, 1516 and more complete in 1532) and *Jerusalem Delivered* (Torquato Tasso, 1581). He also drew on the Arthurian mythos, bringing in the connection between King Arthur and the faerie queen which is also implied in earlier works such as Jean d'Arras' *Melusine de Lusignan* (1393). Spenser and subsequently Shakespeare would change the way that people thought of faeries. Before their work, faerie queens and faeries were not generally thought of as being diminutive, however, as Keightley observed in *The Fairy Mythology* (1833):

> *"After the appearance of the Faerie Queene, all distinctions were confounded, the name and attributes of the real Fays or Fairies of romance were completely transferred to the little beings who, according to the popular belief, made 'the green sour ringlets whereof the ewe not bites.' The change thus operated by the poets established itself firmly among the people; a strong proof, if this idea be correct, of the power of*

*the poetry of a nation in altering the phraseology of even the lowest classes of its society."*

Shakespeare refers to faeries and the faerie queen in a number of his works, possibly illustrating their popularity in the culture of the sixteenth-seventeenth centuries. Some writers point to evidence of the influence of the *Faerie Queene* in Shakespeare's works, Boswell (*Spenser's Allusions*, 2012) includes *Venus and Adonis*, *Romeo and Juliet*, *King Richard the Third*, *A Midsummer Night's Dream* and *King Lear* amongst those with a visible Spenserian influence. Shakespeare is especially significant in the transformation of faerie size, with Queen Mab appearing in a diminutive form ("*In shape no bigger than an agate-stone, On the fore-finger of an alderman*") in a speech by Mercutio in *Romeo and Juliet* (Act I, Scene IV), placing the small faerie figure firmly in the public imagination. Mab would become a popular figure in literature, appearing subsequently in the works of later poets, including Ben Jonson's *The Entertainment at Althorp* (1603), Michael Drayton's *Nymphidia* (1627) and Percy Bysshe Shelley's *Queen Mab: A Philosophical Poem* (1813).

As the stories and myths expressed, encountering a faerie queen could be a fearful, enamouring or deadly experience. By the Middle Ages the faerie queen is seen ruling the realm of the dead, or being connected with the dead. The fifteenth century work *Orfeo* refers to the faerie queen ruling the land of the dead, and Scot's *Discoverie of Witchcraft* (1584) describes the use of a dead spirit to fetch the faerie queen Sibylia. When describing Irish folk tales, Lady Wilde mentions a man who met the faerie queen Oonagh and her King Finvarra on Halloween, who was happy with the faerie gold and wine they gave him, but then was shocked to see that the company they led were all dead when he recognised a long dead neighbour in their midst. The idea of the faerie realm as the land of the dead is echoed in the notion of being trapped there if you eat any food in the faerie world. A precedent for this is seen in the myth of the ancient Greek goddess Persephone, forced to stay a third of the year in the underworld with the god Hades after eating pomegranate seeds. As Persephone became Proserpina in the Roman pantheon with the same myth associated with her, and Proserpina was later seen as a faerie queen, there seems to be a clear progression of motifs from the classical gods to the faerie queens here.

The Germanic faerie queen/goddess Holda was said to keep the souls of newborn children and those who died unnamed in a lake, suggesting water as a gateway between the worlds of the living and the dead, and also the possible role of faerie queens as psychopomps for the souls of the dead. When we also consider the role of Hekate as ruler of the restless dead and guide in the underworld, the role of the Valkyries gathering the souls of the brave, the presence of the dead in faerie courts, and the use of the dead to summon faerie queens in the grimoires, it seems clear that some faerie queens do have a function as psychopomps. Perhaps the best known example of this is the final journey of the mortally wounded King Arthur to Avalon, accompanied by three faerie queens including Morgan leFay and Nimue.

The triplicity motif has occurred since the ancient world in connection with powerful female figures, such as in the three realms of heaven, earth and sky, the three-way crossroads, and hypostases (e.g. Artemis-Selene-Hekate), so it is no surprise to see it is also prominent as a faerie queen emblem. Goddesses who were also seen as faerie queens often have a triple form or triple aspects, as seen with the Roman Diana, Greek Hekate and Artemis, and Irish Morrigan. Spells for such goddesses were often repeated three times to empower them.

Of all the faerie queens, Melusine possibly offers us the most examples of triplicity being emphasised in her tale. Melusine is the oldest of three sisters, there are three beautiful fairy women by the fountain, the three faerie brides (Pressine, Melusine, and the wife of Hervé de Leon), the three forms of Melusine (woman, half-woman and half-serpent, flying serpent), Melusine circling the fortress three times as she, and also appearing three days before deaths and changes of lordship.

Mounds and mountains also feature prominently in connection with faerie queens. In Irish myth, the faerie take their name from the mounds or *sidhe*, which they are said to live in. According to the twelfth century *Lebor Gabála Érenn* (The Book of Invasions), the mounds are doorways to the realms where the faerie race live underground, or in some versions in a parallel realm. The idea of gateways into the earth is an ancient one, and caves were often viewed as gateways to the underworld, e.g. Avernus as the Roman underworld gateway described by Virgil in the epic *Aeneid*, where the Cumaean sibyl dwelt on the shores of the lake.

Melusine trapped her absentee father under a mountain as punishment for abandoning his family, before meeting her future husband Raymondin by a fountain in a forest. There is an element of history repeating itself here, as her faerie queen mother Pressine had met her husband by a fountain as well. The Scottish faerie queen Nicneven was associated with mountains, especially Ben Nevis, the mountain she was named after (Nicneven meaning *'daughter of Nevis'*). The Germanic Holda lived in a cave in a mountain, with a lake nearby. The Greek faerie queen Kalé was known to wander the mountains, as did ancient goddesses like the Greek Artemis and Hekate (who is called *"Ruler, Nymph, Mountain-wandering"* in the Orphic Hymn to her) and the Roman Diana, all of whom have faerie queen associations. Artemis and Hekate both have strong connections with the Phrygian goddess Kybele (*'the Mountain Mother'*), and we can speculate that she is a possible source of the connection between faerie queens and mountains. Kybele was an ancient goddess with roots in pre-history, and was also particularly associated with caves and initiation, like Hekate.

Water has always been viewed as magical by man, so it is no surprise that faerie queens are often connected with water. In the case of some it is their domain, such as the Cornish sea queen Morveren, and the Irish Cliodna and Ounaheencha, whereas others dwell on hidden islands, such as the Arthurian Morgan leFay and the French Queen of the Hidden Isle. Other faerie queens are first encountered near water sources like fountains, as in the case of the French Melusine and her mother Pressine, or lakes, like the Arthurian Viviane, Holda with her lake of souls, and the goddess Diana, with Lake Nemi. The noted German Renaissance magician and physician Paracelsus (1493-1541), who was the first person to write at length on the nature of the different types of elementals, went even further when he linked the faeries to undines, the elementals of water. In his *Anatomy of Melancholy*, (1621) Burton clarified this association, writing, *"The water (as Paracelsus thinks) is their Chaos, wherein they live; some call them Fairies and say that Habundia is their Queen"*.

The lost island or island of Avalon is described as the original home of the faerie queen Melusine, where she and her two sisters were raised by her mother, the faerie queen Pressine. Morgan leFay is described as the Lady of the Lost Isles in *Melusine de Lusignan*, and also as the sister of Pressine, establishing a connection between faerie queens and Avalon, and by extension emphasising the connections in the Arthurian mythos in continental Europe as well as Britain. This connection was clearly used by Spenser in his epic *Faerie Queene*, placing King Arthur in service to the faerie queen Gloriana. Spenser highlighted the association of sovereignty with the faerie queen in his epic work, when the knight Guyon declared: *"She is the mighty Queen of Faerie, ... Throughout the world renowned far and neare, My liefe, my liege, my Soueraigne, my dear"* (*The Faerie Queene*, Book II.ix:4). The bestowing of sovereignty is traditionally associated with Celtic goddesses associated with the faerie, such as the Morrigan, Rhiannon and the Cailleach. However it is also connected to some of the other faerie queens in the tales, such as Melusine with her ability to miraculously create buildings and ensure her lord gained a large expanse of land, and Irish faerie queens like Áine who like Melusine were said to be the progenitors of aristocratic lines.

As well as water sources and high places, forests are another popular haunt of faerie queens, and often surround lakes or contain rivers. Some, like Diana, the Norwegian Skogsrå and Scottish Glaistigs, are particularly at home in forests, and others like Melusine are often encountered by water sources in woods. When we see forest-roaming goddesses like Diana with sacred groves amongst the faerie queens, and the untamed nature of large forests, it is not surprising that these wild and often scary liminal places were seen as a popular place for faeries to roam.

Another place roamed by some faerie queens is the skies. This is noteworthy with Diana, Herodias, Holda and the Valkyries, who would ride through the skies on their horses in their role as psychopomps taking the souls of the bravest warriors to Valhalla to feast and fight until the final conflict of Ragnarok. Diana's role as leader of a skyborne horde is mentioned in the *Canon Episcopi* (chapter 364), in the ninth century CE, as part of the process of demonization of the old gods and ways by the Christian church:

> *"This also is not to be omitted, that certain wicked women, turned back toward Satan, seduced by demonic illusions and phantasms, believe of themselves and profess to ride upon certain beasts in the night time hours, with Diana, the Goddess of the Pagans, and an innumerable multitude of women, and to traverse great spaces of earth in the silence of the dead of night, and to be subject to her laws as of a Lady, and on fixed nights be called to her service."*

The church emphasised the attraction to women held by goddesses like Diana, who in classical times had her following of female nymphs. This theme continued through the witchcraft trials of the Middle Ages, with women being more commonly the victims of accusations of consorting with demons and faeries, and their rulers Satan and the faerie queens. In medieval and Renaissance Scotland, the faerie queen (queen of Elphame or Diana) seems to have been interchangeable with the devil as the patron of covens, a connection which may also be seen in the stories where the faerie folk pay a tribute of souls to hell, such as *Thomas the Rhymer* and *Tam Lin*. This seems to be part of a medieval attempt to place the faerie folk in the Christian cosmology, seen in the rhyme recorded by Evans-Wentz attributing their origins to Lucifer:

> *"Not of the seed of Adam are we,*
> *Nor is Abraham our father;*
> *But the seed of the Proud Angel,*
> *Driven forth from Heaven."*

In *The Elizabethan Fairies* (1930) Latham noted that *"in Scotland, where the terms the Queen of Elfame and the Elf Queen, elf folk and elf boys were used almost exclusively by the common folk in the evidence given in witchcraft trials."*

Indeed, accounts from the Scottish witch trials do frequently mention the faerie queen as the power to whom the witches gave service and acknowledgement. So, e.g. *"In Rye in 1607 Susan Swapper (accused of witchcraft) confessed that she had met the Queen of the Fairies and had been told that if she knelt to her the Queen would give her 'a living' (Gregory 1991, 36)."*

The well known Scottish witch, Isobell Gowdie, even claimed to have gone into a faerie mound for her meeting with the esteemed Faerie Queen, as Latham recounts (1930):

> *"When Isobell Gowdie 'went in to the Downie-hillis' where she met the Queen of Fairies, 'the hill opened, and we cam to an fair and lairge braw rowme, in the day tym.'"*

This role as witch queen is not surprising when we consider the magical powers commonly associated with faerie queens. Additionally, goddesses commonly associated with the role of witch queen, such as Diana, were also later considered faerie queens, showing a clear conflation of these roles. In the nineteenth century Walter Scott in Letter V of his *Letters on Demonology and Witchcraft* (1830) used the names of the faerie queens Nicneven and Hekate interchangeably to describe the head of a Scottish covine of witches practising necromancy.

The popular nature of the faerie queens permeated society from the top to the bottom, and there were those who were happy to take advantage of this popularity. The most infamous of these were John and Alice West in the early seventeenth century, as this description from the period recorded by Latham shows:

> *"The severall notorious and lewd Cousonages of John West and Alice West, falsely called the King and Queene of Fayries, -practised verie lately both in this citie and many places neere adjoyning: to the impoverishing of many simple people, as well men as women', and the arraignment and conviction, on the 14th of January, 1613, of the two impostors whose crime consisted in impersonating the king and queen of fairies, furnishes a significant illustration of the belief in visible and actual fairies at the beginning of the 17th century."*

During this period, with the belittling of faeries to a diminutive size, writings also made the connection of these small faeries to flowers, setting the precedent for the popular Victorian image of flower faeries that has endured to modern times. In *Britannia's Pastorals*, William Browne (1590-1645) wrote:

> *"The dancing Fairies, when they left to play,*
> *Then blacke did pull them, and in holes of trees*
> *Stole the sweet honey from the painful Bees;*
> *Which in the flowre to put they oft were seene,*
> *And for a banquet brought it to their Queene.*
> *But she that is the Goddesse of the flowres*
> *(Inuited to their groues and shady bowres)*
> *Mislik'd their choise. They said that all the field*
> *No other flowre did for that purpose yeeld;"*

As perceptions changed, influenced by literature and social changes, so inevitably perceptions changed and other influences crept in. This is seen in the early nineteenth century in the writings of Howell (1816), who commented on the connection between the faerie queen and Christianity, and observed that:

> *"We also find angels and familiars serving the Queen of the Fairies, fairies and familiars serving God and/or urging the witch to a better*

*Christian faith, and even familiars who are called 'Jesus' and invoked by calling 'Come Christ'."*

The love between mortals and faeries seems to be forever doomed to end in tragedy, as the interaction between the two commonly involving a taboo which must not be transgressed. As a rule, such interspecies romances do not end well, even though they may contain periods of happiness. Both Melusine and her mother Pressine were fated to have doomed romances, with taboos which were broken by their husbands. In the case of Pressine it was not to be disturbed when she was resting in bed, and for Melusine not to be seen on a Saturday when she transformed into her half-serpent form. Melusine's husband Raymondin lost his queen by breaking her taboo, and ended his days as a hermit living in a cave, away from everything and everyone he had loved. In contrast, for Thomas the Rhymer, who honoured the taboo of not speaking whilst in Elphame, he was rewarded with the blessing (or some might say curse) of being only able to tell the truth, and the gift of prophecy. In the tale of *Sir Lanval*, the hero breaks his taboo and speaks of the faerie queen, resulting in her withdrawing her support and Sir Lanval being left penniless and threatened by Queen Guinevere's false accusations. Fortunately for Sir Lanval his lover relents and takes him away to Avalon with her.

Only when a mortal gives up everything does he seem to find happiness in the faerie realm with her faerie queen lover, as with the Cornish faerie queen Morveren and her lovers, perhaps reminding us of the origin of the word faerie being in the Latin *'Fata'* (Fate). To embrace the love of the faerie queen is to honour taboos and surrender to fate, and accept the transformations she brings. This power across realms is a potent reminder of their enduring sovereignty over the liminal places, and Spenser may have unknowingly highlighted this, so that, as Arestad (1947) comments, *"By Faery Land Spenser means Elizabethan England, over which Gloriana (Elizabeth) holds sway."*

The power of the faerie queen as bestower of sovereignty is something which has been played upon by rulers across Europe to justify their positions. By claiming lineage and descent from the otherworldly power of a faerie queen, a ruler strengthened his position of power. After all, if a powerful faerie queen affirmed your right to rule, it meant people were far less likely to challenge your position! This is seen with the various noble houses across Europe claiming connections to Melusine of Lusignan, and in Ireland where various aristocratic families claim faerie queens as their ancestors. Again this continues an earlier practice of divine or semi-divine ancestry, such as the Anglo-Saxon genealogies where the god Woden was claimed as the originator of royal lines, and of course the classical Roman and Greek dalliances of gods with mortals to produce famous rulers.

The term fickle is sometimes used to describe faerie queens, but unpredictable might be a more appropriate word. Predicting the behaviour of a being outside of human comprehension is a challenge, and their motives cannot always be fathomed. *Alison Gross*, a Scottish ballad quoted by Briggs (1977) describes how a faerie queen stopped to remove the spell from a knight who had been transformed into an *'ugly worm'* by a witch:

> *"But as it fell out last Hallow-even,*
> *When the seely court was riding by,*
> *The queen lighted down on a gowany bank,*
> *Not far frae the tree where I was wont to lie.*
> *She took me up in her milk-white han*
> *An she's stroked me three times o'er her knee;*
> *She chang'd me again to my ain proper shape,*
> *An I nae mair maun toddle about the tree."*

Several classic faerie queen motifs may be seen in these words – the queen is riding with her court on Halloween, a traditional time for them to be out, her skin is described as *"milk-white"*, and she strokes the knight three times to break the spell. Another example of the benevolence of the faerie queen towards a random man who she encountered is the tale of *The White Powder*, from the Scottish witch trials, recorded in the seventeenth century. Here a poor man was given a white powder by the faerie queen in her court and used it to heal people, thereby providing a living for his family, and good health to his community. Whenever he needed more powder, he went to the hollow hill she lived in and knocked for entry, whereupon he was given more of the healing concoction.

When Melusine's future husband first meets her by the fountain in the wood, she is in the company of other faerie women. Faerie queens are often accompanied by their court, having a host or train of faeries accompanying them on their travels. This again hearkens back to Diana and her band of nymphs, a point seen in the vitriolic anti-witchcraft tract of King James VI, *Daemonlogie* (1597), who wrote:

> *"That fourth kinde of spirites, which by the Gentiles was called Diana, and her wandring court, and amongst us was called the Phairie"*

The faerie queen and her court might be encountered at different times, often under the light of the moon, and especially on May Day (May 1st) and All Hallow's Eve (October 31st), the two liminal times of the year when the veil between the worlds was said to be the thinnest, and the queen would travel the land with her court. Versions of this are found across Europe, e.g. in Ireland the Morrigan is said to lead her faerie court across the land at Hallow's Eve, and in some tales the faerie court is said to move twice a year at these times between their two palaces. Such faeries are sometimes known as *'trooping faeries'* due to these troops which are often described in local folklore and stories (as opposed to *'solitary faeries'* who do not belong to a court).

ILLUSTRATION FROM THÜRING VON RINGOLTINGEN'S MÉLUSINE, 1477

Moonlight gives a silvery-white radiance to the landscape and those in it, and white is a colour particularly associated with many faerie queens, who are often described as wearing white, and having *'milk-white'* skin. White was the colour worn by the priesthood of many of the goddesses of the Greco-Roman world, and indeed in Egypt before then, where it was considered the colour of sacredness and ritual purity. White is also the colour of snow, and some faerie queens like Holda and the Cailleach are particularly associated with snow and winter as well. The other colour most often linked to faerie queens is green, the verdant green of trees and plants in bloom, emphasising the connection between the faerie queens and the realm of nature.

So when you are out in nature, in the woods or on the hills, by the sea or a lake, if you meet an otherworldly woman, whether young and beautiful or old and knowing, wearing white and green, or on a white horse, by herself, or accompanied by a band of other beautiful women (and men), then you are probably in the presence of a faerie queen. So remember to be courteous, listen carefully, don't break any taboos and don't eat or drink anything you're offered, and you might come out of the encounter transformed by the magic of a faerie queen!

# Bibliography

Arestad, S (1947) *Spenser's Faery and Fairy*. In *Modern Language Quarterly* 8:37-42

Baroja, J.C. (2001) *The World of the Witches*. London: Phoenix Press

Bennett, J.W. (1942) *The Evolution of "The Fairie Queene"*. New York: Burt Franklin

Boswell (2012) *Spenser's Allusions*. In *Studies in Philology*, Vol 109.353-530

Briggs, K.M. (1979) *Abbey Lubbers, Banshees & Boggarts: A Who's Who of Fairies*. Middlesex: Penguin

Briggs, K.M. (1977) *The Vanishing People: A Study of Traditional Fairy Beliefs*. London: Batsford

Briggs, K.M. (1977) *A Dictionary of Fairies*. Middlesex: Penguin

Briggs, K.M. (1977) *The Fairies in Tradition and Literature*. London: Routledge & Kegan Paul

D'Este, Sorita & Rankine, David (2007) *The Isles of the Many Gods*. London: Avalonia

Edwards, Gillian (1974) *Hobgoblin & Sweet Puck: Fairy Names & Natures*. London: Geoffrey Bles

Evans-Wentz, W.Y. (2002) *The Fairy-Faith in Celtic Countries*. London: Dover

Hazlitt, W.C. (1875) *The Romance of King Orfeo. Fairy Tales, Legends and Romances Illustrating Shakespeare*. London: Frank & William Kerslake

Keightley, Thomas (1833) *The Fairy Mythology* (2 volumes). London: Whittaker, Treacher & Co.

Latham, M.W. (1930) *The Elizabethan Fairies: The Fairies of Folklore and The Fairies of Shakespeare*. New York: Columbia University Press

Morris, Matthew W. (1997) *The Romance of Melusine and the Sacralization of Secular Power*. In *Postscript* XIV.14.5, Charleston

Paton, Lucy Allen (1960) *Studies in the Fairy Mythology of Arthurian Romance*. New York: Burt Franklin

Phaer, Thomas (1573) *The whole XII Books of the Aeneidos of Virgill*. London: Thomas Twyne

Rohde, Elizabeth Sinclair (1922) *The Old English Herbals*. London: Longmans, Green & Co

Rankine, David & d'Este, Sorita (2005) *The Guises of the Morrigan*. London: Avalonia

Scot, Reginald (1886, first edition 1584) *Discoverie of Witchcraft*. London: Elliot Stock

Scott, Walter (1888) *Border Ballads*. London: Walter Scott

Thomsett: M.C. (2011) *Heresy in the Roman Catholic Church: A History*. North Carolina: McFarland & Co. Inc.

Waite, A.E. (1888) *Songs and Poems of Fairyland: An Anthology of English Fairy Poetry*. London: Walter Scott Publishing co. Ltd

Wilby, Emma (2010) *The Visions of Isobel Gowdie: Magic, Witchcraft and Dark Shamanism in Seventeenth-Century Scotland*. Eastbourne: Sussex Academic Press

Wilby, Emma (2000) *The Witch's Familiar and the Fairy in Early Modern England and Scotland*, in *Folklore* 111.283-305

Woodcock, Matthew (2004) *Fairy in The Faerie Queene. Renaissance Elf-Fashioning and Elizabethan Myth-Making*. Aldershot: Ashgate Publishing Ltd

# Digging Deeper

## Faery Queens, Death and the Soul

## Emily Carding

*"My lady soon will stir this way*
*In sorrow known*
*The white queen walks*
*And the night grows pale*
*Stars of lovingness in her hair*
*Needing unheard pleading one word*
*So sad her eyes she cannot see"*

- White Queen, lyrics by Freddie Mercury

If you were to ask a selection of people from different walks of life what they pictured when they thought of a Faery Queen, you'd probably find that the responses were as varied as the individuals that were questioned. Perhaps they would think first of beauty, or glitter. They may think of tiny figures in flower petal dresses, or perhaps get the idea mixed up with Disney Faery Godmothers and their *"bibbity-bobbity-boo"* antics. It's possible that nothing at all would come to their minds, or they may think of particularly glamorous drag artists. If you're lucky enough to have chosen someone a little more savvy to interrogate on this subject, they might bring to mind an image akin to Galadriel from J.R.R. Tolkien's iconic *Lord of the Rings*, or Titania from Shakespeare's *A Midsummer Night's Dream*. You are highly unlikely, however, to find the first image to spring to most people's minds to be an ancient and powerful Goddess with as much connection to death and the soul as to life and beauty, yet this is the truth borne out by folklore, myth, and mystical experience.

Literature and mythology brings us a wide variety of Faery Queens. Arthurian Legend gives us a particularly rich vein, with the mysterious Nimue, Lady of the Lake, Arthur's chief challenger, (and hence initiator),

MORGANA BY EMILY CARDING

Morgana Le Fay, and even Guinevere herself, all of whom can be considered to be Faery Queens, as well as many more throughout the tales. As briefly mentioned already, Shakespeare gives us one of our most iconic Faery Queens in the form of his beautiful Titania, wife of the jealous Oberon. The chivalry romance traditions of France gift us with the tale of Melusine, the archetypal Faery bride and matriarch of the noble family of Lusignan who still claim her lineage. These are just a very few of the most familiar examples of powerful and radiant Faery Queens, regal otherworldly figures whose tales are often epic, steeped in beauty, yet tinged with tragedy. It is all too easy to dismiss these figures as being *'simply'* characters in stories, yet in all stories it is truth that is the grit of the pearl of myth. The characters listed above are but the surface manifestation of much deeper forces - forces that are very real and integral to our world. Through examination not only of historical and folkloric material but also through seeking personal contact with the hidden forces of the land, we find that Faery is not a world apart, but intimately connected with our own. But what does this mean for our understanding not only of Faery but also of our own souls?

Scratching away at the topsoil, we can first look at what our Faery Queens have in common. There are often associations with certain animals, and this is more often than not extended to shape-shifting abilities. The most common beastly connections are with crows or ravens, (and other European black birds), serpents, horses, (particularly white horses), and black dogs or wolves. All of these animals have symbolic and mythological associations with death. Faery Queens also tend to be powerful sorceresses with the gift of prophecy, foretelling and influencing the fates of mortals. Many Faery Queens are seen as triple-aspected or triple-formed, and most have a deep connection with the silvery light of the Moon and stars. All of these traits belie their deeper origins in ancient Goddesses, many of whom are now labelled as *'dark'* due to their associations with fate and death. This should not be surprising though, since the very word *'Faery'* comes from the Latin *'Fata'*, meaning *'Fate'*. When we assimilate this concept, we can start to expand our understanding of what is Faery beyond that which is conveniently labelled as such, and hence come closer to comprehending the true significance of the Faery Queens.

Celtic Faery lore shows an intimate connection between Faery and death, to the point where lines become rather blurred. Sidhe or Sidh, (pronounced *'shee'*), was the ancient Irish and Scottish Gaelic name for the Faery race, but it was also the name given to the burial mounds where the bones of the ancestors rested. Both the souls of the dead and the Faery beings are said to dwell in the *'hollow hills'*. The banshee, a spirit who is said to scream and wail when a member of their particular mortal family that they are attached to dies is actually the *'bean-sidhe'*, which simply means *'Faery Woman'*. (There is a parallel to be found here with the French romance of Melusine, who it was said returned in her dragon form to wail at the loss of any of her descendants of the Lusignan ancestral line.) This and other connections, such as spirits of the recently deceased being seen to appear in Faery processions, lead to some confusion. Though in some cases traditions seem to tell us that Faery beings are in fact the spirits of the ancestors, this is not the absolute case, though it is not completely wrong either. This should become clearer later on, as we dig deeper.

> *"... for she had many shapes, and it was in the shape of a crow she would sometimes fight her battles."*- Gods and Fighting Men, Lady Gregory

Morgana le Fay finds her origins in the ancient Celtic myths of the Tuatha de Danann, the pre-Christian Gods of Ireland. The Sidhe were the descendants of these Gods, and one of their number was the triple-aspected Goddess of War and Death, the Morrigan. She was capable of taking many forms, including most commonly that of a raven or crow. Just as Morgana Le Fay was nemesis to her half-brother King Arthur, the Morrigan was both challenger and lover of the great Celtic Hero, Cú Chulainn. Others writing in this anthology will tell of both these figures in greater depth, but the key point is that they are both manifestations of a deeper archetype, a feminine force who personifies the powers of Fate itself, empowering mortals to achieve their true potential, transcending their earthly limits and becoming godlike themselves. When we realise this, it makes sense that three Queens (again, the triple aspect), accompany the dying Arthur on the barge to Avalon, and Morgana is amongst them. There are obvious parallels that deserve to be mentioned with certain figures from Norse mythology. The Norns are Goddesses of Fate who weave and cut the threads of mortal lives and also appear as triple-formed. The Valkyries and their Queen, Freya, can be seen to strongly resemble the Morrigan with their association with corvids and their role as battlefield psychopomps, escorting the souls of the valiant dead to the afterlife. There is also a direct parallel here with Greek Mythology, and the three Moirai, spinners of Fate.

> *"Ill-met by moonlight, fair Titania..."* – A Midsummer Night's Dream

It is not only the Celtic sagas that bring us the idea of Faery beings as descendants of the earliest Gods. Returning to our surface examples of the most famous Faery Queens, Shakespeare hints at this knowledge in his beloved comedy, *A Midsummer Night's Dream*. There is a tradition that the parts of the Amazon Queen, Hippolyta and the Faery Queen, Titania would have been played by the same actor, and often still are in small cast productions today. This is not simply down to frugality, but is an observation of the parallels between the two realms in which Shakespeare gives us many clues as to the true divine nature of the Faery Queen. The play is set in the court of Athens and its rural surrounds, and the conversation of the mortal characters is littered with references to the Greco-Roman Gods, most particularly Diana and her associations with the Moon. In fact moonlight is mentioned so many times during the play that it is almost a character in itself. This becomes more interesting when you consider that the name of the Faery Queen, *'Titania'*, identifies her as the offspring of Titans, the original pre-Olympian Gods of Ancient Greece. The most powerful of the Greek Gods were children of Titans, and Diana herself is the grandchild of a Titan. Shakespeare makes it clear that he is aware of her status as Goddess when he writes this line for Titania:

*"His mother was a votaress of my order..."*

This and the further lyrical interchange between the King and Queen of Faery in which Titania lists the many environmental disasters that stem from their dispute show that Shakespeare felt it was important for us to know just how powerful and important his Faery Queen and King are, not only within their realm of Faery, but also, and perhaps especially, within our own. The equilibrium of the world itself appears to depend upon the balance and peace between this King and Queen, the male and female aspects of Nature itself. Quite deep for what is generally dismissed as a light-hearted comedy! Whilst many may think of the Goddess Diana as a romantic mythic figure, feminine and benign, she and most especially her Greek counterpart Artemis were ruthless, bloody and not to be trifled with. Diana is the female leader of the wild hunt, a role most usually taken by Faery Kings and one certainly to be feared. When the Wild Hunt is heard on the winds it is time to lock up your children safely indoors, light a fire and say your prayers, for death will surely be on their heels.

Staying with the Bard for a short while longer, as he offers us a chance to delve a little deeper, it is interesting to note that at times Diana was also equated with the Goddess Hekate, whose mother was the Titan Goddess of the stars, Asteria. That, combined with the fact that faerys, witches and the dead were almost interchangeable within English folklore, make the addition of Hekate as what appears to be the Queen of the Witches in the tragedy *Macbeth* rather interesting. Though she is usually cut out of modern productions, as she adds nothing to the plot, Shakespeare was no amateur. She is there because for whatever reason, Shakespeare felt her presence was important.

*"Now about the cauldron sing, like elves and fairies in a ring..."* - Hecate, Macbeth

The three witches of *'The Scottish Play'* are firmly established as being utterly otherworldly in nature, certainly not mere mortal practitioners of the Craft. They are described as being able to vanish *"into the air"*, seem to dwell in the wilds, function as a sort of triple-formed hive mind and have hair in unusual places. The general perception is that these beings encountered by Macbeth and Banquo upon the Scottish moors are malignant - but why? Certainly they are not all *'love and light'*, but what do they actually *do*? They merely prophesy events and stir dubious ingredients in a cauldron. They certainly don't urge Macbeth towards bloody deeds, or even plant the idea in his head, yet he instantly starts to plot against Duncan once he hears that he will one day be king. The three witches are not the evil force behind his actions, but rather a manifestation of the forces of Fate. Their appearance awakens Macbeth to his destiny - a *dark* destiny, true, but his destiny nevertheless. In Scottish lore, Hekate was often equated with the Faery Queen of the unseelie court, Nicneven, who dwelt in the mountain Ben Nevis, and Shakespeare would have known this. The three witches, reflecting the triple-formed Goddess of the crossroads and highlighted by the seemingly random appearance of Hekate herself as their Queen are actually more akin to Faery beings.

> *"Now three white ladies, standing still until now, began to dance on the grass before the Fountain..."- The Romance of the Faery Melusine, Andre Lebey, trans. Gareth Knight*

Again and again we find the theme of triplicity occurring, and indeed three is a very important number in Faery lore, but what is its real significance? The concept of *'Maiden, Mother, Crone'* has become very popular in relation to the Feminine Divine, but it is an added surface layer of meaning rather than a revealed deeper truth, an invention of modern neo-paganism. The underlying reason behind the repeating theme of triplicity is a mystery, but one which is well worth spending time contemplating. Do the three forms represent the triple nature of the soul? Celtic tradition holds that the soul is contained within three cauldrons located in the centre, the heart and the head and this draws a parallel with the Platonic concept of the soul consisting of an earthly, intellectual and spiritual component. Similar models of the soul may be found in a number of traditions worldwide, including the Kabbalistic concept of Nephesh, Ruach and Neshamah. Another possibility is that they represent the cycle of life, death and rebirth, a process with which the Faery Queens are intimately involved, or perhaps the realms of Earth, Sea and Sky? All three of these possibilities, (another triplicity!), *may* be considered together as one. It is not hard to see the realms of Earth, Sea and Sky as macrocosmic reflections of the triple aspects of soul and vice-versa, the inner realm of soul and the outer realm mirroring each other. The spark of physical life is our Earth, the mind and emotions our Sea and the higher spiritual part of our soul found in the celestial realm. As the soul is said to pass between these three realms during the process of life, death and rebirth - the relevance of which we will look at shortly - we can see how all three interpretations may be aspects of one underlying truth. A not unrelated further manifestation of the threefold nature of our Faery Queens is that of the Triple Crossroads.

> *"When he had eaten and drunk his fill, "Lay down your head upon my knee,"*
> *The lady sayd, "ere we climb yon hill, And I will show you fairlies three..."*

AQUARIUS BY EMILY CARDING

Hekate, who as we have already discussed counts Faery Queen among her many titles, is perhaps the best known guardian of the triple crossroads, but she is by no means the only Faery Queen to claim this significant role. Within Faery Tradition there are a number of what are considered to be *'initiatory ballads'* in which the usually nameless Faery Queen, or Queen of Elfhame takes a mortal man into the Otherworld for a time. There are many variants of this theme, all featuring crossroads or similarly liminal places. Examples include the famous tale of Tam Lin in which the Faery Queen abducts a young man who must be rescued by his pregnant lover, and the Cornish tale *Cherry of Zennor* which follows the adventures of a mortal *woman* who is taken to the Otherworld by a Faery *King*, thus demonstrating the magical importance of initiation being male to female and vice-versa. But perhaps the best example of this kind of tale is the Scottish ballad of Thomas the Rhymer.

Thomas the Rhymer, also known as True Thomas or by his real name of Thomas Learmonth, was an actual historical figure - a 13th Century Scottish Laird renowned for his gift for rhyming and prophecy that was bestowed on him by the Queen of Faery herself during the events of the ballad. During this epic journey, which sees Thomas leaving the mortal realm for seven years, (abductions or willing visitations to Faery were often for seven days, weeks, months or years of our time), we are given insights not only into his initiation into the Faery Realm but potentially also the journey of the soul after death and therefore the role played in that journey by the Faery Queen. Whilst travelling through the various layers of the Otherworld with the Queen he crosses rivers of tears and blood, partakes of a communion of bread and wine, encounters a mysterious tree with forbidden fruit, and sits at the triple crossroads that lead to Heaven, Hell and Faery. After taking the *"bonny road, which winds about the fernie brae"* that led to *"Fair Elfland"* with the Queen, he then returns to the mortal realm with various gifts, including the traditional Faery gift of prophecy or the *"tongue that tells no lies"*. It is thought that those initiated into Faery in this fashion dwell in the Faery realm after death. Certainly Thomas the Rhymer is by no means the only historical figure that has been encountered as an intermediary within the Faery realm by mystics and magicians in dreams, meditations and otherworld journeys.

A slightly more recent historical figure, (also believed to have been taken into Faery upon his death), is another Scotsman, the Reverend Robert Kirk, who lived in the 17th Century. He observed the Faery race as being of *"a middle nature betwixt man and angel"*, a commonly held view within Christian Celtic Folklore that tells us that Faery beings were Fallen Angels that did not wish to go to Hell but instead settled in the hollow places of the Earth. In other words, they exist *'in-between'* all things, neither in Heaven or Hell, nor fully in this realm. They do however, as we have already noted, have the ability not only to pass between their timeless realm and ours, but to take others with them. In other words, the Faery Queens are psychopomps, keepers of the gates between worlds, weavers of Fate and guardians of the crossroads. As in the tale of Thomas the Rhymer, they guide the disembodied soul to their destination, nourish them with rejuvenating succour of the primal uncorrupted Otherworld, and then return them to either a new incarnation or to their old lives with a new role as Faery prophet.

In the previous Avalonia anthology *Both Sides of Heaven*, I wrote about the significance behind the folkloric connection between Faery beings and Fallen Angels, concluding that Faery beings may indeed have their origins in the celestial realm but perform a very important function in the sublunar realm as conveyers of cosmic energy into the earth and then back into the cosmos. Faery Queens therefore may be seen as regulators of this essential process. If we consider the spirit within all things to consist of this same cosmic energy, then we dig through our final layers to the true depth of significance of our Faery Queens - as agents of, and even manifestations of, the World Soul herself.

> *"On her wedding day, Melusine appeared more beautiful than ever. Her dress seemed more splendid than that of any Queen or Empress, her face more radiant than the silver embroidery on the blue velvet and white gauze, more fresh and clear than the lilies that decorated the altar, more delicate than the rose petals that the children threw before her as she walked."* (The Romance of the Faery Melusine, by André LeBey, translated by Gareth Knight, Skylight Press, 2011)

> *"I am the rose of Sharon, and the lily of the valleys..."* (The Song of Solomon)

Wisdom Goddesses of many cultures throughout the ages have been associated with the concept of the World Soul, and the Faery Queens should certainly be counted amongst their number. Though the term *'World Soul'* was first coined by Plato, the concept of a feminine force that conveys energy from the ultimate cosmic source above into the centre of the planet and radiates that energy into all beings is found in similar form within many philosophies. Just as we have explored the many traits that Faery Queens have in common, so we find that Goddesses perceived as manifestations of the World Soul share similar traits, including the gift of prophecy. They also share a strong connection with the Moon, which was seen as being the *'seat'* of the World Soul and the intermediary lens by which soul is conveyed between the pure spiritual source of the Sun and the Earth. (Since the Moon is ruler of the Sea we can see how this relates to the realms of Earth, Sea and Sky as mentioned earlier in relation to triplicity.) The Fates were also seen as being integral to this process, and we have already learned of the intimate connection between the Fates and the Faery Queens, indeed there seems to be little separating them at all. This understanding certainly brings a new level of depth to the lunar associations of the Faery Queens. Is it a coincidence that Hekate, ruler of the triple realms of Earth, Sea and Sky, is considered within the *Chaldean Oracles* as the World Soul and is within Scottish lore regarded as a Faery Queen?

> *"The Soul, being a brilliant Fire, by the power of the Father remaineth immortal, and is Mistress of Life, and filleth up the many recesses of the bosom of the World."*- The Chaldean Oracles

The World Soul, Shekinah, Holy Spirit, Hekate or whatever name we choose to know her by, is the source of primal light and wisdom that radiates from *within* the world. How better may we describe the Faery Queens? When we view the many threads we have explored regarding our Faery Queens in this context, they start to form a beautiful kaleidoscopic tapestry. Nimue is no longer the cruel enchantress that imprisons Merlin within a tree, but rather the gatekeeper who grants him passage to the land of his restoration. Morgan le Fay is the Morrigan - more than a fearful harbinger of doom but a psychopomp Goddess, initiatrix and weaver of Fate. Shakespeare's beloved Titania is a surface reflection that hints at deeper origins as a powerful Lunar Goddess and Melusine is the cosmic bride, all of them manifestations of the Divine Feminine and World Soul.

The tales by which we know them best are simply a starting point, a signpost at the crossroads, if you will. This essay has only lightly touched on a few points and there is much left to uncover. To experience the Faery Queens this way is simply to look at a picture in a book. To truly know them we must seek them in the landscape and in the dreams of our hearts. We all have a choice- either to stand looking at the signposts and taking in the view, or to follow the path and see where it leads, knowing the world will never look the same again. When you follow the Faery Queen on the *'bonny road'* into Faery, what will you find? Perhaps the most precious jewel of all - wisdom.

## Bibliography

Carding, Emily (2012) *Faery Craft*. Minnesota, Llewellyn Publishing.

D'Este, Sorita and David Rankine,(2010) *The Cosmic Shekinah*. London, Avalonia Books

Gregory, Lady, (2006) *Gods and Fighting Men*. Buckinghamshire, Colin Smythe Ltd.

Jackson, Nigel (1994) *Call of the Horned Piper*. Berkshire, Capall Bann Publishing

Johnston, Sarah Iles (1990) *Hekate Soteira*. Atlanta, Georgia, Scholar's Press.

Kirk, Robert (2008) *The Secret Commonwealth of Elves, Fauns and Fairies*. New York, Dover Publications Ltd.

Knight, Gareth (2011) *The Romance of the Faery Melusine*. Cheltenham, Skylight Press

Matthews, John & Caitlín (1994) *The Encyclopaedia of Celtic Wisdom*. Dorset, Element Books.

Shakespeare, William (1993) *The Complete Works*. London, Magpie Books.

Shrine of Wisdom (ed) (1979) *The Chaldean Oracles*, Godalming, Shrine of Wisdom

# Spirits at the Table

## Faerie Queens in the Grimoires

## Dan Harms

> *This essay would not have been possible without a great deal of work that has been done in the publication of magical texts. With that in mind, I'd like to thank Joseph Peterson, David Rankine, Jake Stratton-Kent, and Ioannis Marathakis for their hard work that made this possible. Thanks also to the British Library, the New York Public Library, and the Folger Shakespeare Library for allowing the reproduction of what appears herein.*

In his autobiography, the famous seventeenth-century astrologer William Lilly spoke of the Queen of the Fairies as follows:

> *"Since I have related of the Queen of Fairies, I shall acquaint you, that it is not for every one, or every person, that these angelical creatures will appear unto, though they may say over the call, over and over, or indeed is it given to very many persons to endure their glorious aspects; even very many have failed just at that present when they are ready to manifest themselves; even persons otherwise of undaunted spirits and firm resolution, are herewith astonished, and tremble; as it happened not many years since with us. A very sober discreet person, of virtuous life and conversation, was beyond measure desirous to see something in this nature. He went with a friend into my Hurst Wood, the Queen of Fairies was invocated, a gentle murmuring wind came first; after that, amongst the hedges, a smart whirlwind; by and by a strong blast of wind blew upon the face of the friend, -- and the Queen appearing in a most illustrious glory, 'No more, I beseech you,' (quoth the Friend:) 'My heart fails; I am not able to endure longer.' Nor was he, his black curling hair*

> rose up, and I believe a bullrush would have beat him to the ground; he was sorely laughed at, &c."[1]

Although the account of the Queen's appearance might take our attention, the statement before it is in fact more interesting. According to Lilly, such an encounter was not unusual for his time. In fact, enough people were calling upon the Queen of the Fairies that it was possible to discuss the common challenges that such individuals experienced.

As with so many other spiritual entities, the queens of the fairies were approached in Europe through the ritual practice pursued outside officially sanctioned religion. Many such practices were likely orally transmitted and lost before they could be recorded. Nonetheless, we do have one genre which has preserved some hints of this tradition: the grimoires, or manuals of ritual magic, that appeared in numerous permutations as their owners and publishers collected, edited, omitted, translated, mistranslated, and rewrote rituals to contact, entreat or compel non-material beings for various ends.[2] Such books usually are steeped in a hierarchical Christian model of spirituality, based upon relationships among God, angels, saints, and demons. Despite this model, rituals dedicated to other beings, including the queens of the faeries, can be found in some works.

In this article we will examine four such figures – Kalé, Micob, Mab, and Sibylia – and their depictions through the magical texts from medieval to modern times. Evidence from these sources is often scanty, so parallels in folklore and other sources will be noted where relevant. Following these, one particular motif arising from these tales – that of the *'table ritual'* – will be explored.

## Kalé

Our first queen began her mythological life an aspect of a goddess: Artemis referred to as *Kalliste*, or *'Most Beautiful'*. In the most commonly known tale, taken from Hesiod, Callisto was considered one of the huntresses of the goddess, whom Artemis turned into a bear when she denied a dalliance with Zeus. The bear later wandered into a sacred precinct of Zeus, and the god chose, instead of having her killed, to place her in the heavens as the constellation Ursa Major.[3] Nonetheless, the second-century author Pausanias describes the tomb of Callisto at Arcadia, with the shrine of Artemis Kalliste at the apex, suggesting that the two might not have been as distinct as it might have been thought.[4]

As time went on and traditions changed, the goddess became the spirit Kalé, or *'Beauty'*, who turns up in the most surprising places. One

---

[1] Lilly, *William Lilly's history of his life and times from the year 1602 to 1681*, 1715:229-231.
[2] Davies, *Grimoires : a History of Magic Books*, 2009.
[3] Hesiod, and Evelyn-White, *Hesiod ; Homeric Hymns ; Epic Cycle ; Homerica*, 1936:69.
[4] Pausanias, Jones, & Wycherley, *Pausanias Description of Greece,* 1918.4:77.

prominent example is a manuscript dating between the fifth and eighth centuries of the *Alexander Romance*. Alexander the Great has journeyed to *'the land of the blessed'* with his retinue. While he is away from camp, the cook washes the king's meal of fish in a local stream, only to find that the fish returns to life and swims away. The cook, seeing such a wonder, drinks some of the water, becoming immortal. Upon Alexander's return, the cook tells him only that the fish had returned to life, and the king punishes him for his carelessness. Acting out of revenge or love, the cook approaches Alexander's daughter Kalé and convinces her to drink of the water as well. When the king learns of this additional transgression, he becomes envious. He hangs a millstone around the cook's neck and tosses him into the Adriatic Sea. As for his daughter, he names her *Nereida* and banishes her to the mountains, where she becomes a daimon or spirit who will live there for all time. Why exactly Alexander himself did not drink the water is not explained.[5]

Kalé survived the Greek transition to Christian belief quite easily. Within the tradition of the Laments of the Virgin for the death of Jesus, she sometimes appears as the questionably-appointed *'Saint Kalé'*. Despite her holy title, she criticizes Mary during the time of her grief, in response to which the Virgin curses her:

> *"Away, and may they build for you a church out in the oceans,*
> *that neither priest may chant a liturgy nor deacon sing a psalm for you…*
> *Instead, may you become a pen for lambs, a pen for sheep,*
> *and may the crows on the bell towers look down upon you!"*[6]

Despite the virgin's disapproval, Saint Kalé did come to have several tiny chapels on the rocks off the Greek coast dedicated to her.[7]

This can only touch upon a few aspects of the figure of Kalé, belief in whom lasted until the nineteenth century. The folklorist John Cuthbert Lawson, while travelling on the Aegean Sea, met a shepherd who claimed that he had met the *'good lady of the mountains'*. She was seen as a capricious being accompanied by a train of nymphs.[8] In other stories, the *'Good People of the Mountains'* are said to seek Kalé out each September 1, although they never find her.[9] Nonetheless, it is best to narrow our scope to the literature of magic.

Kalé is not always a beneficent figure in the magical literature. One fifteenth century prayer against sickness mentions her with both the Nereids

---

[5] Cook, "A Watery Folktale in the Alexander Romance: Alexander's Byzantine Neraïda," *Syllecta Classica* 20(2009).
[6] Alexiou, Yatromanolakis & Roilos, *The Ritual Lament in Greek Tradition*, 2002:75.
[7] Loukatos, *Personifications of Capes and Rocks in the Hellenic Seas*, 1973:471-72.
[8] Lawson, *Modern Greek Folklore and Ancient Greek Religion: a Study in Survivals*, 1965:162-171.
[9] Alexiou, Yatromanolakis & Roilos, *The Ritual Lament in Greek Tradition*, 2002:221.

and Onoskelis, the donkey-legged demon from the *Testament of Solomon*, as a potential cause of an affliction.[10] Nonetheless, she could still be called upon to help others; one spell to cure animals calls upon the Virgin Mary, John the Baptist, and Kalé to cure sheep[11].

Perhaps one of the most influential works of magic is the *Hygromanteia*, a Byzantine work detailing numerous methods of contacting spirits. This work was later translated into Latin, in which it became the *Clavicula Salomonis*, or the *Key of Solomon*. The processes of manuscript transmission and translation omitted some material that was present in the Greek, with one instance being the ritual to call Kalé to oneself. Ioannis Marathakis translates it as follows:

> *"At the first of August put honey and pine kernels in a bowl, take various coloured silken pieces of cloth and write the following words on a parchment: Linōmo, Kouōrō. Take all these things and go to a mountain at the same day. Place them on a firm rock at noon and hide. The Lady of the Mountains will come and say: 'Who did this good thing to me?' Then respond and say: 'I did so, and I want such and such a thing'. She will say, 'Go, and may your wish be fulfilled'."*[12]

KALE, FROM BONONIENSIS 3632, REPRODUCED IN ANECDOTA ATHENIENSIA, DELATTE, 1927:600

---

[10] Cook, *A Watery Folktale in the Alexander Romance: Alexander's Byzantine Neraïda*, 2009:121.
[11] Loukopoulos & Roumeles, Athena,1930:205.
[12] Marathakis (trans. & ed.), *The Magical Treatise of Solomon or Hygromanteia*, 2011: 131-33.

The cloth on the table, we are assured, may be used after the ritual is finished to make a horse run more quickly. One manuscript from this tradition, Bononiensis 3632, includes a drawing of Kalé, a woman with a row of eyes around her middle, the tail of a serpent, and a crown on her head.

## Micob/Micol/Mical/Mycob

As references to Kalé had been omitted as the *Key of Solomon* moved west, magicians had a wide variety of names for the queen of the fairies. One notable mention of a *'lady to the queen'* appears in the 17th century manuscript Sloane 1727, just after a list of four names of spirits assigned to *'treasures of the earth'*: Florella, Mical, Tytan, and Mabb.[13] At least three of these names are referred to elsewhere as fairy queens – Tytan being a variant of Titania, and Mical and Mabb turning up in the magical literature at various points. We will look first to Mical and her variants, as she appears under different names in the grimoires.

First, Micol is mentioned only a few pages from the list of the four ladies in Sloane 1727. A spirit called *'Micol'* who is *'queen of the pygmies'* can be summoned via a Latin incantation beginning, *"Micol o tumicoll regina pigmeorum deus Abraham: deus Isaac: deus Jacob…"*.[14] Although no context is given as to how the spell should be used, William Lilly mentions a similar invocation being used to call Micol into a crystal owned by *"Ellen Evans, daughter of my tutor Evans"*.[15]

Sloane MS 3824 includes a treasure-finding ritual, conducted on seven nights from eleven at night to two in the morning, to call *"these spirits there are too who are Set over the Hierarchy, as the Supream head thereof, whose names are Mycob and Oberion"*.[16] The king and queen themselves do not appear, but they are asked to send one of the seven sisters who serve them – Lilia, Rostilia, Foca, Folla, Africa, Julia, and Venulla – to accede to the magician's demands. This ritual is unique, insofar as it is the only one in which both the queen and king of fairies are invoked.[17]

Another variant of this name, Mycob, appears alongside the king of fairies, Oberion, in Folger MS. V.b.26 at the end of an Officium Spirituum, or *'Offices of the Spirits'*. These were lists of spirits that appear in many medieval and early modern works, detailing the spirits that a magician could summon for various purposes. The most recognizable example of this

---

[13] Sloane MS. 1727, fo. 37.
[14] Sloane MS. 1727, fo. 28.
[15] Lilly, *William Lilly's History of his Life and Times from the year 1602 to 1681*, 1715:229.
[16] Sloane MS. 3824, fo. 98v; published in Elias Ashmole and David Rankine, *The Book of Treasure Spirits*, 2009:109.
[17] Oberion himself has a rich tradition of being summoned. See Arthur Gauntlet and David Rankine, *The Grimoire of Arthur Gauntlet: a 17th century London Cunning-man's book of charms, conjurations and prayers*, 2011:261-262; Frederick Hockley and Dan Harms, ed. *Experimentum potens magna in occult philosophy arcanorum*, 2012:24-32.

genre is the *Goetia* transcribed by MacGregor Mathers and published (without credit to Mathers) by Aleister Crowley.

Her inclusion is of great interest: at least one author thought of the queen and king of the faeries as beings that might be considered alongside such figures as Lucifer, Satan, and Astaroth. Nonetheless, she appears as an unnumbered entry at the end of the main list, suggesting that she sits apart from the rest[18].

Mycob is said to appear as a meek lady dressed in green and wearing a crown. She provides a ring that gives invisibility and teaches medicine and the natural magic that lies within trees, herbs, and stones. She has seven followers – variants on those given in Sloane MS. 3824 – who perform many of the same functions. The nineteenth century occultists John Palmer and Frederick Hockley, both of whom had contact with the manuscript, copied this material for their own purposes, indicating that its influence extended even to their times.[19]

The same fairy turns up earlier in the manuscript, in a ritual to acquire a ring of invisibility. The magician draws a circle used for operations of love on the day and hour of Jupiter – an unusual combination, as Venus is typically the planet of love. After doing so, he[20] calls upon three spirits, Micol, Titam (Titania, once again) and Burfex, to appear. The spirits appear, lay a rich table, and offer the magician wine. To acquire the ring, the magician must be prepared to kiss the most beautiful member of their company.[21]

## Mab

Mab is a common name for the queen of the fairies in literature, most notably in the speech of Mercutio from *Romeo and Juliet*, Act I, Scene IV, who *"comes / In shape no bigger than an agate-stone / On the fore-finger of an alderman."* Some would link her to Queen Medb of Irish legend, so it is disappointing that she has yet to appear in any other sources than Sloane 1727. William Lilly assures us that another spell calling upon her for crystallomancy did exist in his time:

> *"There was, in the late times of troubles, one Mortlack, who pretended unto Speculations, had a crystal, a call of Queen Mab, one of the Queen*

---

[18] Folger MS. V.b.26, p. 81.
[19] Campbell (ed.) *A Book of the Offices of Spirits, the occult virtue of plants & some rare magical charms & spells, transcribed by Frederick Hockley from a sixteenth century manuscript on magic & necromancy by John Porter*, 2011:27.
[20] In general, ceremonial magic texts assume the operator is male, so I use a male pronoun when discussing ceremonial rites. This is done to convey the historical sense of these rites, not to suggest that women were never mentioned as operators, or that they cannot or could not work such magic. Indeed, we will see otherwise shortly.
[21] Folger MS. V.b.26, pp. 38-39. A more detailed examination of this passage will appear in *The Book of Oberon*, forthcoming.

*[sic]* of Fairies; he deluded many thereby: at last I was brought into his company; he was desired to make invocation, he did so; nothing appeared, or would... at last he said he could do nothing as long as I was in presence.'[22]

## Sibyllia / Sympilia

If we were to look for the most influential faerie queen of the magical literature, however, that honour would be visited upon one who has been hitherto unmentioned: the lady Sibyllia.

In Greek and Roman belief, the Sibyls were women of great mystical power, most particularly the ability to divine the future. The most famous of these figures is the Cumaean Sibyl, who led Aeneas on his trip into the Underworld.[23] Pausanias calls our attention to the first Sibyl who gave prophecies at Delphi, and who was said to have been the offspring of Zeus and Lamia, daughter of Poseidon.[24] Lamia was said to be a sea-being similar to a shark, evoking similarities with the figure of Kalé. The 10th century Byzantine lexicon the *Suda* lists ten different Sibyls, corresponding to different areas of the world.[25]

Perhaps the earliest sources of magic that discuss this figure is, as with Kalé, the *Hygromanteia*. One rite calls for a young boy to skry into a mirror set up against a black-handled knife, which has been used to inscribe a circle *'like a grave'* into the ground. The boy then views a cook on a public road, who he dispatches to obtain and butcher three lambs. After a rich table is set, the Queen Sympilia arrives. The magician calls upon her to send a servant to King Solomon, to obtain a talisman on which she will swear to answer the magician's questions truthfully. After the queen has finished answering, she and her followers may eat.[26]

The most famous mentions of Sibylia appear in a later English work, Reginald Scot's *Discoverie of Witchcraft* (1584). Scot's book was a treatise attacking all manner of targets – Roman Catholics, magicians, proponents of witch-trials, and charlatans. He republished several spells, many of them from a manuscript written by one T. R. and John Cokars, in the hope of both discrediting magic and highlighting its ties to Catholic imagery and practice. Within this work we find two different spells directed toward Sibylia.

---

[22] Lilly, *William Lilly's History of his Life and Times from the year 1602 to 1681*, 1715:234.
[23] Virgil & Fairclough, *Eclogues ; Georgics ; Aeneid I-VI ; [Aeneid VII-XII ; The Minor poems]*, 1934.1:509.
[24] Pausanias, Jones & Wycherley, *Pausanias Description of Greece*. vol. 4, p. 431.
[25] Suda On Line and Suda Consortium, "Suda On Line: Byzantine Lexicography,"
http://www.stoa.org/sol/. A detailed look at such beings can be found in Jake Stratton-Kent, *Geosophia: The Argo of Magic*, 2 vols, 2010.1: 64-90.
[26] Marathakis, *The Magical Treatise of Solomon or Hygromanteia*. 2011:128-129.

The first spell for Sibylia requires a dead man to serve as intermediary. After three days of fasting, abstinence, and prayer, the magician should travel at 11 o'clock at night to the grave of a person who died an unnatural death. (It is even suggested that the magician make a deal with a criminal beforehand who is soon to be executed, to guarantee co-operation.) The experiment should be conducted with a companion, who carries a crystal stone and a candle. At the grave, the spirit will be conjured into the crystal in the form of a twelve-year-old child. After its appearance, the ghost is sent to fetch the spirit Sibylia.

The magician and his companion then re-pair to a nearby room, drawing two magical circles without any holy name or adornment. The magician places a parchment shield-shaped talisman on his chest and stands in one circle with his companion. The magician calls for Sibylia to appear *"by the king and queene of fairies, and their vertues, and by the faith and obedience that thou bearest unto them"*.[27] Although Sibylia's station as one of these rulers may have slipped since the *Hygromanteia*, she still is noted as being associated with them.

After citing all manner of holy names and events, the magician finally states his purpose:

> *"I conjure thee Sibylia by all their vertues to appeare in that circle before me visible, in the forme and shape of a beautifull woman in a bright and vesture white, adorned and garnished most faire, and to appeare to me quicklie without deceipt or tarrieng... For I will choose thee to be my blessed virgine, & will have common copulation with thee."*[28]

This sort of pursuit of sexual favours of a spirit might be illuminated via an example from Sweden, in which a fisherman gains a magical book and the power to use it via sexual relations with a water spirit.[29] Given that the two circles for magician and fairy are four feet apart, however, the logistics of any such act might be difficult to negotiate. The magician seeks to bind her to answer his questions and to seek treasure as well, which might be more achievable goals.[30]

Sibylia turns up again a few pages later in Scot in a different ritual entirely. In this case, the magician spends nine days in a private room. After that, he places clean water and boils it over a charcoal fire in the middle of the room. He then circles the fire with a virgin wax candle in one hand while calling out to the three sisters Milia, Achilia and Sibylia to bring him a ring of invisibility. Soon it becomes apparent that Sibylia is once again

---

[27] Scot, *The Discouerie of Witchcraft*, 1584:406.
[28] Ibid.
[29] Johnson, *Tidebast och Vändelrot : Magical Representations in the Swedish Black Art Book Tradition*, 2010:103.
[30] A longer excursus on the possible significance of this ritual, in light of ancient Greek ritual practice, appears in Stratton-Kent, *Geosophia: The Argo of Magic*. vol. 1:91-101.

the focus of the rite, for the magician dismisses the other two spirits before lying down on a bed, with a silk kerchief around his head so the ring might be placed on his finger.[31]

*The Discoverie of Witchcraft* was not received as its author would have preferred, as it soon became a common source of charms for cunning folk and was later expanded in 1665 with even more rituals.[32] As with Scot's other writings on magic, the rituals of Sibylia made their way from his sceptical work back into other popular traditions in other ways. The first ritual is repeated verbatim in the grimoire of the seventeenth century London cunning man Arthur Gauntlet (now Sloane MS. 3851).[33] The second appears in the popular English Faust-book *Second Report of Doctor Faust*, in which the three fairy maidens Millia, Achilya, and Sybilla, provide a miraculous horse with a ring of invisibility so a magician might awaken a maid who has been shocked into a swoon.[34]

The queen also appears in the same manuscript from the Folger Shakespeare Library that includes the list of spirits with Micob at its end. We find her in a convoluted ritual to create a fairy ointment, placed in the eyes to view spirits. The magician must first slaughter seven different types of animals, retaining the blood and fat for each in vessels. After washing his hands with rose water, he places the seven types of fat and a sliver of bay wood therein, mixing it together while calling on another seven sisters, most notably Delforia, in the name of *"Inferiours & servants to the Emprice & princes of all fayres Sibilis"*.[35] By the end of the incantation, Delforia herself has been promoted to the rank of empress, and the mixture is prepared to be placed on a fairy throne to derive the virtue that will make it efficacious. This work, too, was one of those Palmer and Hockley selected to copy.[36]

Near the end of the same manuscript is another ceremony to call Sibilia. In this case, the magician need merely hold a new wax candle in his or her right hand and say a Latin incantation calling upon her to appear in a pleasant human form in the flame. Such a rite, we are assured, is particularly useful for finding treasure and locating stolen goods.[37]

Not only was Sibylia's influence more profound than those of her sisters, it would last longer. The Liverpool-based galvanist and astrologer William Dawson Bellhouse included an anti-witchcraft charm in his personal book of charms in 1852. In that work, the name *'Sibilia'* is a name of power to be written on a figurine to be used to combat the witch's power.[38] Over a

---

[31] Scot, *The Discouerie of Witchcraft*. pp. 408-410.
[32] Davies, *Popular Magic: Cunning Folk in English History*, 2007:126-27.
[33] Gauntlet and Rankine, *The Grimoire of Arthur Gauntlet*, 2011:237-243.
[34] Thoms, *Early English Prose Romances, with bibliographical and historical introductions*, 1858.3:358.
[35] Folger MS. V.b.26, fo. 139.
[36] Campbell, *A Book of the Offices of Spirits*. pp. 46-51.
[37] Folger MS. V.b.26, fo. 228-229.
[38] Bellhouse, "A Complete System of Magic," in *Miscellaneous Manuscripts*, 1852:43. Thanks to the New York Public Library Manuscripts Division for permission to quote this information.

century later, an abbreviated form of Scot's ritual for invisibility appeared in an article from the U. S. radical feminist group W.I.T.C.H (Women's International Terrorist Conspiracy from Hell) as *"a must for prospective underground goers"*.[39] Even if we see this as satiric, it confirms that Sibylia had an impact well into the twentieth century.

## The Rite of the Table

I have refrained from commenting on the parallels between the rites above until now. We have some of the usual language and procedures of ceremonial magic, but underlying these are a few other elements that do not turn up consistently, but nonetheless often enough to bear comment. I would particularly point out the connection of such figures with the dead, the use of skrying in mirrors, crystals, or candles to contact them, and their usage for a recurring set of goals: invisibility, divination, and treasure hunting. The most striking, however, is a ritual in which a feasting table is provided for the spirits, who partake of food and drink in return for providing the magician with some benefit. Even in the rites of Queen Symphilia in the *Hygromanteia*, which are otherwise unremarkable rites of divination using a child skryer, involve a meal being set for the queen.

The *'table ritual'*, as we might call it, might be considered less a point of analysis than a collection of similar phenomena that I have placed together for the purposes of comparison. I make no claims as to the validity of the sources used, the date at which they might have originated, or whether the practices described diffused from one location or sprung up in multiple regions. Scholars have only mentioned these rituals rarely, and then only to note the parallels between two or three and remark upon their uniqueness. It is hoped that this collection of material might lead to more investigation as to the history and relations of this particular set of rituals.

The table ritual is not exclusive to the fairy queens. Instead, it is used here to describe a broader set of rituals in which a table is laid, for spiritual beings mostly outside a traditional Christian hierarchy, who partake of refreshment before offering their services. The roots likely lie in traditions of leaving offerings to ward off ill fortune from spiritual visitors, yet here those beings are explicitly called upon to bring about a desired result. Contrary to usual ceremonial practice, a magical circle and protective rituals appear rarely in such rites, and even then might be considered optional. Previous scholars have noted examples of the table rituals, usually as anomalies that contrast with the usual corpus of ceremonial magic. Nonetheless, an examination of all of these disparate sources suggests that they represent a tradition of magical practice that has a wide geographical range and coincides closely with certain areas of witchcraft and folk life.

---

[39] "Survival", *Off Our Backs* 1.12:19 (1970).

Perhaps the earliest example we have of such a rite appears alongside the rites for Kalé in some copies of the *Hygromanteia*. This rite is intended to call the *'black demon'* Mortzē. Inside the house, the magician sets up a table bearing peeled fruit, a censer, and two candles. The magician draws three circles around the table with a black knife, then plunges the knife into the table to summon the creature.[40]

Even outside the Greek context, such rites have become part of the canon of ceremonial magic. We might look at the *Fourth Book of Occult Philosophy*, attributed (likely spuriously) to Henry Cornelius Agrippa:

> *"There is another kinde of Spirits which we have spoken of in the third book of Occult Philosophy, not so hurtful, and neerest men; so also, that they are affected with humane passions, and do joy in the conversation of men, and freely do inhabit with them: and others do dwell in the Woods and Desarts…"*[41]

Pseudo-Agrippa states that these spirits should be summoned with sweet smells and beautiful music. Exorcisms and threats can be used, but fearlessness and single-mindedness are more important. He ends with the procedure:

> *"you ought to prepare a Table in the place of Invocation, covered with clean linen; whereupon you shall set new bread, and running water or milk in new earthen vessels, and new knives… But let the Invocant go unto the head of the Table, and round about it let there be seats placed for the Spirits, as you please; and the Spirits being called, you shall invite them to drink and eat. But if perchance you shall fear any evil Spirit, then draw a Circle around it, and let that part of the Table at which the Invocant sits, be within the Circle, and the rest of the Table without the Circle."*[42]

The last admonition shows how far we have come from the usual model of ceremonial magic, in which the magician and the spirit are strictly divided.

In addition to the rite that Scot collected in his work, we also have a work in e. Mus. 173 for calling three sisters to the table. This one varies slightly from the others, insofar that the magician must extract a substance from water in a fairy-haunted chamber with which to anoint the eyes. After this substance is obtained, one should

---

[40] Marathakis, *The Magical Treatise of Solomon or Hygromanteia*. 2011:118-119.
[41] Heinrich Cornelius Agrippa von Nettesheim et al., *"Henry Cornelius Agrippa his fourth book of occult philosophy of geomancie, magical elements of Peter de Aban : astronomical geomancie ; the nature of spirits ; Arbatel of magick ; the species or several kindes of magick,"* Printed by J.C. for the Rooks … p. 65.
[42] Ibid., p. 66.

> *"the next night following come to the same house agayne before II of the clocke at night, making a good fyre with sweet woods and sett upon the table a newe towell or one cleane washt and upon yt 3 fyne loaves of newemangett,[43] 3 newe knyves with whytehaftes and a newe cuppe full of newe ale, then sett your selfe downe by the fyre in a chaire wyth your face towards the table..."*[44]

Another such procedure appears in Sloane 3824, shortly before the call to Mycob and Oberyon mentioned above:

> *"...the place which is appointed or set apart for action must be Suffumigated with good Aromatick Odours, and a Cleane Cloath spread on the Ground or a table nine foot Distant from the Circle, upon which there must be Either a Chicken or any Kind of small joynt, or peice of meat handsomely Rosted, and a white mantlet, a Basin or little Dish like a Coffe Dish of fair Runing water, hafe a pynt of Salt in a botle, a bottle of Ale Containing a Quart, Some food and a pint of Cream in a Dish... and some have used noe Circle at all... but onely being Cleane washed and apparreld..."*[45]

We can also find parallel rituals in other classic grimoires from outside Greece and England. The French work the *Grimorium Verum*, bearing the date 1517 but likely dating to the nineteenth century, includes its own ritual to set a table to bring three unnamed women to one's bedchamber – or men, if the operator is a woman.[46] One of these spirits remains to discuss all manner of arts and sciences, to divulge the location of treasure, and to provide a ring that allows for invisibility and instant seduction.[47] Some Italian editions of the *Grand Grimoire* also have a ceremony that is greatly similar to this, save that the ring is useful for seduction and gaming.[48] Both are quite similar to Scot's second rite, as outlined above.

Another variant appears in the rites of the pygmies in the German work *Magia naturalis et innaturalis*, one of the oldest grimoires attributed to the infamous maker of demonic pacts, Johann Faust. These juxtapose the setting of a tiny table with honey, bread, butter, water and wine, atop a green hill in a pleasant setting, with the bloody sacrifice of a hen or pigeon, the blood of which is scattered to various directions. Apparently this does not dissuade the two small men who come to partake in the feast. After two more, they willingly come to serve the magician, granting knowledge of

---

[43] Probably manchet bread.
[44] Briggs, "Some seventeenth-century books of magic," *Folklore* 64, no. 4:460 (1953).
[45] Sloane MS. 3824, 98v; published in Ashmole and Rankine, *The Book of Treasure Spirits*, 2009:109.
[46] It has been suggested that the mention of a female operator means that it is of recent origin. This might not be the case, as we shall see.
[47] Peterson, *Grimorium Verum*, 2007:44-45. A fictional depiction of this rite appears in Bowen, "One Remained Behind," in *Kecksies and other twilight tales*, ed. Marjorie Bowen, 1976.
[48] e.g. Rudy & Del Rabina, *The Grand Grimoire* (Seattle, Wash.: Trident Books : Ars Obscura, 1996).

hidden things, so long as their master does not swear in their presence or fornicate.[49]

Yet were these rites practiced in reality, or did they remain intellectual experiments? We have a few examples of their practice that have come down to us. Similarities might be found, for instance, to some accounts of women who fly at night with Diana, Herodias, or other female goddesses or spirits, most prominently made in the *Canon Episcopi*. Although it was hardly universal, it was believed that leaving out food and drink for this figure and her train would lead to good fortune.[50] William of Auvergne, Bishop of Paris, describes food and drink simply being left uncovered so that the spirit Satia or Abundia and her train might grant a household good fortune, but the setting of a table for the spirits also appeared in other cases.[51] Perhaps the earliest mention of this appears in Burchard of Worms' *Confessor*, a manual of questions for priests to ask during their confessions, written in the eleventh century:

> "Have you done as some women are wont to do at certain times of the year? That is, have you prepared the table in your house and set on the table your food and drink, with three knives, that if those three sisters whom past generations and old-time foolishness called the Fates should come they may take refreshment there, and... [do you] believe that those whom you call "the sisters" can do or avail aught for you either now or in the future?"[52]

Another version appears in the *Golden Legend*, a collection of popular legends on saints compiled by Jacobus de Voragine around 1260. In one particular tale regarding St. Germain of Auxerre (c. 370 – c. 448), the saint was visiting a household in which the table was set again after the meal for the *'good ladies'*. The saint remained and discovered that the purported guests were actually devils in disguise.[53] This bears parallels to the work of William of Auvergne, Bishop of Paris, who recorded similar practices in his time. Even if this is a legend dating well after the saint's death, it still indicates that something similar to a table rite was being practiced in Europe in the thirteenth century.

A fifteenth-century manuscript from a German monastery refers to a similar ceremony conducted for the Germanic goddess Perchta or Perhta and her cohorts. Between Christmas day and Epiphany, householders

---

[49] Faust and J. Scheible, *Doktor Johannes Faust's Magia naturalis et innaturalis, oder Dreifacher Höllenzwang, letztes Testament und Siegelkunst*, 1849:140-148. Peuckert believed that this rite could be connected to a ritual in honour of Jupiter in the *Picatrix* which also calls for a table with food and drink. Will-Erich Peuckert, *Pansophie : ein Versuch zur Geschichte der weissen und schwarzen Magie*, 1976:438-439; Greer & Warnock, *Picatrix: The classic medieval handbook of astrological magic*, 2010:188-189.
[50] N. Cohn, *Europe's inner demons: an enquiry inspired by the great witch-hunt*, 1975:210-219.
[51] William of Auvergne, *Guilielmi Alverni Opera Omnia*, 1963.1:1036, 1066.
[52] Kors & Peters, *Witchcraft in Europe, 400-1700: a Documentary History*, 2001:66.
[53] Voragine & Graesse, *Legenda Aurea : Vulgo Historia Lombardica Dicta*, 1846:449.

would set a table covered with bread, meat, eggs, cheese, water, wine and milk, for these women, to bring them domestic prosperity and success in worldly matters.[54]

A few centuries later, we find Johann Praetorius' 1669 account of one Paul Creuz of Nuremberg. Creuz was said to hold feasts for the little mountain people, very similar to those described in the Faustian rites described above. He became so much in their favour that their king appeared and granted him leave to read a book with a great deal of mystical wisdom within, through which he obtained secret knowledge.[55]

One curious English pamphlet published in 1613 deals with the con games of Alice and John West, who were particularly fond of using the King and Queen of the Fairies in their frauds. One such attempt, aimed at Thomas Moore of Hammersmith, involved as *"the first rites that must be performed"*, *"a very great banquet which must be prepared for this royall king and Queene of Fayries, then all the chamber must be hunt with the richest linnen…"*[56] Caution in using this particular piece of evidence is warranted, as those who practiced it were not actually seeking contact with these beings. Nonetheless, we might propose that the two hucksters sought a model that already existed in folk culture to accomplish their goals.

Until recently, a similar rite was conducted in rural Greece for the Fates when a child was born, to ensure it health and a happy life. Lawson describes the tableau for the Fates as follows:

> *"The house-door is left open or at any rate unlatched. Inside a light is kept burning, and in the middle of the room is set a low table with three cushions or low stools placed round it – religious conservatism apparently forbidden the use of so modern an invention as chairs, for at the lying-in-state before a funeral also cushions or low stools are provided for the mourners. On the table are set out such dainties as the Fates love, including always honey; in Athens formerly the essentials were a dish of honey, three white almonds, a loaf of bread, and a glass of water."*[57]

---

[54] Schmeller, Frommann, & Kommission Bayerische Akademie der Wissenschaften. Historische, *Bayerisches wörterbuch*, 1872.1:271.
[55] Praetorius, *Der abenteuerliche Glückstopf*, 1669:177-178. The Grimms later incorporated this into their massive work on German folklore; see Jacob Grimm and Wilhelm Grimm, *Deutsche Sagen*, 1816.1:48-49, or the partial translation in E. M. Butler, *Ritual magic*, 1949:171.
[56] *The seuerall notorious and levvd cousnages of Iohn V Vest, and Alice V Vest, falsely called the King and Queene of Fayries practised very lately both in this citie, and many places neere adioyning, to the impouerishing of many simple people, as well men as women: who were arraigned and conuicted for the same, at the Sessions House in the Old Bayly, the 14. Of Ianuarie, this present yeare, 1613*.Printed at London: [By William Stansby] for Edward Marchant, and are to be sold at his shop [.], 1613.
[57] Lawson, *Modern Greek Folklore and Ancient Greek Religion: a Study in Survivals*. p. 125.

During their fieldwork in rural Greece in 1962, Richard and Eva Blum came across a similar rite in which sweets were left on a table for three nights so that the Fates would give a child good fortune.[58]

Yet the most striking example of the use of these rituals appears in the records of the Spanish Inquisition. Between 1579 and 1651, during the Spanish occupation of Sicily, the inquisitors placed a curious group of folk healers near Palermo on trial. These individuals were part of a company that overlapped the boundaries between fairies and witches, being considered one or the other at different times. When people unwittingly offended such a powerful being, manifesting a condition called a *'witch-touch'*, a healer was called for to free them from the affliction. The healer would decorate the sick person's room and set out a table with jugs of water and wine, and with sweetmeats, five loaves, five napkins, and a honey-cake, a cup and other eating utensils. *"[And that she] covered the sick person's bed with a red cloth and perfumed the whole room [sweet-smelling incense]..."*[59]

Such rituals were carried out for the purposes of healing both men and beasts, with the latter rites being conducted in a stable. Yet, it should be noted that these were not merely rituals passed down through simple training. Most of their practitioners claimed to have learned them as members of a secretive organization. This august company that, on three nights a week, would pass through the towns and villages, dancing and eating at each house. The leader of this *'White Sabbath'* was an impressive figure known by various titles – *'The Queen of the Fairies'*, *'The Greek Lady'*, and *'La Sabia Sibylia'*.[60]

## Bibliography

Agrippa von Nettesheim, Heinrich Cornelius, Robert Turner, Petrus, and Collection Early English Books Online Ebook. *"Henry Cornelius Agrippa His Fourth Book of Occult Philosophy of Geomancie, Magical Elements of Peter De Aban : Astronomical Geomancie ; the Nature of Spirits ; Arbatel of Magick ; the Species or Several Kindes of Magick."* Printed by J.C. for the Rooks ...

Alexiou, Margaret, & Dimitrios Yatromanolakis, & Panagiotis Roilos (2002) *The Ritual Lament in Greek Tradition*. Lanham, MD: Rowman & Littlefield.

Ashmole, Elias, & David Rankine (2009) *The Book of Treasure Spirits : A 17th Century Grimoire of Magical Conjurations to Increase Wealth and Catch Thieves through the Invocation of Spirits, Fallen Angels, Demons and Fairies*. London: Avalonia.

---

[58] Blum & Blum, *The Dangerous Hour: the Lore of Crisis and Mystery in Rural Greece*, 1970:100.
[59] Henningsen, "'The Ladies from Outside': An Archaic Pattern of the Witches' Sabbath," in *Early modern European witchcraft : centres and peripheries*, ed. Ankarloo & Henningsen, 1990:200-201.
[60] Ibid. Henningsen did not follow up on this work, so it awaits another researcher to further explore the trial records for the Inquisition. Henningsen pursues the possible links between his fairy cult and the witches' sabbats in this article and in "The White Sabbath and Other Archaic Patterns of Witchcraft," *Acta Ethnographica Academiae Scientiarum Hungaricae* 37, no. 1-4 (1991). Whether the material herein could alleviate any of the author's concerns regarding the geographical overlap between the two motifs remains to be seen.

Bacon, Rogerus, & Michael-Albion Macdonald (1988) *De Nigromancia : Sloane Ms. 3885 & Additional Ms. 36674*. Gillette, NJ: Heptangle Books.

Bellhouse, William Dawson (1852) *"A Complete System of Magic."* In *Miscellaneous Manuscripts*. New York: New York Public Library.

Blum, Richard H. & Eva Marie (1970) *The Dangerous Hour: The Lore of Crisis and Mystery in Rural Greece*. New York: Scribner.

Bowen, Marjorie (1976) *"One Remained Behind."* In *Kecksies and Other Twilight Tales*, edited by Marjorie Bowen, 141-66. Sauk City, Wis.: Arkham House.

Briggs, K.M. (1953) *"Some Seventeenth-Century Books of Magic."* In *Folklore* 64.4:445-62.

Butler, E.M. (1949) *Ritual Magic*. Cambridge [England]; New York: University Press; Cambridge University Press.

Campbell, Colin (ed.) (2011) *A Book of the Offices of Spirits, the Occult Virtue of Plants & Some Rare Magical Charms & Spells, Transcribed by Frederick Hockley from a Sixteenth Century Manusript on Magic & Necromancy by John Porter*. York Beach, ME: The Teitan Press.

Cohn, Norman (1975) *Europe's Inner Demons: An Enquiry Inspired by the Great Witch-hunt*. New York: Basic Books.

Cook, Brad L. (2009) *"A Watery Folktale in the Alexander Romance: Alexander's Byzantine Neraïda."* In *Syllecta Classica* 20:105-34.

Davies, Owen (2009) *Grimoires: A History of Magic Books*. Oxford: Oxford University Press.

——— (2007) *Popular Magic: Cunning Folk in English History*. London: Hambledon Continuum.

Faust, & J. Scheible (1849) *Doktor Johannes Faust's Magia Naturalis Et Innaturalis, Oder Dreifacher Höllenzwang, Letztes Testament Und Siegelkunst*. Stuttgart: J.Scheible.

Gauntlet, Arthur, & David Rankine (2011) *The Grimoire of Arthur Gauntlet : A 17th Century London Cunning-Man's Book of Charms, Conjurations and Prayers : Includes Material from the Heptameron, the Arbatel, the Discoverie of Witchcraft; and the Writings of Cornelius Agrippa and William Bacon*. London: Avalonia.

Greer, John Michael & Warnock, Christopher (2010) *Picatrix: The Classical Medieval Handbook of Astrological Magic*. n.p.: Adocentyn Press.

Grimm, Jacob & Wilhelm (1816) *Deutsche Sagen*. Berlin: Nicolaische Buchhandlung.

Henningsen, Gustav (1990) *"'The Ladies from Outside': An Archaic Pattern of the Witches' Sabbath."* In *Early Modern European Witchcraft : Centres and Peripheries*, edited by Bengt Ankarloo & Gustav Henningsen, 191-215. Oxford [England]: Clarendon Press.

———. (1993) *"The White Sabbath and Other Archaic Patterns of Witchcraft."* In *Acta Ethnographica Academiae Scientiarum Hungaricae* 37.1-4:293-304.

Hesiod, & Hugh G. Evelyn-White (1936) *Hesiod ; Homeric Hymns ; Epic Cycle ; Homerica*. Cambridge, Mass.: Harvard University Press.

Hockley, Frederick & Harms, Dan (ed.) (2012) *Experimentum Potens Magna in Occult Philosophy Arcanorum*. Hinckley: Society for Esoteric Endeavour Publications.

Jacobus de, Voragine, & Johann Georg Theodor Graesse (1846) *Legenda Aurea : Vulgo Historia Lombardica Dicta*. Dresdæ [Dresden]: Arnold.

Johnson, Thomas K. (2010) *"Tidebast Och Vändelrot : Magical Representations in the Swedish Black Art Book Tradition."*.

Klaassen, Frank (2011) *"Three Early Modern Rituals to Spoil Witches."* In *Opuscula* 1.1:1-10.

Kors, Alan Charles & Edward Peters (2001) *Witchcraft in Europe, 400-1700: a Documentary History*. Philadelphia: University of Pennsylvania Press.

Lawson, J.C. (1965) *Modern Greek Folklore and Ancient Greek Religion: A Study in Survivals*. New York: University Books.

Lilly, W. (1715) *William Lilly's History of His Life and Times from the Year 1602 to 1681*: Reprinted for C. Baldwin.

Loukatos, Demetrios (1973) *"Personifications of Capes and Rocks in the Hellenic Seas."* In *The Realm of the Extra-Human : Agents and Audiences*, edited by Bharati Agehananda, 467-74. The Hague; Chicago: Mouton ; Distributed by Aldine.

Loukopoulos, Demetres (1930) *Poimenika Tes Roumeles*. [Athena]: Kentrike Polesis, Vivliopoleion I.N. Sidere.

Marathakis, Ioannis (trans. and ed.) (2011) *The Magical Treatise of Solomon or Hygromanteia Also Called the Apotelesmatike Pragmateia, Epistle to Rehoboam, Solomonike*, Sourceworks of Ceremonial Magic. Singapore: Golden Hoard Press.

Meyerstein, Edward Harry William (1959) *Some Letters of E.H.W. Meyerstein*. London: N. Spearman.

Pausanias, W. H. S. Jones, & R. E. Wycherley (trans.) (1918) *Pausanias Description of Greece*. Cambridge, Mass.: Harvard University Press.

Peterson, Joseph H. (2007) *Grimorium Verum*. Scotts Valley, CA: CreateSpace.

Peuckert, Will-Erich (1976) *Pansophie: Ein Versuch zur Geschichte der Weissen und Schwarzen Magie*. Berlin: E. Schmidt.

Praetorius, J. (1669) *Der Abenteuerliche Glückstopf*. s.n.

Rudy, Gretchen, & Antonio Venitiana Del Rabina (1996) *The Grand Grimoire*. Seattle, Wash.: Trident Books: Ars Obscura.

Schmeller, Johann Andreas, G. Karl Frommann, & Kommission Bayerische Akademie der Wissenschaften. Historische (1872) *Bayerisches Wörterbuch*. München: R. Oldenbourg.

Scot, Reginald (1584) *The Discouerie of Witchcraft: Wherein the Lewde Dealing of Witches and Witchmongers Is Notablie Detected, the Knauerie of Coniurors, the Impietie of Inchantors, the Follie of Soothsaiers, the Impudent Falshood of Cousenors, the Infidelitie of Atheists, the Pestilent Practices of Pythonists, the Curiositie of Figure Casters, the Vanitie of Dreamers, the Beggerlie Art of Alcumystrie, the Abhomination of Idolatrie, the Horrible Art of Poisoning, the Vertue and Power of Naturall Magike, and All the Conueiances of Legierdemaine and Iuggling Are Deciphered: And Many Other Things Opened, Which Have Long Lien Hidden, Howbeit Verie Necessarie to Be Knowne. : Heerevnto Is Added a Treatise Vpon the Nature and Substance of Spirits and Diuels, & C*. Imprinted at London: By William Brome.

*The Seuerall Notorious and Levvd Cousnages of Iohn West, and Alice West, Falsely Called the King and Queene of Fayries Practised Very Lately Both in This Citie, and Many Places Neere Adioyning, to the Impouerishing of Many Simple People, as Well Men as Women: Who Were Arraigned and Conuicted for the Same, at the Sessions House in the Old Bayly, the 14. Of Ianuarie, This Present Yeare, 1613*. Printed at London: [By William Stansby] for Edward Marchant, and are to be sold at his shop.

Suda On Line, and Suda Consortium. *"Suda on Line: Byzantine Lexicography."* http://www.stoa.org/sol/.

Stratton-Kent, Jake (2010) *Geosophia: The Argo of Magic.* 2 vols, Encyclopedia Goetia. n. p.: Scarlet Imprint.

"Survival." (1970) *Off Our Backs* 1.12:19.

Thoms, William John (1858) *Early English Prose Romances, with Bibliographical and Historical Introductions.* London: Nattali & Bond.

Virgil, & H. Rushton Fairclough (1934) *Eclogues; Georgics; Aeneid I-VI; [Aeneid VII-XII; the Minor Poems].* Cambridge, Mass.; London: Harvard University Press ; W. Heinemann.

William of Auvergne, Bishop of Paris (1963) *Guilielmi Alverni Opera Omnia.* Frankfurt am Main: Minerva.

# WRITING FAERY

## A Tale of Viviane

## JACK WOLF

One of the most subtle members of the Faery Courts of Britain and France, whose mythos is often overshadowed and even, on occasion, conflated with that of her more famous, or infamous cousin Morgan le Faye,[61] Viviane,[62] also known as Neyve, Nimue and Ninianne, has fascinated me as a writer and a fan of Faerie ever since I first encountered her under a starry sky whilst reading for my English degree. Dark and fair, true and false in equal measure, Viviane is a fascinating, ambiguous and in the end highly sympathetic figure who has inspired and touched the hearts, minds and stories and brushes of writers and artists for almost a millennium. She is well known in literature and popular culture as the manipulative faerie seductress who wilfully steals, or cons, the knowledge of magic from the infatuated Merlin and then turns it against him; the power hungry seeker after forbidden mysteries.

In the French Vulgate Romance tales, which were written in the thirteenth century, Viviane is the beautiful young Faerie who enchants the enchanter Merlin in the Forest of Briosque, learning his secrets in exchange for the – assumedly false – promise of her love and the freedom of her body. [63] In the earliest version, however, the *Histoire du Merlin*, the love Viviane gives is genuine, if somewhat obsessive; she seals Merlin in a beautiful tower where he will lack for nothing in order to keep him entirely to herself. In the continuation, the *Suite du Merlin*, the relationship is much more sinister; when Merlin reveals to Viviane a lovers' tomb, she seals him

---

[61] An example of this occurs in the John Boorman film *Exacalibur* (1991) where Morgan Le Fay steals the dragon-spell from Merlin, and having done so entraps him in a pillar of ice.
[62] I am using the name and spelling "Viviane" throughout although some of the writers mentioned will have used other variations.
[63] H. Oskar Sommer, ed. *The Vulgate Version of the Arthurian Romances*. (Carnegie Institute of Washington, 1908. Reprinted University of Toronto, 2011.)

inside it alongside the lovers to die a slow death. In Malory's *Merlin*, which is the opening tale of the *Morte d'Arthur*, she first appears unnamed, an arm rising from the water: the Lady of the Lake. Later in the Cycle she is the innocent virgin whom Merlin ruthlessly pursues, who fearing the possibility of rape by him, persuades him to go by himself into a wondrous cave beneath a great stone – into which cave he had been trying to entice her – and magically imprisons him within it so effectively that *"he never come oute for all the craufte he could do"*.[64] Malory, interestingly, has a more sympathetic attitude toward Viviane- whom he calls Neyve - than may be expected, given that his sources would have included the *Suite du Merlin*, but it is important to remember that his story is about Arthur, and the fate of the old magician does not seem to have inspired as much dismay in him as it did in earlier writers. Although his Neyve is directly responsible for Arthur's loss of his most important councillor, she cannot be blamed for protecting herself against a sexual predator; and if that were not mitigation enough, Malory gives her the chance to redeem herself. She twice saves Arthur from attempts upon his life by Morgan le Fay, and eventually, by means of her magic, punishes the lady Ettarde for her mistreatment of Pelleas, and achieves a happy ever after ending for herself with the handsome young Knight.[65]

Leap forward to the Victorian period, and the poet Matthew Arnold, in the final section of his *Tristram and Iseult*, has Viviane entrap Merlin in his sleep by waving *"the fluttering wimple round"* nine times, in order to set herself free from a lover of whom she has become weary.[66] Tennyson, in *Idylls of the King*, distinguishes her from the benevolent Lady of the Lake, who gives Arthur his sword, and makes her into a villainous and cunning seductress, determined to gain complete power over her lover and mentor, which she uses to imprison him forever in a hollow oak.[67] Yeats describes her in less than complimentary fashion as The Witch Viviane, and has her lose her life in a dice game played against Time itself, which she cannot, of course, win, as Time cannot be defeated.[68] Viviane, naturally, tries anyway.

From a feminist perspective, of course, Viviane's refusal to behave herself, to know her place as Merlin's student, and her desire to be powerful turns her into the epitome, not of malevolence, as Tennyson would have it, but of the strong woman who must be punished, or censured because of her presumption. And indeed, despite the fact that the position of women in modern European society is – thankfully – unlike that of Mediaeval or

---

[64] Thomas Malory: "The War with the Five Kings", in Malory: *Works*, (OUP, 1971.) Malory does not quite say that Merlin would have raped Neyve, simply that he would not leave her alone and desist in his unwelcome attempts to "have hir maydynhode".
[65] Ibid, "Gawain, Iwain and Marhalt"
[66] Arnold, Matthew: "Tristram and Iseult" in *The Poems of Matthew Arnold 1840-1867* (reprinted Kessinger Publishing LLC 2004)
[67] Tennyson, Alfred Lord: *Idylls of the King* (Penguin 1996)
[68] Yeats, WB. "Time and the Witch Vivien" in *Collected Works of WB Yeats, Vol 1, The Poems, 2nd Edition* (Scribner, 1997)

Victorian times, in very few tales, from the Middle-Ages right up to the present day, does she receive much sympathy from the writer. For instance, in the recent U.K. BBC Television series *Merlin,* viewers will have encountered her as Nimue, the wicked sorceress who plots the downfall of Camelot and meets an end – though I doubt a final one – at the hands of the young Merlin, in a clever plot device that turns the story upon its head and returns to Merlin's hands the power that was stolen from him in – and in a sense, by - the earlier Merlin-Viviane stories.

In examining Viviane's modern mythos from a feminist perspective, it is of course appropriate – if not obligatory – to take a brief look at Marion Zimmer Bradley's Arthurian Novel, *The Mists of Avalon*[69]. In this vast, impressive and influential novel, which can be read as a lament for a putative pre-Christian past in which Goddess worship constitutes the primary religious spirituality of Britain, Zimmer Bradley tells the Arthurian story through the eyes of its many female protagonists. Like Tennyson, she divides the character into three: Viviane is depicted as the ruling Priestess of Avalon, a position which carries the title of Lady of the Lake, whilst Nimue and Niniane become the names of younger priestesses who independently enact different parts of the Viviane-Merlin story. Despite Zimmer-Bradley's focus on the feminine aspects of the story, and her refusal to condemn any of her Priestesses as being self-centredly power hungry or malevolent, all three priestesses still, meet unhappy ends: Viviane is killed by her son's foster brother, Balin; Niniane by her lover, Mordred; whilst Nimue kills herself in guilt after her seduction of Kevin, the Merlin of Britain, betrays him to Morgaine and to his death. Avalon falls, and with it both British Paganism and the right of women to be political and religious rulers. Goddess spirituality is to be absorbed into the figure of Mary and safeguarded by that most male dominated of organisations, the Catholic Church. All very sad; and once again, Viviane has unfortunately become the author's victim, whether Zimmer Bradley quite intended it to work out this way or not. [70]

Mary Stewart, writing just a few years before Zimmer Bradley, at the end of the seventies, takes a refreshingly different tack from all of this and does not cast Viviane (Niniane in this version) as a figure of malice; Merlin's loss of his power is depicted as almost a natural consequence of the increase in hers rather than an act of theft or treachery on her part. Their love is mutual and benevolent, but ultimately their relationship still founders upon its power inequality.[71]

---

[69] Zimmer Bradley, Marion: *The Mists of Avalon.* (Knopf, 1983)
[70] Although I do not imagine she intended to reinforce the message that a woman who seeks power must be punished, Zimmer Bradley's novel is set in the context of a world in which a Goddess religion *has* fallen to a patriarchal system, and from that point of view Avalon's fall, and that of the Ladies of the Lake, is tragically inevitable.
[71] Stewart, Mary, *The Last Enchantment*, (1979)

As a writer, I have taken it upon myself in my forthcoming novel *The Tale of Raw Head and Bloody Bones*[72] to create a psychological and literary space in which the Faery witch-woman Viviane can reveal herself without the distorting pressure of the literary trope that dictates that she must always, in one fashion or another, lose. Unlike Tennyson, I have sympathy for her as a character and a Faery being, and like Malory and Stewart I do not accept the logic that has seemed to dictate that a female character who shows spirit, or who refuses the advances of a man who is, quite frankly, out of order, must be punished. Unlike Zimmer Bradley, I do not see in the Lady of the Lake an inevitably tragic figure or a symbol of the fall of a pre Patriarchal golden age. I believe that she can instead function psychologically, ritually and on a literary level as a symbol of the woman who does not define herself by her relationship to any man. I do not by this mean to imply that Viviane is necessarily Dianic – her willingness to share her body with Merlin, whether out of love or ambition, gives the ready lie to this – but I do intend to suggest that this willingness does not grant any form of ownership over her body and her sexuality to the man she shares it with. Viviane belongs only to herself. My Viviane, then, (as much as she can be mine) is a lady who is allowed the narrative space and freedom to speak her mind, and to exist within her own power rather than having to steal it from a male Merlin.

Channelling Viviane in this way, allowing her to appear freely as she so desires, and to speak in her own voice without my attempting to constrain the woman or to disempower the witch, has been simultaneously revealing, fascinating, and liberating. I have tried to take her on her own terms, without prejudice, to examine what she really stands for and reject any moral yardstick that unthinkingly condemns her as wicked seductress or sorceress. The Lady who has emerged out of this process into my consciousness and onto the pages of my literary work has proved herself capricious, clever, acquisitive, sexually assertive and sly; at the same time generous, honest, untameable and possessed of a peculiar, childish innocence; in other words, the complex feminine intelligence of a real woman, and a veritable Queen of Faerie easily the equal of Titania, or her own narrative rival, Morgan le Fay.

Although I have primarily been dealing with Viviane as a character, both in this essay and throughout my interaction with her via my creative work, where she takes a speaking role, it seems clear that as a Faerie entity her presence in the narrative and in my own psyche whilst I am writing contributes energetically to the process of writing itself and the texture of the work produced. Nor does her effect stop there. Faeries are beings of change and flux, movement and instability, and any writer who allows them inside his or her writing must be prepared for surprises on many levels and

---

[72] Wolf, Jack, *The Tale of Raw Head and Bloody Bones* (forthcoming: Chatto and Windus, 2013) Although Viviane has a pivotal role in this narrative, as she does in Malory's, the novel, which is set in the seventeen fifties, is not a reworking of any of the Arthurian tales.

in unexpected places.[73] Viviane, in bringing her energy to my work, also brought it into my life and taught me a great deal about the unpredictability of creativity whilst upsetting my presumptions about women, men, manipulation, power, and love. Whilst writing her, I encountered, gave, and ran away from, obsessive love; I experienced from both ends power dynamics in relationships that were unhealthy and manipulative; I learned, in the end, that the only viable basis for love between two people is complete honesty, and the strength of will on both sides to let the loved one be who he or she wishes to be.

What I am describing is of course the process of encountering an archetype and coming to view it without cultural baggage and prejudice, to comprehend it as closely as possible to its essence and to integrate its teaching, in a positive way, into one's psyche and life – a difficult thing to attempt, but not impossible. Faerie exists upon the edge of consciousness, where archetype blends into entity and the boundaries between self and other become blurred. Psychologically, it is important to establish a relationship with archetypal parts of the self that is honest, fair, and unmediated by cultural norms and prior expectations of what is acceptable and what is not. A vision of archetypal Viviane seen through traditional eyes would be intensely negative and potentially terrifying – for the wrong reasons. Worse still would be an identification on an ego level with this vision, as that could lead to ones acting out destructive behaviour toward self and others. For any sort of creative artist, however, and especially a writer, encountering the Faerie and archetype Viviane has another inherent danger, and that is the formation of an ego identification not with her, but with Merlin.

The act and illusion of writing, and especially that of writing Faerie tales, is intensely magical. The writer creates, seemingly, a tangible something – a story – out of nothing – his own imagination; but in fact there is nothing tangible about a tale, and it does not spring out ex nihilo. A fiction is an illusion of being something, a glamour, in much the same way that a picture of a thing is not the thing it depicts. To create it, the writer must draw upon many different elements and sources, and alchemically muddle them all up in order for them to produce something new. He is the magician, mixing elements together in a crucible as does the figure depicted on the second major arcane card of the tarot.[74] Like the magician, or the shaman, he travels upon his imagination into the borderland where elements of faerie brush up against the limits of human consciousness.

---

[73] There are many books describing methods by which humans may contact the Faerie Realm. Wendy Berg's *Red Tree, White Tree* (Skylight Press, 2010) explains how Faeries and humans may work in partnership, while Hugh Mynne's *The Faerie Way* (Llewellyn, 1996) has many tips and exercises for anyone wishing to make Faerie contacts.
[74] I am thinking primarily here of the Thoth Tarot, as this is the deck with which I am personally familiar. The image, however, is archetypal.

Identification with Merlin, in a creative or a psychological context, can lead one into a situation where he or she, for women are not immune to the risk, becomes enchanted by one's own glamour and begins to believe himself more powerful than he or she really is. I am not exempt from this danger; however, when I catch myself daydreaming that I am superman I remind myself that Merlin's own loss of power at Viviane's hands can be interpreted as exactly this sort of warning: even the greatest magician made an ass of himself, behaved badly, and ended up stuck beneath a stone. The archetype of the magician, (with a capital M) therefore, has remained my unfulfillable fantasy and a part of my writerly psyche rather than coming to dominate my ego.

It is my belief, that when dealing with the Faerie Realm, whether as a writer, a magician or simply an individual who wishes to tune in to the energies and archetypes that dwell within, that any suggestion of uncontained egotism is highly likely to work to the detriment of the mental health of the human doing the dealing. Faeries, quite simply, enjoy bursting bubbles. However, even if this risk is avoided, the Faerie Realm has its own inherent dangers, which are harder to see simply because they are so obvious. Faery-land is beautiful; it is vast, compelling; it holds infinite potential; it can drive a human mad with both despair and delight, if he or she stays there too long. Again the warning implicit in Merlin's entrapment shouts aloud: we who make our magic with the Fae must beware falling into the eternal otherworldly trap of neurosis, narcissism or emotional disconnection from the prosaic and mundane human society in which we live.

The stories we write, or the pictures we paint, or the otherworldly contacts we establish, rewarding though they are, are not more important than the ordinary world of human beings in which we live. We must take responsibility, in the real world, for our actions and feelings, value the human people who surround us without attempting to manipulate or possess them, and try to understand them as real and subtle people, fair and dark in equal measure. We must try not to love them obsessively, as do both Merlin and Viviane in different versions of their story, but allow them freedom. We must resist the temptation to identify in real life with negative presentations of Merlin or Viviane, and to act out a pernicious relation toward our lovers and our selves that is more stereotype than archetype. Imprisonment, by our own carelessness, in a crystal tower can mean more than loss of power, whether this power be magical, psychological, emotional or physical; it can mean loss of self.

# Maids of Ice and Meadows

## Cliff Seruntine

In the highlands of Nova Scotia the early spring wind is yet cool, and as it passes over the low mountains it gathers many voices. From the spruce forest it collects whispers that sough like rangy ghosts. Through ancient maples it rattles, yet bare branches that creak and groan secrets like ornery old men. It brushes over the brambles and grasses of meadows gathering the susurration of innumerable Earth spirits. And for all that, there is more. It passes over ancient graveyards riddled with cracked, half-sunk tombstones and perhaps gleans mysteries from the wind-hum of those forlorn monuments. It blows by abandoned farmsteads where decaying cottages and sagging barns guard tales of the lives of the rural Gaels who settled here long ago. And here and there in this wild, rolling land it touches upon a home where it might even come by voices of ordinary folk. The ancient wind of spring hears so much. It is very wise. It has stories to tell, of things gone by, of forbidden mysteries, of perilous secrets that might yet wish to be known again . . . at least among the intrepid.

I believe it is so, for I have often roamed this wild country and listened to the wind, straining to catch its words. They are always elusive and the hearing of them, well, that is a thing one needs more than ears for. One needs another way of perceiving. One needs quiet, erudition and perhaps someplace green. And if one is very still and very cunning, one may just overhear one of the wind's oldest tales, that of the *glaistig uaine*: the green-clad lady.

To perceive the true depth of her tale, one would have to listen very close to the wind—for it seems the glaistig uaine has been many places, and known by many names, and her story is so old that it is faded and crisscrossed by wrinkled details that often seem to run counter to one another. In some places and at some times she was thought to be a tutelary spirit who stayed with families and oversaw their welfare. In other tales she was a being of the land and looked after the welfare of herbivores, most often cattle, ever a prized beast of the old Gaels. In a few odd, rare tales she is a bloodsucking creature, antithetical to mortal folk, though the wind says she looked kindly upon children and the affable dim-witted. But here in the highlands of Nova Scotia, a place where Gaelic is still spoken and some folk are still cautious of faerie rings in the deep forests, she is thought of as a keeper of deer and a warden of the farmstead, that is, if she is remembered at all. And among the Gaels of old Scotland and Ireland the glaistig is both a helper of shepherds and vengeful sprite. Whatever else, she is most certainly a complex being.

But wait. This anthology is a study of faerie queens, and clearly the glaistig is a rural being, a mere helper sprite, some have said. The folklorist John Campbell, who perhaps wrote most about her in his books *Superstitions of the Highlands & Islands of Scotland* (1900) and *Witchcraft & Second Sight in the Highlands & Islands of Scotland* (1902), stated: *"[The] glaistig and her near relation the brownie are among the most harmless [faeries]."*[75] He would seem to want to tell us she is just a tutelary being, or as we learn if we delve more deeply into the tales he recorded, a noble woman given an elfin nature by the Good Folk as a result of her great love for them. In either event, the glaistig is certainly nothing regal, right? Listen to the tales borne by the spring wind, a wind that passes at the crossroad of winter and summer, old and new, decay and rebirth, and perhaps a different picture shall emerge. If one studies deeply, and listens closely, I believe one will hear in the spring wind the tale of an entity that is far, far more than she seems . . . perhaps among the greatest of faerie queens.

Perhaps the first thing to ask of the wind is who are the faeries? The legends of faerie beings trace back millennia. In the *Colloquy of the Ancients* there is a tale of an encounter between St. Patrick and the shade of Caeilte. During their dialog a beautiful young faerie woman passes by. Patrick seems to sense the many years upon her and does not understand how she yet possesses such beauty and youth. Caeilte explains that she is of the Tuatha de Danann, the enchanted race who inhabited Ireland long before the children of Mil came and conquered it. Caeilte says that while mortal folk fade the Tuatha do not. Like gods, this otherworldly folk are immortal. Yet in *The Book of the Dun Cow* and *The Book of Leinster*, we are informed that the faerie folk are not gods. They are something between mortal and god, for the faerie folk share traits of both. Like people, they eat and drink, work and play, live and make love. Like gods, they are immune to time's entropy. And Campbell relates that they are something else, too—they are the sithchean, the silently moving people who traipse through the world as deftly as spirits, venturing about the countryside or just as easily into mortal dreams.

---

[75] Campbell, *Superstitions of the Highlands & Islands of Scotland*, 1900.

To be fair, Campbell was careful to use wording that described the sith not so much as spirits but as just another kind of people. He wrote they are *"the counterparts to mankind in person, occupations and pleasures"*. Campbell was a Christian minister, and the cosmology he had been indoctrinated into had no room for spirit entities beyond the biblical view. Spirits were either of the Hebrew god or of diabolic origin. But Campbell, himself a Gael, knew the Scots faerie mythology well, and he was only too aware that the faeries are portrayed in that mythology as complex beings: some good, some bad, and some indifferent. And the faerie mythology was very ancient, originating long before the first Christian myths ever came into being far in the East. The faerie mythology, having nothing to do with Christian concepts, could never fit comfortably into the biblical cosmology, and various entries by Campbell indicate he wrestled earnestly with that fact. For example, he wrote: *"[The fairies'] interference is never productive of good in the end, and may prove destructive. Men cannot therefore be sufficiently on their guard against them."* Such a statement is clearly in favour of the biblical cosmological notion that any spirit being not originating from and aligned directly with god is malignant. And yet in other entries he writes in defence of the faeries, noting they sometimes take care of forgotten children and persons who have wandered into dangerous places. Despite his solidly Christian education, he was compelled to be fair toward the faeries and wrote: *"[There] is observably a desire to make the Elves contemptible and ridiculous."*[76]

We see the same phenomenon — a compulsion to cast the faeries as undesirable despite a clear admiration of them—in the work of the seventeenth century minister-cum-folklorist, Robert Kirk, most famous for his book, *The Secret Commonwealth of Elves, Fauns and Faeries* (1691), and his later legendary abduction by the faeries. In the first chapter of *The Secret Commonwealth* Kirk likewise says that faeries are something between men and spirits, *"as were daemons thought to be of old"* — a clearly disapproving statement — but later in chapter nine, Kirk writes admiringly of the ancient faeries: *"As Birds and beasts, whose bodies are much used to the change of the free and open air, foresee storms; so those invisible people are more sagacious to understand by the Books of Nature things to come, than we, who are pestered with the grosser dregs of all elementary mixtures, and have our purer spirits choked by them."* (Transliteration to modern English, mine). Kirk, like Campbell, clearly admired the sithchean, and yet due to religious constraints often felt compelled to write of them in a darkly critical manner. It's an old, myopic pattern that is often seen when a new religious perspective overtakes an old. The beings of the old are diminished, sometimes made out to be wicked, and over the generations are relegated to the dark domains of the imagination. Certainly, if we look into the most ancient myths of faeries, past the Christian template of diminution and disdain, we see them become great and honourable beings full of enchantment and essential to the order of the natural world.

---

[76] Campbell, *Superstitions of the Highlands & Islands of Scotland*, 1. 1900.

But Campbell was, in the end, a man of truth, and so he felt compelled to write truthfully of their spirit natures: *"[They are] unsubstantial and unreal, ordinarily invisible, noiseless in their motions, and having their dwellings underground, in hills and green mounds of rock or earth".* He was describing the preternatural traits of spirit entities, though the biblical taboos of his time prevented him from merely calling them spirits lest he should be forced to equate them with devilry.

The spring wind has encountered faerie myths throughout time and all around the world. The aboriginals of the American far north call them Inuqun, and the Mi'kmaq (Mee*Mah) aboriginals of the Canadian Maritimes thousands of miles away call them Megumoowesoo. The Acadians of Canada's Maritime provinces and the American state of Louisiana call them les feys. Even if we look to a culture as far away and alien to the West as that of Japan, we find an ancient awareness of the faerie folk. Shinto - the Japanese spirituality - teaches that all Nature is rife with wights similar to elves, hobgoblins and other sprites. They call these entities Kami, a term that describes deific beings and minor spirits alike. The minor Kami, like the faerie folk, abide in the elements: the land, water and wind. Practitioners of Shinto recognize that while they are everywhere, some places are especially enchanted, nexuses where Kami and mortals may intermingle. These sacred places often become shrines or are designated sacred natural spaces. And we find evidence of faerie belief in the myths of modern day survivals of primitive cultures and in virtually every extinct culture around the world. Faerie lore is a universal phenomenon that traces back as far as our awareness.

Back in the Old World of the Gaels, in Ireland and Scotland, there were very ancient myths of an old sith (shee) dame called the Cailleach, a Gaelic word meaning old woman or hag. Deer were very precious to her, making her something of a shepherdess, for MacKenzie tells us in *Scottish Folk Lore and Folk Life* (1935) that deer were a kind of faerie cattle, when he writes: *"On milk of deer I was reared. In milk of deer was I nurtured. On milk of deer beneath the ridge of storms. On crest of hill and mountain."*[77] In fact, many animals, including those from which milk could be drawn, were precious to her, for MacKenzie also writes, *"[The Cailleach] had great herds and flocks to which she gave her protection—nimble footed deer, high horned cattle, shaggy grey goats, black swine, and sheep with snow-white fleeces. She charmed her deer against huntsmen and when she visited a deer forest, she helped them to escape from the hunters."* The Cailleach looked after her wild and domestic flocks throughout the landscape and warded them from overly opportunistic hunters and poachers. In many tales the Cailleach punished overzealous hunters for pursuing deer into forests and glens she considered hers (a recollection of the inviolate sacred groves of European pagan faiths long gone). As we can see, this old fey woman was an ardent protector of many creatures.

---

[77] Mackenzie, *Scottish Folk Lore and Folk Life*, 1935:204.

But the old woman had more to her than shepherding. The legend of the Cailleach Bhéarra tells us she was so old she could not remember her own age. Her origins traced back into the most distant racial memory of the Gaels and beyond, and the deeper down that way we look, the greater she appears. We discover in those ancient myths that she was a keeper of winter. Numerous legends tell how the Cailleach would come forth in late winter to make or unmake the season. It was said that she would go out a-gathering firewood in late February and you could tell how long she would maintain winter by the fineness of the day. If she meant to gather much firewood, she would make the day clear to help her work along. But if the day were bitter, it meant she had little need of more firewood so spring was sure to come soon.

There are many other myths affirming the jurisdiction of the Cailleach over the elemental power of cold. It was said the Cailleach possessed a slachdan, a wand or staff that carried cold within it. If she should strike the ground with the slachdan frost would form there. Nothing would grow again at that spot unless she willed the cold away. But she did not yield up that cold easily. Each spring she fought a battle with the waxing warmth and one legend has it that she did not relent until she was herself turned into a cold stone around which moisture collected. Only when she became a stone could the summer season of growth recommence.

The tales of the spring wind indicate the Cailleach is a goddess of ice, and her heyday may well have been a far more ancient era when great glaciers covered vast regions of Europe. In that era was she even then perceived as old? Perhaps she was in her prime, the sexual goddess portrayed in Ice Age and Stone Age Venus figurines found throughout Europe. A fertility goddess is a creative being, and the Cailleach's creativity may well be expressed in the legends describing how she shaped the landscape. It was said she could become gigantic, so large that rocks dropped from her skirt's pockets and became the hills and mountains of the landscape. Her skirts may be a metaphor for the long-gone glaciers that once dominated the land. Glaciers are great rivers and oceans of ice, and though ice seems solid it is in fact plastic and flows, far too slowly for the eye to perceive but glaciers indeed march slowly across the land by only inches or feet each year. In the far north of Alaska, I often saw the slow but inexorable progress of glaciers while sailing off the southern coast. Those glaciers flowed between the mountains, cutting vast gorges, and when they reached the coast from time to time huge chunks broke away, hundreds of thousands of tons of ice crashing into the sea with a sound to rival thunder, raising waves that coursed miles across the water. When this happened it was said the glaciers were calving.

As the glaciers moved over the land they broke away and carried vast quantities of stone, and wherever the land descended there the glaciers gathered to melt over time, leaving piles of detritus in the form of huge rocks, gravel and finely ground up stone silt. Over time, such deposits could become hills of immense proportions. If the Cailleach is Old Lady Winter, might we not liken the glaciers to her skirts? Then we can easily understand the myths telling us how stones spilled from her skirts to become features of the landscape. The prolific mythologist, Donald MacKenzie, also remarks in *Scottish Folk-lore and Folk Life* that glaistigs formed land features in such ways.

Some legends add that the Cailleach carried a hammer which she used to reshape the land. If the legends are an ancient recollection of a powerful Ice Age goddess, they also indicate very ancient peoples understood glaciers' awesome power to destroy and remake geography. As they flow, they press whole landscapes flat, drop massive boulders called '*erratics*', carve valleys out of rises and even sheer away whole faces of mountains. There is a huge mountain in the Chugach range in the state of Alaska, not far from the village of Glacier View, that resembles a massive dark pyramid. The unusually shaped mountain was created by the action of great Ice Age glaciers miles high flowing obliquely along it, sheering away the irregularities of its surface as they went. In a metaphorical sense, the hammer of the Cailleach, Keeper of Winter, is ice. Whether we speak of the American north or post-glacial Europe, the effect of glacial ice is the same. These great flowing skirts of ice dropped entire hills of stone and smashed the land, reforming it entirely. This makes the Cailleach a kind of creatrix. Not a true creator deity, but something vastly powerful—a primal force of Nature. Yet between god and mortal and spirit, she must be a faerie being.

But the spring wind knows well how times change, and it carries with it an ancient truth: winter must inevitably give way to summer. And likewise, the Ice Age gave way to a new warm era—the Holocene Age which started 12,000 years ago and continues to the present. If the Cailleach was indeed Old Lady Winter, she diminished as the springtime of the world progressed. And as she did, she transformed from the giantess creatrix to something smaller, lesser. She had to make way for a more fecund deity of warmth and growth. Some mythologists say she yielded to Brighde, a creatrix who ruled summer. But Brighde is a great goddess while the Cailleach is only a faintly remembered shadow. They are mismatched. Perhaps we should look to another entity as her counterpart, something likewise diminished. But speaking of diminishment . . .

The Ice Ages had fostered the evolution of huge creatures called megafauna like the cave bear, the dire wolf, and the Irish elk. As an example of the size of these creatures in comparison to their modern descendants, consider the Irish elk. It looked very much like the red or whitetail deer, but it was as big as a moose with a rack of antlers two to three yards broad. The legends of the Cailleach to this very day are so strongly consistent that she was a protectress of animals that it is not hard to imagine she may have been a warding Nature goddess to Ice Age peoples, a being whose task was to oversee the wildlife upon which they were so dependent even as she brought balance to the action of ice, at once a destructive and creative force on the land and essential to the survival of the megafauna.

But many things diminished with the passing of the glaciers. Dire wolves vanished, leaving behind only the smaller gray wolves. Cave bears became a memory, and only brown bears and black bears harkened back to them. And the great Irish elk perished, leaving in their shadow only their smaller kindred deer. In this era of diminution, even elder myths were reduced. In the far north, giants gave way to the anthropomorphic Scandinavian gods of more human proportions. The great ice goddess who shaped the land and warded the megafauna became the much frailer Cailleach. Even mortal folk shrank. From Cymru comes the *Mabinogi* which records *The Dream of Rhonabwy*, wherein we read that Arthur perceived the folk of Britain had become *"little men"* after his era. The trend is clear: with the march of time into the present, on the physical and mythological planes, the world was becoming a lesser place.

\* \* \* \* \* \* \* \* \*

At some point in the history of the Gaels, the glaistig appears. Known as the Glaistig Uaine, pronounced GWAHSH\*chik AHN\*ya, her story is so ancient its origins are unclear . . . much like the Cailleach. But the myths of her turn up in Scotland, Ireland and the Isle of Man, and probably elsewhere under other names. And though some folklorists believe the lore of the Glaistig did not follow the Gaelic pioneers across the sea to their settlement in Nova Scotia, the wind whispers of her appearance in stories from the Scots-Canadian island of Cape Breton where she turns up as a tutelary spirit, looking after families, warding forest creatures and showing interest in homes where beloved family members have passed away. One story related to me by a Nova Scotia Gaelic teacher tells of a tall, pale lady who lived about the lands and forests of a rural dwelling in Cape Breton. No one was sure what this being did exactly, but she seemed to have an interest in the wild creatures and perhaps the cattle, and she showed a special interest whenever members of the household passed away, at which times she might be seen wandering near the house, as if trying to listen in on the family mourning within the dwelling.[78]

Sometimes, when the glaistig appears in myth as a fuath, a part earth/part water spirit, she is wicked and intends harm toward humans. In those legends it is said she might try to lure persons into her clutches whereupon she will suck their blood or kill them through some other gruesome means. However, John Campbell, in *Superstitions of the Highlands & Islands of Scotland*, leaves no doubt that it is a mistake to perceive the glaistig as malevolent. More often, when the glaistig appears, she is a benevolent being who is kind to children and the mentally infirm, and concerned for the welfare of animals. She is a tutelary being who looks after the land and develops attachments to the families that live where she dwells. Campbell

---

[78] From the oral tradition of Nova Scotia Gaels, related to the author by a native Gaelic speaker and teacher with the Oifis Iomairtean na Gàidhlig, 2012.

notes the glaistig *"had sympathy with the tenant"*, but as one would expect of a Nature entity, if the family left, she stayed with the land.

Campbell adds that the glaistig was one of the human race *"who had a Fairy nature given to her."* It is curious, therefore, that many of her legends indicate her allegiance would be focused upon the land, wild creatures, even certain old structures. Aside from looking after children and impaired adults, she appears to feel little obligation toward humans. When she wards a family's cattle, it is for some kind of recompense, such as milk, and if she does not get it she is quick to abandon her post. Her myth is, then, a kind of transformation story—changing from mortal perspective to Nature-centric perspective. Such a myth would indicate that a love of Faerie necessitated adopting sith values, behaviours and their intimate concern for the natural world.

The glaistig might sometimes look after a dwelling much in the way of a bruanighe, tending the chambers and even engaging in spinning and woodworking. She might just as well tend the barn and the farm's creatures. Often she undertook tasks such as keeping the young animals away from cows and does in milk, a needful occupation as any keeper of dairy animals can attest, for the young will attempt to drink the mother's milk long after it is necessary and when the dairymaid attempts to milk the animal in the morning she will find only an empty udder. Some of what she does, she does for love of the labour. For some of her labours, she expects trade, usually in the form of milk or some other reward directly related to her work. And in the way of faeries, if mere payment as opposed to trade is rendered, she is finished with the work and is never seen again. Often this odd behaviour - as if taking offense at payment - has stymied students of faerie lore, but it seems to say clearly that faeries, in the way seen among aboriginals throughout the world, shunned the human invention of economy. They worked gladly for practical trade, i.e., labour for milk. Payment, though, as in money or a suit for service in the field, was abstract and confounding . . . so much so it drives them off.

While the word Cailleach refers to a haggardly woman of immense age, the Glaistig legends often refer to a young woman partial to the wearing of green dresses. Like a satyr, her upper body might appear to be that of a beautiful maiden but her feet might appear as cloven hooves and her legs might even be that of a goat or deer. It is uncertain if this description is a post-Christian insertion into the myth—an attempt to make the glaistig appear sinister. As earlier noted, in the Christian cosmology any spirit entity not linked directly to the biblical cosmology was diabolic and cloven-hooved beasts were strongly associated with the devil in the Western European mind. But if the description is accurate to the pre-Christian concepts, it would show a powerful link between the glaistig and grazing and browsing herbivores. This might explain, in part, her penchant for looking after them. It would also reflect her own character as a Nature being and ward.

When we consider the Cailleach's deep wintry origins as a creatrix shaper of the land who diminished to become a much lesser keeper of animals and cold, we see a being who has gone from goddess to faerie. And if we examine the glaistig closely, we see a being of ancient origin who also wards animals and who is herself part deer or goat, things sacred to the Cailleach, but who has gone from mortal noble woman to faerie. It is as if the forces of myth contrive to bring the Cailleach and glaistig to the same nexus: a meeting of mortal, spirit and divine transformation and a melding of elemental forces, with the Cailleach as the winter element and the glaistig—keeper of verdant farms and productive cattle—the summer element. They would, in fact, seem to be two faces of the same coin. And enveloped in myths of deity and nobility . . . their origin myths strongly indicate regality.

From folklore recorded as early as the seventeenth century, like *The Secret Commonwealth*, to the last great collections published in the early twentieth century, such as Evans-Wentz's *The Fairy Faith In Celtic Countries*, we can develop a solid sense of the late Celtic perception of faerie character. And of all the things that might be noted of the character of the Cailleach and glaistig, what seems to stand out most is the reason in the way of aboriginals or even animals. Campbell illustrates this with numerous stories of chance encounters with them. One, *The Wife of Ben-Y-Ghloe*, tells of a pair of hunters who seek shelter from a sudden snowstorm and receive benevolent care from a strange, silent hag (cailleach) described as having two bare arms of great length, a grizzled look and a terrifying visage. The hag not only shelters them, she abides Gaelic custom and shows hospitality by feeding them. Yet in the tale of *Donald Son of Patrick*, we see a mortal mistreating the Cailleach. Upon nightfall, the Cailleach approaches Donald, a fox hunter, to ask for shelter in his bothy and a bit of the venison he has roasted over a fire. Donald obstinately turns her away and even allows his dogs to snap and snarl at her. Here the Cailleach is longsuffering in the same way as many animals, persisting in her entreaties while failing to understand human greed and obstinacy, and come sunup she departs without so much as an ill word. In still another tale, *Mac Ian Year*, we read of the glaistig visiting a legendary highland thief and his brother, Ronald, at their camp. Ian was napping while Ronald roasted venison, and she asked for some but Ronald selfishly refused. Ian intervened on her behalf and ever after she showed unwavering favour to him, but after Ian passed away many years later she left Ronald without a backward glance. In all these tales we see the Cailleach and glaistig reason with kindness where possible, incomprehension of human avarice and unswerving loyalty to goodness. Sadly, such reasoning is far more characteristic of wild animals and even domestic dogs than humans. And such common reasoning reflects the same heart and mind—another reason to believe the Cailleach and glaistig are but different faces of the same coin.

Like all old things, the Cailleach and the glaistig are complex. Like all vast things, they present many faces depending on the time and place they are witnessed. Attempting to understand them through the hazy media of myth and folklore gives an apparently contradictory picture, for it leaves us in the position of the three blind men who tried to apprehend an elephant: one perceiving its legs like pillars, another its trunk like a snake, yet another its flank like a wall. But these entities, quite possibly the dual faces of a single queen of summer and winter, depending on her aspect... perhaps it is inevitable they are so enigmatic to us. Apart from their great age, they are through and through beings of Nature, and the human mind is far from Nature in this era. The ways of wind and cold and deer, and all the other old, wild things that are so much a part of her are all but forgotten. And so maybe the real way back to understanding her is not through evermore far ranging attempts to decipher dimly remembered myths, but to engage, like the shamans and witches of old, the wild and enchanted side of ourselves that is also, at heart, regal and fey.

## Bibliography

Bollard, John K. (2006) *The Mabinogi*. Llandysul: Gomer

Campbell, John (1900) *Superstitions of the Highlands & Islands of Scotland*. James MacLehose; Glasgow

D'Este, Sorita & David Rankine (2009) *Visions of the Cailleach*. London: Avalonia

Gimbutas, Marija (2006) *The Language of the Goddess*. London: Thames & Hudson

Kirk, Robert (1691) *The Secret Commonwealth of Elves, Fauns and Faeries*. Aberfoyle

Mackenzie, Donald (1935) *Scottish Folk-Lore and Folk Life*. London: Blackie & Son

Ono, Sokyo (2004) *Shinto: the Kami Way*. Ph.D.

O'Grady, Standish Hayes (trans) (2008) *The Colloquy With the Ancients*. USA: Evergreen Review Inc.

# TRANSATLANTIC FAIRY QUEEN

Helen Adam's Fairy Inspiration, Masks and Veils

## KATIE STEWART

Rather than mere myth, the otherworld of fairy was a reality for the Scottish-born poet Helen Adam (1909-1993). Its queen appeared in Adam's work, particularly in her reinvention of the ballad tradition, but also in hybrid form in the pantheon of regal, bold, and often deadly female characters that Adam created in her forays into theatre and the visual arts. Adam's own fairy qualities – her sense of play, spectacle and non-conformity – aided her in the creation of a unique persona which helped her navigate a path through the literary and art worlds of San Francisco and New York. This essay stands as both a recovery of an individual artist and a revision of the lineages of the magical and irrational in poetry and art.

Outside the poetry community which supported Adam through friendship, collaboration and publication after she settled in the United States, Adam remains relatively unknown. But since the mid-1990s her status has been under revision with Adam's work being read as a part of the San Francisco Literary Renaissance[79] and in the field of women writers of the Beat Generation.[80] The main scholar of Adam's work to date is Kristin Prevallet, who worked directly in the Helen Adam Archive at the University of Buffalo to compile *A Helen Adam Reader* (2007), which included poetry, prose, correspondence, interviews and other previously scattered material.[81] The late Scottish makar Edwin Morgan provided a rare response from the Scottish poetry establishment when he commented at a lecture in 1999 that

---

[79] See Michael Davidson. *The San Francisco Renaissance: Poetics and Community at Mid-century*. 1989.
[80] Adam appeared in the *'precursors'* section of Brenda Knight. *Women of the Beat Generation: The Writers, Artists and Muses at the Heart of a Revolution*. 1996.
[81] Most of the biographic details I include are sourced from Prevallet's introduction to the reader.

Adam was a writer who had found her poetic voice only after leaving Scotland: *"Adam is possibly unique in the sense that she would never have made anything of her poetry, even though she wrote a lot of it, if she remained in her native place. She was a latent poet who needed the jolt of an entirely different environment to bring to the surface what was subterraneanly there."*[82] Morgan's view points to the influence of the poet's movement across the Atlantic and west across the American continent to the nurturing literary and arts community of San Francisco.

Adam was born in Glasgow in 1909 into a financially-secure and culturally-privileged environment. Her father was a Presbyterian minister, which afforded the education, mobility and connections which would enable Adam's literary career. She cites her earliest experiences of poetry and song as nursery rhymes,[83] the works of William Blake,[84] the Scottish hymn book[85] and the old ballads.[86] With these external resources and what would prove to be amazing internal creative resources, Adam began reciting original poetry to her mother Isabella, who acted as scribe. Thus her first book of poetry – *The Elfin Pedlar and Tales told by Pixy Pool* was published in 1923 when Adam was fourteen years old. It consists of poems Adam wrote between the ages of four and twelve which contemplate nature, the fairies and a Christian God. The poems are written in the English *lingua franca* with the occasional Scots word adding a rustic sheen, and utilises self-consciously literary devices typical of Victorian verse. Themes such as nostalgia and romantic enchantment appear uncanny coming from a writer so young.

The influence of Adam's mother on the book's authorship can only be speculated. But the exceptionality of young Adam's achievement is noted in a foreword to the book written by a family friend, the Rev. John A. Hutton. The feat is *"so remarkable that it has been felt that someone should stand sponsor for its bona fides".*[87] Hutton suggests that there exist *"elect minds, so delicate and rare that they can mediate between us and the Father of Light in Whom is no darkness,"*[88] highlighting the Christian influence but failing to anticipate the developing thread of divine feminine influence that would characterise Adam's oeuvre. Hutton draws attention to the vital maternal lineage when he reports that Adam's *"mother's people had [...] a noted gift of verse".*[89] Prevallet notes that the work fitted snugly into the *'kailyard'* vision of Scottish literature which gave sentimental portrayals of rural Scottish life and indeed, the book was

---

[82] Edwin Morgan. *Scotland and the World: Edinburgh Book Festival Post Office Lecture.* 1999. PN Review, 26.2 (Nov-Dec), pp. 14-23. The post of Scots Makar is equivalent to that of poet laureate.
[83] Adam 2007:331.
[84] Ibid, 2007:335.
[85] Adam states that *'it does have good tunes, set to preposterous travesties of the gorgeous Biblical language [...] there are only two hymns I remember as poetry'* (2007:335). She is likely referring to *The Scottish Hymnary*, published in 1898 and going through various editions thereafter.
[86] Adam states she was *'practically brought up on the old ballads'* (2007:335).
[87] 1923:vi.
[88] 1923:vii-viii.
[89] 1923:viii.

commercially well-received and established Adam as a child prodigy on the literary scene.[90] It also resonated with the fashion for fairy, which was a vestige of the popularity of Victorian romance and fantastic literature, and also stemmed from the *'Celtic Twilight'*, the literary and art movement initiated in Ireland.[91]

Adam was exposed to the different landscapes of Scotland due to her father's peripatetic work and on family holidays. She stated that: *"all my strongest memories are of Scottish countrysides, and the extraordinary unearthly quality in the lonely places, in the moors and glens [...] that weird quality that Scotland has, when you're really alone"*.[92] These memories would offer a point of stability – a landscape where the physical and non-physical intersect to draw upon in her work, particularly in the ballad form, but also a foundation which to exploit for the creation of a personal mythology. While she was studying at the University of Edinburgh, a second book of verse, *Shadow of the Moon*, was published which developed the early fairy themes into more mature gothic and biblical imagery including a long poem *'The Caravan of Stars'*, which depicts Satan collaborating with the stars in order to steal the moon.[93] Only Lilith is accepted by Satan in exchange for the moon's return, but the terms of the pact ensure that the standard patriarchal marital relationship will be threatened by external influence: *"He shall hunger for the earth's dark breast"*.[94] Adam later commented: *"I became so horrified by the rubbish I had written that I stopped writing and didn't start again until I was about thirty"*,[95] thereby effacing her early feats of imagination, craft and discipline.

After their father died the family unit of Adam, her sister Pat and their mother moved to London in 1933, with the sisters pursuing their respective careers in writing and illustration. They would continue to live together and have a creative partnership for the rest of their lives, and neither would marry. The facts as presented by Prevallet suggest a parasitic relationship, one that enabled Adam's literary production to the detriment of Pat's freedom and aspirations. Pat was the one who kept a steady job, although she was a published novelist. She was interested in men, but Helen reportedly *"scared away all her suitors"*.[96] Photographs of their arrival in New

---

[90] 2007:7. The term *'kailyard'* literally means *'cabbage patch'* and after appearing in the literary press in 1895 became synonymous with Scottish Victorian literature as a whole, that which is *'characterised by a provincial outlook, a predilection for romance over realism, an excessive focus on rural as opposed to urban settings, and a tendency to evade social and industrial issues'* (Nash 2007:14). Still in use over a hundred years later, the term is often used to refer to what critics deem to be *'wrong ways of writing about Scotland, whether this be at the level of style, content or outlook on Scottish life'* (ibid, 2007:14).
[91] See W. B. Yeats. 1893. *The Celtic Twilight: Men and Women, Dhouls and Fairies*. London: Lawrence and Bullen and Lady Gregory. 1904. *Gods and Fighting Men: The Story of the Tuatha de Danann and of the Fianna of Ireland*. London: John Murray. The former work contains folk tales collected by Yeats and the latter puts Irish fairy lore into context by tracing the epic battles of Irish founding myths.
[92] Adam 2007:335.
[93] Adam, Helen Douglas. 1929. *Shadow of the Moon*. London: Hodder and Stoughton.
[94] Adam 2007:398.
[95] Prevallet 2007:10.
[96] Ibid, 2007:54.

York encapsulate their different personalities: Pat has a natural beauty, smiling as she poses while embracing her mother; Helen poses alone, dressed in a sundress and sunbonnet, her right hand held aloft behind her head in a theatrical gesture as she surveys the panorama of New York Harbour and, metaphorically, contemplates the American dream.[97]

The family had travelled to United States to attend a wedding in 1939, but the outbreak of war in Europe meant that they decided to stay. They lived variously on the East Coast but settled in San Francisco in 1949. Adam had been working with ballad material since her return to poetry and she began to attend workshops at the Poetry Center led by one of the leading lights of the poetry community, Robert Duncan. This inaugurated a decisive relationship for both, what Beat generation luminary Allen Ginsberg referred to as a *'mystic marriage'*.[98] Duncan credited Adam with creating a link to the visionary tradition of William Blake and the Romantic poets, and he in turn promoted Adam as a *'Nurse of Enchantment'*.[99] Prevallet argues that he *'partly invented'* Adam *"by projecting onto her [his] desire for some authentic link to the ballad tradition"*, and thus she *"gradually began to perceive herself as a kind of medium of the 'authentic' ballad form"*.[100] Her younger contemporary, the poet Ruth Weiss recalls Adam being *'given more respect'* by the poetic authorities in San Francisco in the 1950s because of her age.[101] Her sexuality posed no threat to the largely gay poets she befriended.

Despite the incongruity of a balladeer in the midst of a group of experimental, free verse aficionados, Adam resonated with them. This was due to her interest in folk material as subject matter, the stories and myths of the people, and as style through her use of the vernacular.[102] But it was also due to her *'attention to performance'*,[103] her insistence on poetry as an embodied, dynamic utterance with a power comparable to that used in ritual or incantation. Both these elements come together in the ballad form. Rather than the English verse of her early work, Adam was using the Scots tongue – but it was a form appropriated from the ballads rather than the language spoken in her family. In her essay *'A Few Notes on the Uncanny in Narrative Verse'* Adam throws the fairy realms of Scotland into relief and provides a source for her study of ballads.[104] Adam notes that *"the world of the*

---

[97] See Prevallet 2007:13. Adam dressed with style and flair, careful of the image she presented to the world. She loved dressing up, and as she got older added a few esoteric touches - a turban, an art deco brooch, or a billowing fabric with a cosmic pattern – to create a unique image.
[98] Naropa Poetic Audio Archive, 2001. Helen Adams and Robert Duncan reading – Part 1 (June 9, 1976). [online] Available at:
<http://www.archive.org/details/naropa_helen_adams_and_robert_duncan> [Accessed 5th February 2012].
[99] Prevallet 2007:20.
[100] Ibid, 2007:21.
[101] Grace and Johnson 2004:73. The poet weiss chooses to present her name in lower case.
[102] Adam had a liberal attitude to poetic diction and in addition to using Scots and English, she experimented with American speech patterns and slang in what she referred to as her 'blues ballads'.
[103] Prevallet 2007:3.
[104] First published in The Poetry Society of American Bulletin, (Spring 1980), 70:3-15.

Border Ballads *is almost entirely Pre-Christian, with its stern 'eye for an eye, and tooth for a tooth' sense of revenge, and its wonderful come-and-go with Nature. Birds talks to maidens, seals doff their skins and become men, Elf Land is as near as the green wood, and ghosts are as real, and as taken for granted, as human beings'*.[105] She includes a version of *Tam Lin*, the tale of mortal Janet's rescue of her lover, the eponymous enchanted knight, from the Queen of the Fairies. Tam recalls his first encounter with the queen:

> *There blew a wind out o' the north*
> *A bleak wind and a snell,*
> *A drowsiness came over me*
> *And frae my horse I fell;*
> *The Queen o' Fairies she took me*
> *In yon green hill to dwell.*[106]

He admits it is *'pleasant'* in the subterranean fairyland, but has the fear that he will be given to Hell by the fairies as their next due levy or *'tithe'*.[107] Adam suspects that if Tam had not feared this threat he would have been quite happy to stay with the queen. In the ballad the queen has an intangible presence, she speaks *'out o' a bush o' broom'* which Adam likens to God speaking to Moses from the burning bush.[108]

Adam's attitude to the Scottish fairy world is revealed in a saying which she quotes: *'If a man tells you he has seen the Fairies, look if he be shaken, / If he be not terrified be sure he has not seen'*.[109] They are *'dangerous, proud, often terrible spirits, akin to the Pagan gods of the heath and the forest'*, more menacing than *'the playful and mischievous elves of England'*.[110] She cites the following lines which depict Janet's wait for the fairy host as among the most magical lines in literature: *'About the dead hour o' the night/ She heard the bridles ring'*.[111] Indeed, the ring of the horses' bridles seems uncannily vivid. It is an example of what Adam called *'the grue'*, which was a *'spine-tingling shudder'*, an unearthly feeling created by true poetry and experienced in the body rather than the mind.[112] It was this feeling Adam sought in her study of ballads and which she attempted to translate in her writing and performance.

---

[105] 2007:352.
[106] Adam 2007:359. When Adam states that she was 'practically brought upon on [...] the Border Ballads of Scotland' (352) it is unclear whether it is an oral or textual source she is referring to. Her version of *'Tam Lin'* resembled that one presented as *'The Young Tamlane'* in Child (1859), vol. 1. A source for many of Child's ballads was Walter Scott's *Minstrelsy of the Scottish Border* (1802).
[107] Ibid.
[108] Ibid, p. 363.
[109] Ibid.
[110] Ibid. Adam is perhaps generalising here, but it would be of interest to contrast the Scots fairy mythology which came from a Germanic or Scandinavian source, as Scott (1802) does, with the depictions of the supposed gentler fairies of England.
[111] Ibid.
[112] Prevallet 2007:23.

Adam also delights in the ballad *Thomas the Rhymer*, which tells the story of a hero who willingly journeys into fairyland after meeting its queen. Rather than a voice speaking out of a bush of broom, she has a tangible and enchanting physical form:

> *Her shirt was o' the grass-green silk,*
> *Her mantle o' the velvet fyne;*
> *At ilka tett of her horse's mane,*
> *Hung fifty siller bells and nine.*[113]

He mistakes her for the *'Queen of Heaven'*, but she answers that she is the *'Queen of fair Elfland'*, with *'Elfland'* or *'Elphame'* being a rendering of fairyland in Scottish and northern English folklore.[114] Adam hears magic in this ballad's description of their journey, quoting these lines in her essay:

> *On they rade on and further on,*
> *And they waded rivers abune the knee,*
> *And they saw neither sun nor moon*
> *But they heard the roaring of the sea.*
>
> *It was mirk, mirk, night,*
> *There was nae star light,*
> *And they waded through red blood to the knee,*
> *For a' the blood that's shed on earth*
> *Rins through the springs o' that country.*[115]

The depiction of their entry into fairyland, wading through a river of blood, surely contains the chilling, visceral quality of the *'grue'*. By examining several of Adam's poems I will place them in context of her reading of traditional Scottish ballads.

*The Birkenshaw* is a ballad written by Adam in Scots which takes place in ancient space and time. The Birkenshaw is a magical realm inside a hill encircled by trees with silver branches, which Adam locates beside Badenoch in north-east Scotland.[116] Inside the hill the Elf Queen resides, lonely in her *'heather-bell bed'*, so she hunts with her maidens in the misty, haunted surrounding glen for the hearts of men.[117] The queen is ruthless and unforgiving:

> *Their Queen has a hert like a crystal wave,*
> *A wave o' the murderous sea.*

---

[113] Child 1859, vol. 1:227.
[114] Ibid.
[115] 2007:364.
[116] The subterranean fairy dwelling echoes the Irish mythology presented by Gregory in which the Tuatha de Danann escaped into parallel worlds or in simpler terms, underground, after their defeat at the hands of the Gael. The Celtic fairy folk or sidhe are believed to be their descendants. See Gregory op. cit.
[117] Ibid, p. 94.

> *She'll ha' nae mercy on any young man*
> *Nae matter how braw he be.*[118]

A magical human harper named Robin o' Leith appears, boasting of having once played his music in Atlantis, hinting at Adam's reading of the occult. The queen offers him gold to play in The Birkenshaw, but Robin's music cannot be bought. So the queen and her fairies hunt Robin through earth and heaven, and in the traditional ballad conceit he transforms into a variety of forms – a tom cat, an eagle, a seal – to escape her clutches.[119] Robin is captured and taken into The Birkenshaw where the queen vows to keep him there in a tithe of a thousand years. But as a true match for her magic, he transforms himself into a holy harp that she dare not touch. In this form he sings *'the truth o' love'*, which he evidently learned in Atlantis, a language the Queen evidently does not speak.[120] The dynamics of unrequited desire are played out as Robin is unattainable to the queen, though held captive in her realm where *'A thousand years are but as a day/And a day a thousand years'*.[121]

A more obscure view of the fairy realm and its elusive queen is presented in Adam's *In and Out of the Horn-beam Maze*. The poem is written in standard English but contains the pulse of the ballad meter in its telling of the story of four children who played in a *'Troy Town'* maze:

> *They felt no fear, for the maze was small.*
> *Its horn-beam hedges not very tall,*
> *And the huge, hot sun shone high over all,*
> *Over the maze, the maze.*[122]

Three children in turn run into the centre of the maze, with each one experiencing a different dark omen – Lenard sees a *'cloven hoof print on the sand'*; Nancy sees *'a great hawk moth'* soar up from *'soft, whispering grass'*; Jason encounters *'cold, shivering mist'* which kisses his mouth.[123] Yet Flora dances into the centre of the maze singing *'a half forgotten song/In the Queen of Elfhame's praise'*:

> *When she reached the centre nothing was there.*
> *Nothing! Nothing! nowhere, nowhere!*
> *Only silence, and radiant air.*
> *She never ran out of the maze.*[124]

---

[118] Ibid.
[119] This occurs in *'Tam Lin'* as Tam is turned into a variety of forms (a lizard, snake, wild deer and hot iron bar) while held in Janet's arms, but she remains resolute and wins her lover from the Queen.
[120] Adam 2007:97.
[121] Ibid
[122] Ibid, p. 119.
[123] Ibid.
[124] Ibid p. 120.

Her friends search *'for a year and a day'* but only Flora's hair ribbon and silver ring can be found.[125] Evidently the Queen of Elfhame favoured the lovely girl who sang to her, and with her *'bright hair loose, and her ring tossed down'* Flora has been transported by the labyrinth to the fairy realm. The centre of the maze that Flora encounters is a void and beyond description – only *'silence'* and *'radiant air'*. With the eerie *'huge, hot sun'* shining overhead the monastic stillness of a Zen garden is conveyed, perhaps an image from the Beat generation world Adam frequented, and is a novel point of contrast to the poem's nursery rhyme lyricism.

The title and refrain of another poem *Anaid si tearg (Great is Diana)* at first appears to be written in Scottish Gaelic but is actually a reversal of an exultation to Diana. Thus, it does not exist as a paean but as a denial of the moon goddess. First published in 1962, it imagines man's conquest of the moon: *'There'll be rockets going up like rattle snakes,/And signs saying Eat at Edie's Place,/On the biggest craters of the full moon's face'.*[126] The Diana of the poem is a synthesis of moon goddess, witch and fairy queen: *'Your cats vanish/Over all the earth'*, *'the wings of your elves wither'*[127] and *'your nymphs forsake you'*.[128] The tone of the poem is marked by both regret, yet also accusation, mimicking the voice of technology's judgement as Diana is portrayed as a *'jealous virgin'* spying on Earth's lovers.[129] The song of the women of Earth is used to bring down the goddess who once aided them: *'Sing women o' the Earth/Sing down the mune/Sisters she's bound tae fa'/Sudden and sune'*.[130] The result of her demise is that *'not a heart on Earth/Remember love'*.[131] The poem ends with the droning refrain, *'And there shall be no more moonlight'* which segues into *'And there shall be no more opposites/Over all the Earth'*.[132] The movement into non-duality appears oddly ambivalent. It is both a vision of the demise of female power, but also an end to the oppositions that have defined and subjugated women, typically in the Christian tradition.

The movement toward non-duality also shows Adam's reading in Eastern religion. Adam's was a hybrid, scholarly spirituality. She has written of her rejection of Western individualism and a Christian afterlife, rather *'if the ancient Eastern notion that life is a cosmic game in which the Eternal plays at becoming all forms and creatures of Time is true (and I believe it is), then nothing, not even the grimmest of human fate, is at all tragic'*.[133] Cindy McMann refers to Adam's *'decidedly un-Christian'* spiritual leanings and relates that notebooks belonging to Adam were filled with learning about *'magical theory and practices, folklore and mythology'*, with Adam being *'most drawn to ancient Egyptian and*

---

[125] Ibid.
[126] Ibid p. 207.
[127] Ibid.
[128] Ibid p. 208.
[129] Ibid.
[130] Ibid.
[131] Ibid.
[132] Ibid p. 209.
[133] Ibid p. 374.

*hermetic traditions, although she culled from other classical Greek, Roman, medieval, and contemporary Scottish sources'.*[134] Adam stated in interview that she did not belong to any occult society or association.[135] Yet perhaps building a community rather than working and researching in a solitary manner would have grounded her and provided protection, not only from those that put her on a shaky pedestal, but from her own ego. Anecdotal evidence suggests irresponsibility and perhaps ignorance of the power of negatively charged words in magical terms. For example, she spoke of threatening a critic of her beloved Robert Duncan – *'if I ever meet this character I am going to put a spell on it to rot its bones'.*[136]

The musicality of Adam's writing is evident in *Anaid si taerg*. She stated she found it impossible to write poetry unless she was working with a tune,[137] and she would compose while walking or riding her bicycle[138] in order to experience the rhythm in her body. There is a musicality to her speaking voice and it was described as *'shrill in a charming way'* and compared to that of Glinda, the Good Witch of the North, portrayed by Billie Burke in the 1939 MGM production of *The Wizard of Oz*.[139] When Adam allows the inherent musicality of the material and her speaking voice to flow, the effects are often spellbinding, as a recording or Anaid si taerg from the *'Poetry as Magic'* workshop highlights.[140] But for most of her performances, Adam would consciously *'sing'* the poem. Friends regarded her as *'quite tone deaf'*,[141] and indeed, there is an irregularity of key and tone with only the pulse of the metre and her passion driving the poems. There is the tendency to enunciate every syllable, and therefore the results sound laboured. By consciously *'performing'* as was common in the Victorian parlour and the British music hall tradition, Adam destroys any conventional beauty of the ballad material that folk singers are so effective at translating. Comedy is achieved, which undermines the ability of the poet to channel the *'grue'*. The results are more successful when the material is intentionally comic, for example the blues ballad, *Cheerless Junkie's Song*, a tale of a suburban youth's slumming and resultant demise which incorporates the American street slang of the day: *'Let rat tails write my epitaph / Brother! He died high!'*[142] As a musician, her performance style resonates with the American primitive

---

[134] n. pag. I think it unwise to underestimate the Christian influence on Adam, and further study could highlight the influence of the Christian hymns of her youth on her sense of song and melody or her creation of monstrous female figures as a reaction to Christian rationalism and duality.
[135] 2007:333.
[136] McMann 2009, n.pag.
[137] Adam 2007:337.
[138] Ibid, p. 348.
[139] Adam 2007:331.
[140] Poetry Center Digital Archive, 2011. Jack Spicer's Poetry as Magic Workshop: June 9th, 1957. [online] Available at: <https://diva.sfsu.edu/collections/poetrycenter/bundles/191225> [Accessed 5th February 2012].
[141] Prevallet 2007:23.
[142] Adam 2007, p. 220. For the performance see: Wizzyd 2006, 2007, Helen Adam. [video online] Available at:<http://www.youtube.com/watch?v=t9b7RhTYUKE>[Accessed 3 February 2012].

musical tradition – like art naïf its freakish qualities developed because of its isolation – and in the following decade Adam was embraced by the New York art punk world, opening shows for Patti Smith.[143]

Song is fundamental to her play *San Francisco's Burning*, a *'ballad opera'* set in the city prior to the earthquake and subsequent fire devastation of 1906, with the lyrics co-written by Pat Adam. The action takes place in the first world of grand parlours and mansions of San Francisco society and in the underworld of waterfront gambling dens; but also by extension in the spaces inhabited by a strange cast of sleepwalkers, lost souls and narcissists fallen prey to the mirror. Presiding over such in-between spaces is the spectral and monstrous Worm Queen, a grotesquely tall figure dressed in black, wearing a head-dress of twigs and black veils. She sits in the Hanged Man's House playing a game of *'Worm Queen Patience'*, deciding the fate of the sailors, drug-eaters and gamblers with a flourish of the Ace of Spades and the inevitability of the route to her bed:

> *My crown is crusted with carrion flies*
> *And my head is bald and wet,*
> *But the loveliest women of living flesh*
> *With me you will quite forget.*
>
> *I am the Fair Forgetfulness*
> *Whom men seek only in pain.*
> *Who sleeps in the bed of the Worm Queen*
> *He never will weep again.*[144]

Sex is equated with oblivion and with death – death not as an end but as an entry into a limbo of sorts. The role was played by Adam in its various productions, relishing in the character's over-stated apparel and songs, and represents the crone figure in Adam's creation myth of the fairy queen.

After their mother Isabella died the fairy trinity was broken and the sisters moved to New York in 1965 in the hope the play would be produced off-Broadway. In another example of Adam's irresponsibility in her magic practice, she sent a letter and giant Ace of Spades to a critic who had given *San Francisco's Burning* a bad review, boasting *'I have never before been in such a splendid position to curse'* in a letter to Duncan .[145] Adam refused to shorten the play and cull its innumerable songs as suggested by her collaborators and producers so that it would translate to mainstream theatre. Instead she would make numerous revisions of the original material that had so pleased audiences in San Francisco, apparently lost in a creative limbo.

---

[143] Prevallet, p. 52.
[144] Adam 1985:18.
[145] Prevallet 2007, p. 50.

Adam's interest in using masks and veils in order to fashion a persona extends to her experimentation in visual arts. *Daydream of Darkness* is a film made in collaboration with cameraman and editor William McNeill based on *Anaid si tearg* and the images mirror the poem to build an impressionistic dream tapestry. Adam adopts a sylvan queen character, capering in San Francisco's Golden Gate Park and controlling the fates of the film's mortal false and true lovers by proffering tarot cards. Correspondences are made between real and fantastic realms in a twinning of characters and junk shop figurines. In fairy head-dress, Adam kisses a Classical statue of the female form.

She also engaged with images of female physical perfection in a series of photographic collages, in which images of glamorous women sourced from ladies magazines of the day fraternise with large-scale images of insects, lizards and rodents. For example, a woman in an evening gown stares blankly ahead while cradling a pair of bats who nuzzle against her bare skin. The juxtaposition of their papery black wings and her luminous white flesh suggest a merging of forms. She ignores a friend who turns to engage with her at the soiree, with a caption alluding to her thoughts: *'Perhaps no one will notice them'*.[146] The simplicity and immediacy of the medium, the impact of its startling dual juxtaposed forms – beauty and the beast, real and imaginary, rational and irrational – allow multiple, ironic meanings to resonate.

After Pat's death in 1986, Adam's lifelong support structure was gone, and she became increasingly isolated from friends. Her health deteriorated and she died a ward of state in a care home in Brooklyn in 1993. Yet to look back on her life, we see a lifelong engagement with the otherworld of fairy and the poet contemplating its queen as through a veil. The queen is always just out of reach – across the red river of *Thomas the Rhymer* and in the *'bush o' broom'* of *Tam Lin* in the ballads she treasured, and at the centre of the Hornbeam Maze and within The Birkenshaw in Adam's modern revisionist storytelling. The other world could be glimpsed in fleeting moments, as when one experiences the *'grue'*, which Adam skilfully translated in her poems. Although she defined the fairy world as a dark place, based on her reading of Scottish folklore, she also manifested the lighter side of fairy through the creation of an eccentric and playful persona. Adam stands as an important practitioner and investigator of the magical and irrational in poetry, existing in the lineage of Blake, W.B. Yeats and Robert Duncan. The body of work Adam left us is unique in that it straddles the cultural, mythic and geographic landscapes of either side of the Atlantic, bridging the Victorian and postmodern eras, and therefore she has created a vast web of veiled entry points from the mundane, physical world into the otherworld of imagination, dreams and fairy.

---

[146] Prevallet 2000, n. pag.

# Bibliography

Adam, Helen Douglas (1923) *The Elfin Pedlar and Tales told by Pixy Pool.* London: Hodder and Stoughton.

Adam. Helen (1974) *Selected Poems and Ballads.* New York: Helikon.

Adam, Helen (1985) *San Francisco's Burning: A Ballad Opera.* Brooklyn: Hanging Loose.

Adam, Helen (2007) *A Helen Adam Reader.* Ed. Kristin Prevallet. Maine: National Poetry Foundation.

Child, James Francis (ed.) (1859) *English and Scottish Ballads.* 8 vols. Boston: Little, Brown and Company.

Davidson, Michael (1989) *The San Francisco Renaissance: Poetics and Community at Mid-century.* Cambridge: Cambridge University Press

Grace, Nancy M. & Johnson, Ronna C. (2004) *Breaking the Rule of Cool: Interviewing and Reading Women Beat Writers.* Jackson: University Press of Mississippi.

Hutton, John A. (1923) Foreword in: H. Adam. *The Elfin Pedlar and Tales told by Pixy Pool.* London: Hodder and Stoughton. pp. vi-viii.

Knight, Brenda (1996) *Women of the Beat Generation: The Writers, Artists and Muses at the Heart of a Revolution.* Berkeley: Conari.

McMann, Cindy (2009) *Helen Adam and the Feminist Gothic Imagination, in The Irish Journal of Gothic and Horror Studies,* 6, [online] Available at:

<http://irishgothichorrorjournal.homestead.com/HelenAdamandtheFeministGothicImagination.html [Accessed 25 November 2011].

Nash, Andrew (2007) *Kailyard and Scottish Literature.* Amsterdam: Rodopi.

Prevallet, Kristin (2000) *Helen Adam's Sweet Company*, Riding the Meridian—Lit[art]ure, [online] Available at: <http://www.heelstone.com/meridian/adam4b.html> [Accessed 16 November 2011].

Prevallet, Kristin (2007) Introduction. In: Adam. H. *A Helen Adam Reader.* Maine: National Poetry Foundation. pp. 3-62.

Scott, Walter (1802) *Minstrelsy of the Scottish Border.* 2 vols. London: Cadell and Davies.

# MELUSINE

## Enduring Serpentine Queen

## DAVID RANKINE

> *"And I believe that the marvels found throughout the earth and all Creation are the most true, such as the things said to be fairy, and a variety of others."*[147]

Since Jean d'Arras penned *Melusine de Lusignan* in 1393, the epic tale has captured the imagination of authors and poets across Europe for more than six hundred years. The story of Melusine is a bold and beautiful work, replete with numerous motifs found in folklore across Europe, and serves as a tapestry of myth from the medieval period and earlier. I shall begin by recounting the tale, and then explore the key motifs in the tale, and consider their significance and other examples which shed further light on this tragic fairy queen, and their influence in subsequent esoteric teachings.

### The Tale of Melusine of Lusignan

To distract himself from the grief he felt at the death of his wife, King Elinas of Scotland (called Alba or Albany and mistranslated in some later versions to Albania) used to hunt frequently. One day, desperately thirsty, he approached a fountain, where he heard a woman singing. The woman was the beautiful fairy queen Pressine, who agreed to marry him as long as he never visited her when she was lying-in in bed. Elinas agreed and they had triplets, Melusine, Melior and Palatine (or Palestine). Nathas, the King's son, rushed to tell his father, who without thinking rushed into his wife's chamber as she was bathing their new daughters. Pressine cried that he had broken his word, and so now she had to leave, and disappeared with their daughters.

---

[147] d'Arras, *Melusine de Lusignan*, 1393:2.

Pressine reared her daughters on the Lost Island, also called Avalon, which could only be found by chance by man, no matter how often a person visited it. When Melusine and her sisters were fifteen, she asked her mother what their father had done wrong. When she was told, she concocted a plan, and with her sisters went to Scotland, and used a charm to enclose him and all his wealth in a high mountain called Brandelois.

When Pressine found out what they had done, she cursed Melusine to become a serpent from the waist down every Saturday until she met a man who agreed to marry her on condition that he never saw her on a Saturday, and kept his promise. The other two sisters received less severe punishments in accordance with their lesser roles following Melusine's lead.

Melusine travelled the world looking for the man who could break the curse. Arriving at the forest of Colombiers, in Poitou, she was told by the local fairies that they were waiting for her to rule them.

Now it happened that a man called Raymondin, who had accidently killed his uncle, the wise Count Aimery with his boar-spear whilst hunting, was wandering in the forest. Before his death, Aimery had predicted from the stars that a man who killed his lord in that hour would gain great fortune and success. He arrived at the fountain known as the Fountain of the Fairies, or the Fountain of Thirst, famous for its miraculous occurrences. Melusine and two other fairies were dancing in the light of the moon at the fountain, and he was quickly enamoured of her beauty and manners.

Melusine soothed Raymondin, concealed his deed, and married him, on his oath that he would never see her on a Saturday. Melusine stressed to him that if he broke his oath she would have to leave, and they would both know unhappiness for the rest of their lives. With her magic and wealth as fairy queen, she built the castle of Lusignan, near the fountain, as well as other places including Cloitre Malliers, Larochelle and Mersent.

Melusine and Raymondin's children were affected by the curse on her, and were born deformed, but this did not diminish Raymondin's love. However, Raymondin's brother (or cousin) whispered malicious gossip in his ear and suggested his wife was having an affair on Saturdays. Raymondin hid himself and saw Melusine in her half-serpentine form with grey, sky-blue and white scales. Raymondin kept silent, not wanting to lose his wife.

The curse was not to be undone, and one of their sons, Geoffroy with the tooth (with a boar's tusk protruding from his mouth), burned an abbey full of monks and his brother Freimund to the ground killing them all. Raymondin reproached Melusine, saying *"Out of my sight, thou pernicious snake and odious serpent! Thou contaminator of my race!"* Melusine fainted, and on waking sadly told him that she must now depart and wander the earth as a spectre in pain until the day of doom.

As she departed, she left the impression of her foot in one of the stones. Her final words to her lover were that only when one of her race died at Lusignan would she be visible. She warned that her appearance at Lusignan would presage the death of the lord that year, and that she would still be visible at the Fountain of the Fairies. For a period of time afterwards, Melusine returned to the castle unseen to feed her two youngest sons. After her departure, Raymondin later died as a hermit at Montserrat.

PRESSINE'S CURSE, MELUSINE DE LUSIGNAN OF D'ARRAS, LATE C14TH (ARS MS FR 3353 FO.14V)[148]

## The Origins of Melusine

Jean d'Arras did not pull his work *Melusine de Lusignan* out of thin air, but drew on an existing tradition, and set it against the backdrop of a Europe that was at threat from the Ottoman Empire and seeing a number of deaths and successions in royal courts (in 1393). A clear predecessor was recorded several decades earlier, circa 1355, when Pierre Bersuire (1285-1362) the prior of the abbey of St. Eloi, wrote in his *Reductorium morale*:

> *"They say that in my country the solid fortress of Lusignan was founded by a knight and a faery he married, and that the fairy is the ancestor of a great number of nobles and great persons, and the kings of Jerusalem and Cyprus, as well as the Counts of la Marche and Parthenay, are her*

---

[148] Note the dragon facing Melusine indicating her fate. The dragon is shown next to her throughout the manuscript to emphasise her hybrid nature.

> *descendants ... But the faery, they say, taken by surprise, naked, by her husband, transformed into a serpent. And today they still tell how when the castle changes master the serpent shows itself in the castle."*

Many of the motifs found in D'Arras may be found in the *Otia Imperialia* (Diversions for Emperors) of Gervaise of Tilbury (c.1152-1234). Indeed d'Arras quoted from this earlier work (written circa 1211-12) to illustrate his own:

> *"... faeries take the form of very beautiful women, and various men have married them. They made them swear to various stipulations: some had to swear never to see them naked, others never to inquire into their actions on Saturdays ... As long as they followed these stipulations, they enjoyed an elevated condition in life and great prosperity. But as soon as they betrayed their oaths, they lost their wives, and luck abandoned them little by little. And, of these beings, certain ones changed into serpents on one or several days of the week."*

Another source for the Melusine tale may be seen in the Anglo-Norman tale of *Henno cum dentibus* (*'Henno with the Teeth'*) in *De Nugis Curialum* (*'Of Courtier's Trifles'*) written by Walter Map during the period 1181-1193. In this story, the fairy wife who always avoids the beginning and end of Mass (and hence the holy water and communion wafer) is seen by her mother-in-law bathing in the form of a dragon. When she is sprinkled with holy water by a priest she jumps through the roof and disappear with a howl, never to be seen again.

In addition to French sources, earlier tales in other languages contributed to this tradition of the hybrid fairy queen (serpent/dragon maiden), such as the late twelfth or early thirteenth century 9400 line poem *Lanzelet* of von Zatzikhoven (which contains a dragon maiden episode), the Middle English *Lybeaus Desconus* written in the mid-fourteenth century, and the Italian *Carduino* of 1375.

There is a major difference between Melusine and earlier European serpent/dragon women, which is their relationship to the Church. The benevolence of Melusine is repeatedly stressed, overlaying her fairy roots and cursed nature:

> *"And Melusine caused many churches to be founded and endowed in the region, and many other good works that should not be forgotten"*[149]

Whereas earlier fairy shapeshifters are anathema to the Church, Melusine insists on the full sacraments and emphasises her role within God's creation. Nowhere is this more poignant than towards the end of the tale, when Raymondin berates her, and she mourns her loss of mortality and

---

[149] d'Arras, *Melusine de Lusignan*, 1393:80.

a Christian burial, instead condemned by his actions to be the doomsayer of their family line.

Serpentine women with the lower body of a snake were an ancient concept found in many cultures, such as the Gnostic wisdom figure of Edem, the Greek monster Echidna, the Egyptian goddess Isis-Hermouthis, and the Anatolian goddess Shahmeran. They are also seen in the Indian Nagas, of whom there is an entire tradition of literature and folklore. Some of these tales contain a number of parallels to the story of Melusine, e.g. in *"The Sakya youth who married a snake-maiden and became king of Udyana"*, the hero meets the Naga princess by a lake (water source) and becomes king through her aid (gains kingdom), he chops off her dragon crest and as a result their children are cursed to suffer head afflictions (the disfigurations of the children).[150]

Irrespective of the roots of her ophidian or draconian nature, Melusine's name is also the source of speculation. Jean d'Arras in his tale explains that Melusine means *'marvel or marvellous woman'*.[151] Modern writers have proposed alternative roots, with Morris suggesting that Melusine is derived from *'Mere Lusine'*, i.e. Mother of the Lusignans, and Charpentier proposing that she had Celtic roots, and was the consort of the Gallic fire and air god Lug, with her name of Lugine, hence Mere Lugine becoming Melusine, and Lusignan being her sacred place.[152]

## Exploring the Story

The tale of Melusine contains the structural motif found in many fairy tales of the three sections – the mysterious meeting, the pact, and the transgression. The idea of triplicity is found throughout the story, from Melusine being the oldest of three sisters, to being one of three beautiful fairy women by the fountain, the three fairy brides (Pressine, Melusine, and the wife of Hervé de Leon mentioned in the full version of the tale), the three forms of Melusine (woman, half-woman and half-serpent, flying serpent), Melusine circling the fortress three times when she leaves, and also appearing three days before deaths and changes of lordship to presage the events.

> *"Melusine came to Lusignan and circled it three times, shrieking woefully in a plaintive female voice. Up in the fortress and in the town below, people were utterly amazed; they knew not what to think, for they could see the form of a serpent, yet they heard the lady's voice issuing forth from it."*[153]

---

[150] Bogel, *Indian Serpent Lore of The Nagas in Hindu Legend and Art*, 1926:123-125.
[151] d'Arras, *Melusine de Lusignan*, 1393:47.
[152] Morris, *The Romance of Melusine and the Sacralization of Secular Power*, 1997:62-3.
[153] d'Arras, *Melusine de Lusignan*, 1393:260-261.

The boar motif is an interesting one, which hints at Celtic roots in the story. Boar hunting is found in several stories (most famously in the Welsh *Culhwch and Olwen*), often as a metaphor for the otherworld, as the boar was considered an otherworldly animal. The death of the Count at the hands of Raymondin's boar-spear is echoed later in the tale by the emphasis on their son Geoffroy with the Great Tooth, who has a boar's tusk coming out of his cheek.

Geoffroy is the catalyst for the destruction of the family, for although he is a noted giant-slayer, he also burns the monastery of Maillezais full of monks and his brother Fromont, leading to Raymondin's outburst which reveals the breaking of his oath. Although this initially seems shocking, Melusine describes this as an act of divine vengeance, to punish the corruption of the monks in question (a point supported by the Pope granting absolution to Geoffroy). In so doing, Melusine emphasises that it is Raymondin who is the oath-breaker, and who has condemned her to never die and receive Christian funerary rites, and their family to dwindle in power and fame. This act of Geoffroy burning the abbey, which is the axis of the whole Melusine tale, was a historical act occurring in 1232, and as such is an example of the liminal merging of history and myth found in this tragedy.

A peripheral point which fixes the story firmly in the mythic world is the reference to Pressine's sister, *'the Lady of the Lost Isles'*. This is a discrete reference early in the story to Morgan le Fay, and indicates that Melusine (Pressine's daughter) is her niece, and on a wider scale, that a large number of noble families in Europe could thus claim a connection to Avalon.

Another Celtic theme seen in the story is the woman as bestower of sovereignty. Melusine builds a castle for Raymondin near the fountain where they met, and other dwellings, making him the ruler of the land, having explained to him how he can win the land through gaining a charter which she will magically fill. The comment made by Melusine at their meeting also emphasises the power she wields, when she declares, *"I am second only to God in being able to advance your interests in this world of mortals"*.

It is interesting to note that Raymondin's father Hervé de Leon also had land granted to him by his fairy wife when he founded the County of Forez. At some point he offended this wife and she left, so he remarried and had several sons by his second wife, the third of whom he named Raymondin, who was extremely handsome, charming and gifted.

An obvious reason for the level of Celtic mythological backdrop in the tale beyond the Norman setting is the Scottish origins of Melusine, and the doom-saying life which Melusine is condemned to has its parallels in the Celtic tradition of the washer at the ford. Combining the meeting at a liminal watery location with foretelling of death and (in some instances) association with a particular noble line, we see parallels in various Celtic figures like the Irish Banshee (*'fairy woman'*), the Welsh Gwrach-y-Rhybin ('*hag of the mist*') and the Scottish Bean Nighe ('*washing woman*').[154] The stricture laid on Melusine by her mother in the original tale is quite specific and combines the motif of three with the presaging of death and change:

> "*You will appear three days before the fortress which you shall build and endow with your name is to change lords, as well as when one of your descendants is about to die.*"[155]

THE TEMPTATION OF EVE, C14TH GERMAN MS (HARLEY MS 4996 FO. 4V)

## Mirroring the Old Testament

As a product of its time, it is inevitable that the tale of Melusine should reflect significant and religious events. Particularly noteworthy is the implied echoing of biblical events through the tale of Melusine, such as the murder of Abel by Cain (Geoffroy killing Fromont), the mark of Cain (the various facial marks of the children, but especially Geoffroy's boar tusk), and the Fall from Eden (the discovery of Melusine's hybrid form when she hides on Saturdays and associated decline of the family line).

---

[154] For more on the comparative qualities of these fairy beings, see Rankine & d'Este, *The Guises of the Morrigan*, 2005:113-121.
[155] d'Arras, *Melusine de Lusignan*, 1393:13.

Indeed the medieval images of Melusine, where she is shown at times with a small dragon next to her hinting at her nature, or in hybrid form with a serpent's tail, or in full dragon/winged serpent form, mirror depictions of the serpent on the tree from this period, shown with a female face. Such lamia-like figures thus suggest a connection between Lilith (known as a lamia from the ancient world) as the temptress of Eve, and Melusine as the temptress of Raymondin.

## Continuing the Tradition

A few years after the prose of d'Arras, Coudrette produced *Le Roman de Parthenay* (The Romance of Parthenay) a verse version of the myth in 1401. In both instances the plays contained an element of dynastic justification, having been commissioned to glorify and raise the origins of aristocratic houses. Of note is the inclusion of Alexander the Great as an ancestor of King Elinas, and hence of Melusine. This common practice of claiming divine origins was seen in earlier and contemporary cultures, including the ancient Greeks, the Saxons and Vikings, as seen in myths and genealogical documents. Colwell notes that:

> *"The Mélusine romances attained wide popularity with the noble French and Flemish audiences amongst whom the extant 20 poetic and 15 prose romance manuscripts are known to have circulated during the fifteenth and early sixteenth centuries"*[156]

However Melusine's popularity was such that the tale would spread all across Europe:

> *"The story of Mélusine was later transmitted into several other languages. There is, for example, an anonymous Middle English prose version written around 1500, a Middle Dutch version first printed in 1491, and a German prose version written by the Swiss Thüring von Ringoltingen in 1456. The Middle English and the Middle Dutch version are based on that by Jean d'Arras, whose popularity is attested by the twenty-two times the version printed by Steinschaber was reprinted in the next hundred years. The German Melusine is a translation of Coudrette's version, equally popular, and was printed in 1474 in Augsbourg. In the next hundred years, another twenty-four editions of this text, and translations into other languages, such as Flemish, Danish, Swedish, and Spanish, followed."*[157]

Germany, with its traditions of Rhine-Maidens and Undines would prove a particularly popular haven for Melusine, and *Die Schöne Melusine* (*'The Fair Melusine'*), based on Coudrette's tale, was written in 1456 by the mayor

---

[156] Colwell, *Patronage of the Poetic Mélusine Romance*, 2011:216.
[157] Zeldenrust, *When a Knight meets a Dragon Maiden: Human Identity and the Monstrous Animal Other*, 2011:45-46.

of Berne Thüring von Ringoltingen for the Margrave of Hochberg. In this first German version of the tale, Melusine has the mermaid form seen in many later descriptions and in heraldry. This image shows Melusine as a mermaid with a twin split tail, and holding a tail in each hand. It is found in heraldry as a symbol of eloquence and enlightenment, where this mermaid image is appropriately known as a *'melusine'*. As with France, the tale was perpetuated through the centuries by numerous German writers:

> *"Die schöne Melusine, printed in Thüring's version in 1474, became the theme of a popular Volksbuch and was frequently reprinted in the 16th c., 17th c., and even 18th c. It was dramatically treated by Hans Sachs and Jakob Ayrer and, with variants, by the Viennese K. F. Hensler (Das Donauweibchen, a comedy in two parts, 1798) and F. Grillparzer (see Melusina, 1833), and in the narratives Sehr wunderbare Historie von der Melusina (1800) by L. Tieck, Undine (1811) by Fouqué, and Die neue Melusine (published in two parts in 1817 and 1819) by Goethe, who included his story in Wilhelm Meisters Wanderjahre."*[158]

That versions of the story have spread across Europe, is seen in a Greek version of the tale (note the returning mother motif found in the original tale):

> *"There are also some legends narrating the noble origin of Greek families, for example the Vretoi family (vretos: found), well-known since the nineteenth century. According to them, the founder of the lineage once met a most beautiful blue-eyed neraïda, married her, and had several children with her. She was dumb and never spoke to him ... Then the husband one day seized her child and threatened to burn it in the oven, making the neraïda speak, or cry very loudly to stop him. But finally the fairy left her human mate. She continued caring for her children though, going back to them in order to feed them."*[159]

The Romanian tale of *The Prince and the Fairy-Queen of the Fairies* also contains elements of the Melusine story, with the faerie queen extracting a promise from her husband on their marriage bed to never question her actions, no matter how bizarre they seem, for they will not be evil. He agrees, and does not respond when she claps and a lamia appears (note the serpentine connection), or when she throws their daughter into a fire (possibly recalling the Greek goddess Demeter and her treatment of Demophon to immortalise him). However, when she deprives his army of its provisions before a war he challenges her, and she disappears.[160]

---

[158] Gallagher, *Metamorphosis. Transformations of the Body and the Influence of Ovid's Metamorphoses on Germanic Literature of the Nineteenth and Twentieth Centuries*, 2009:340.
[159] Angelopoulos, *Greek Legends about Fairies and Related Tales of Magic*, 2010:218.
[160] Bezza, *Paganism in Roumanian Folklore*, 1928:80-81.

## Along came Paracelsus

Melusine figures in a number of Paracelsus' writings, especially *De Vita Longa* (The Book of Long Life), and *Liber de Nymphis, sylphis, pygmaeis et salamandris* (The Book of Nymphs, Sylphs, Pygmies and Salamanders). Indeed, as well as mentioning Melusine, Paracelsus also popularised an idea found in her tale, that of the gaining of a human soul through marriage to a human:

> *"The power of your father's seed would have drawn you and your sisters towards his human nature, and you would have left behind the ways of nymphs and fairies forever."*[161]

MELUSINE AS PHILOSOPHICAL MERCURY C17TH CZECH MS

Although images of Melusine commonly showed her with the body of a serpent, some also depicted her with a mermaid's tale. Her complex and powerful nature saw her equated to the philosophical mercury of the alchemists. This is seen in images such as those found in Marcus Bonacina's seventeenth century tractate *Compendium de praeparatione auri potabilis veri* (MS Skeny XI C 42).

---

[161] d'Arras, *Melusine de Lusignan*, 1393:12.

This attribution of Melusine to the philosophical mercury may derive from Paracelsus, who Cazenave quotes as saying:

> *"Melusine is the correct name for the alchemist's aquaster ... the aquatic star, which is related to the silver of the moon and, beyond that, to androgynous Mercury, at once aerial and aquatic, solar and lunar."*[162]

## The Children of Melusine

In the story, most of Melusine's sons go on to positions of high status, including three kingships. Much of the tale is focused on the deeds of her sons, so that the saga of Melusine and Raymondin is set at the beginning and end of the text, with the central corpus being full of battles against Saracens, unfaithful vassals and giants.

| *Son* | *Deformity* | *Destiny/Position* |
|---|---|---|
| Urien | one red eye and one green, extra large mouth and ears | King of Cyprus |
| Eudes | red face shining like fire | Count of La Marche |
| Guy | one eye lower than the other (otherwise handsome) | King of Armenia |
| Antoine | lion's claw birthmark on his cheek | Duke of Luxembourg |
| Renauld | only one eye, but it has exceptional sight | King of Bohemia |
| Geoffroy | one large tooth/tusk protruding from his mouth | Inherits Lusignan after slaying giants and Saracen kings |
| Fromont | furry patch on his nose | Becomes a monk and is killed by Geoffroy in fire |
| Horrible | three eyes and evil disposition | Killed on Melusine's orders to prevent destruction of all her works |
| Raymond | - | Count of Forez |
| Thierry | - | Lord of Parthenay |

---

[162] Cazenave, *Encyclopedie des Symboles*, 1996:403.

Significantly, the two sons who are still infants when Melusine is forced to leave are the two who bear no physical deformity. Melusine visits them for a while to nurse them, unseen by anybody, emphasising the link between her and these last two.

## Divine Ancestor?

Melusine as the divine ancestor is a key theme in the Melusine tales. This is seen early in the Coudrette version, when the Lord of Parthenay addresses his chaplain, instructing him:

> *"'Do it,' he said, 'at your leisure,*
> *For the entire day is yours.*
> *The castle was built by a fairy,*
> *From whom I am descended,*
> *So they say everywhere,*
> *Both me and all of my lineage*
> *Of Parthenay; have no doubt about it'."*[163]

Morris lists the extent of the lands containing noble families who subsequently declared descent from Melusine:

> *'In all the lands where the Lusignans founded a dynasty and in all those lands in which certain families could attach themselves to this illustrious house (Poitou, Saintonge, Marche, Lorraine, Agenois, Forez, Dauphine, Languedoc, Burgundy, Alsace, Luxemburg, Bohemia, England, Armenia, Cyprus), the descendants of Melusine, true or pretended, swelled with pride over their supposed supernatural origin.'*[164]

King Edward IV (1442-1483) married Elizabeth Woodville (1437-1492) in 1464, whose mother Jacquetta of Luxembourg (the duchess of Bedford) traced her ancestry to Melusine.[165] Bingham notes of Elizabeth, described as the most beautiful woman in Britain, that she was *'Famously beautiful with 'heavy-lidded eyes like those of a dragon','*[166] and it is surely no coincidence that such a term should have been used in describing her.

It is curious to note that Edward and Elizabeth had ten legitimate children, mirroring the ten children of Melusine and Raymondin, and to further add to the continuation of the mythic theme, on Edward IV's death, his brother, who became King Richard III, had the marriage to Elizabeth declared illegitimate and subsequently claimed the throne for himself. He was the last of the Plantagenet line, which died with him, in the manner that Melusine had predicted her line would die out.

---

[163] Coudrette, trans. Morris *Le Roman de Parthenay*.
[164] Morris, *The Romance of Melusine and the Sacralization of Secular Power*, 1997:66.
[165] Gosman, MacDonald, & Vanderjact, *Princes and Princely Culture 1450-1650* Volume 2, 2005:118.
[166] Bingham, *The Cotswolds: A Cultural History*, 2009:66.

As a final twist, King Edward IV was described as having the demonic spirit Birto conjured for him (in Sloane MS 3824). The conjuration includes the use of two magic circles, with a dragon marked on the floor between them,[167] which is in exactly the same style as the images of Melusine flying from Lusignan found in the early copies of Melusine de Lusignan (i.e. in Paris MS Arsenal 3353 fo 155v).

## What happened to the Sisters?

The fates of Palatine and Melior are also described in the tale of Melusine, and we must not ignore these as they are both also indicative of the power and curse of the fairy bride.

Palatine was cursed to guard her father's treasure in the mountain of Conigo in Aragon until a knight of their lineage came to take the treasure to use it in conquering the Holy Land.

Melior had to guard the Castle of l'Espervier (Sparrowhawk) in Armenia and grant gifts to any who could remain awake there for three nights around the eve of 25th June. She could grant any gift but her body, but if a person failed the vigil they were imprisoned there forever. One of Guy's descendants succeeds in this quest, but insists on Melior's hand in marriage, leading her to curse the kings of Armenia to suffer great misfortune and lose their kingdom after nine generations. After telling him that she was his aunt, she disappeared and he was given a severe beating by an invisible force before leaving the castle.

## The Return of Melusine

It is clear that Melusine embodies wisdom and transformation in the motif of the fairy queen as an ancient union of woman and serpent (and later as siren). The popularity and influence of Melusine remained undiminished through the ages, and in 1833, Mendelssohn composed *Das Märchen von der Schönen Melusine* (*The Fair Melusine*), opus 32. Beyond music, Melusine also found expression in the writings of Carl Jung, who observed that, *"In alchemy, the spiritus mercurii that lives in the tree is represented as serpent, salamander, or Melusina."*[168]

Melusine also found expression as the influential and inspirational muse, as seen in A.S. Byatt's Man Booker Prize winning work *Possession: A Romance* (1990), which includes an epic poem on the tale of Melusine as one of its foci.

Of course, the ultimate demonstration of the survival of Melusine can be found when you go to buy your coffee – in the Starbucks logo (originally

---

[167] Rankine, *The Book of Treasure Spirits*, 2009.
[168] Jung, *The Collected Works* Vol 1, 1953:458.

based on a 16th century *'Norse'* logo which is clearly derived from the medieval Melusine images)!

Ultimately Melusine enhances the best aspects of man and also provokes the jealousy of the worst aspects – it is up to you to approach her from the right direction!


## Bibliography

Alban, G.M.E. (2003) *Melusine the Serpent Goddess* in A.S. Byatt's Possession and in Mythology. Oxford: Lexington Books

Angelopoulos, Anna (2010) *Greek Legends about Fairies and Related Tales of Magic. In Fabula* Vol 51:3/4:217-224

d'Arras, Jean & Vincensini, Jean-Jacques (tr.) (2003) *Mélusine ou La Noble Histoire de Lusignan: Roman du XIVe Siècle.* Paris: Librairie Générale Française

Beza, Marcu (1928) *Paganism in Roumanian Folklore.* London: J.M. Dents & Sons Ltd

Bingham, Jane (2009) *The Cotswolds: A Cultural History.* Oxford: Oxford University Press

Cazenave, Michel (ed) (1996) *Encyclopédie des Symboles.* Paris: Librairie Générale Française

Colwell, Tania M. (2011) *Patronage of the poetic Mélusine romance. Guillaume l'Archevêque's confrontation with dynastic crisis. In Journal of Medieval History* Vol 37.2:215-229

Dobenek (1698) *Histoire de Melusine, tiree des Chroniques de Pitou.* Paris

Gallagher, David (2009) *Metamorphosis. Transformations of the Body and the Influence of Ovid's Metamorphoses on Germanic Literature of the Nineteenth and Twentieth Centuries.* Amsterdam: Rodopi B.V.

Gosman, M. & MacDonald, A. & Vanderjact, A. (2005) *Princes and Princely Culture 1450-1650* Volume 2. Leiden: Brill

Jung, Carl (1953) *The Collected Works* Vol 1. London: Routledge & Kegan Paul

Keightley, Thomas (1833) *The Fairy Mythology* Vol 2. London: Whittaker, Treacher & Co

Krell, Jonathan F. (2000) *Between Demon and Divinity, Melusine Revisited.* In *Mythosphere* Vol 2.4:375-396

Maddox, Donald & Sara Sturm (eds) (1996) *Melusine of Lusignan. Founding Fiction in Late Medieval France.* Athens: University of Georgia Press

Morris, Matthew W. (2007) *A Bilingual Edition of Jean d'Arras's Melusine or L'Histoire de Lusignan.* Lampeter: Edward Mellen Press

Morris, Matthew W. (1997) *The Romance of Melusine and the Sacralization of Secular Power.* In *Papers from the 1996 PAC conference*, Postscript Vol XIV:57-68

Rankine, David (2009) *The Book of Treasure Spirits.* London: Avalonia

Rankine, David, & d'Este, Sorita (2005) *The Guises of the Morrigan.* London: Avalonia

Sax, Boria (1998) The Serpent and the Swan. The Animal Bride in Folklore and Literature. Virginia: McDonald & Woodward Publishing Co.

Sigerist, H.E. (ed) (1941) *Paracelsus: Four Treatises.* Maryland: John Hopkins Press

Vogel, J. (1926) Indian Serpent Lore of The Nagas in Hindu Legend and Art. London: Probsthain

Williams, G.S. (2002) *Defining Dominion. The Discourses of Magic and Witchcraft in Early Modern France and Germany.* Michigan: University of Michigan Press

Zeldenrust, Lydia (2011) *When a Knight meets a Dragon Maiden: Human Identity and the Monstrous Animal Other.* Masters Thesis, Utrecht

# HOLDA

## Winter's Faerie Queen

## CERI NORMAN

*"The Snow Queen passed our way last night,*
*Between the darkness and the light,*
*And flowers from an enchanted star,*
*Fell showerlike from her flying car"*
(Radford, 2004:14).

The Snow Queen is a fearsome figure, hard as ice, with a cold heart to match. She is an antithesis to life and to growth as she creates an artificial winter, or even ice age, in her wake. Utterly lacking in compassion the Snow Queen, or White Queen, is a tyrannical, cruel, ruler with a penchant for enchanting and kidnapping children. At least that is the image of Wintery Queens that many of us are familiar with from popular culture, from Hans Christian Andersen's *The Snow Queen* and from C.S. Lewis' *The Lion, the Witch and the Wardrobe*. However, this is a corruption of the true nature of an ancient Faerie Queen and Goddess of Winter known as Holda or Frau Holle. This Faerie Queen does have her dark side, but she is not, as some may have us believe, intrinsically evil. As with many other Goddesses, Holda was demonised to turn her faithful Pagan followers away from her.

Holda is a very complex figure, and the stories and information that surrounds her can often be contradictory. The archaeologist Marija Gimbutas considered Holda an ancient supreme Mother Goddess of Neolithic Europe, who predated the later Germanic and Viking deities such as Odin and Frigga – with whom Holda would later be associated (2001:195). Certainly Holda appears in a variety of guises in stories from all over Western Europe, which does suggest a common, ancient origin. To the mythologist Jacob Grimm, Holda was an aspect of Frigga, the wife of Odin (2004:III:927), and this was evidenced by the fact that one of her German bynames was *"Frau ('Mrs') Woden/Odin"*.

The earliest written records of Holda are several Latin inscriptions, from Germany and the Netherlands, dating from the late 2nd and early 3rd centuries CE. In these inscriptions she is referred to as *Deae Hlvdanae* – *'Goddess Hludana'* (CIL XIII:8830). In the 13th century Icelandic poem *Völuspá* (*'Prophecy of the Seeress'*), we find a similar name, Hlóðyn, given as a byname of the Goddess and giant, Jörð (Dronke, 1997). Jörð is best known to us today as the mother of Thor, whose father was Odin, but it is important to remember that Jörð is not a byname of Frigga. Nerthus, or Hertha, is the name of another Germanic Goddess who is associated with Holda, primarily because both Nerthus and Holda are associated with pools and carts that travelled around blessing the land (Waschnitius, 1913:89). The names of these Goddesses - Hludana, Hlóðyn, Jörð and Nerthus/Hertha - all derive from words for *'earth'*, suggesting she is indeed an earth Goddess, known by many different names. Holda may also be closely linked with Perchta, a Goddess found in Southern Germany, as Perchta is found where Holda leaves off and the two do share many traits (Grimm, 2004.I:272 & 282). The more recent form of her name, Holda, is cognate with the German for *'loyal'* (Duden, 1989) or *'merciful'* (Ellis Davidson, 1993:115), suggesting that Holda is a title rather than an actual name, which could help explain why the same Goddess appears under different names and guises.

Other than as the Snow Queen, Holda is best known to us today as *Frau Holle* or the witch in the well in the tale recorded by the Grimm brothers (Grimm, 2009:67-69): A mother had two daughters; the oldest was lazy and utterly spoilt and the youngest was ignored and forcibly overworked. One day the youngest daughter was sitting spinning by the well outside the cottage when she pricked her finger on the spindle and accidentally dropped it into the well. Knowing she would be punished for losing the spindle she jumped into the well after it, where she met Holda and acted as her maid until she became homesick. Holda was very pleased with the girl's industriousness and sent her back to the mortal world covered with gold. Seeing this, the older sister deliberately pricked her finger on her spindle, threw it in the well and jumped in after it. Despite a promising start - fuelled by greed - the elder daughter soon fell into her usual lazy ways. Holda was less than impressed with the girl's work, so she was sent home covered in tar or bad luck, depending on the translation!

*Frau Holle* is just one of the many stories that she appears in, but it helps show us many of Holda's areas of influence; she is a Goddess of spinning, domestic life, agriculture, magic and sacred wells e.g. Snow Well in Greenwich Park, UK, (Geddes-Ward, 2006:91) and the Frau Holle Pond in Meißner Gebirg, Germany (Altmann, 2006:211). Wells are traditionally portals into the Otherworld, and children were said to be born into the world via wells (Schrijnen, 1977:246). Unlike the Snow Queen, Holda is, on the whole, not cruel to children. Her act of *'taking'* away children's souls could be interpreted as an act of compassion, for in the Germanic culture it was thought that a child's soul was not properly affixed to their family until they were named at nine days old. If a child died before that time their soul was *'lost'*, so by collecting these lost souls, Holda gives them a home that they would not otherwise have.

Holda's was the kindly hand that rocked the cradle, but it was also the monstrous hand that dragged naughty children into her pools, if they wandered too close (Altmann, 2006:212). Parents used the tales of Holda or Frau Holle to threaten and chastise their children into good behaviour; if they were naughty, Holda might come along and do something very unpleasant to them. In *Frau Holle*, as well as other tales, Holda does not simply punish people because she is evil or tyrannical; there is always a clear reason for the punishment. In particular she penalises those who are lazy in their house-keeping or who break the taboos of spinning, which varied from area to area. Yet Holda was also known to help and teach those who were hard-working and in this she is very much like the Faerie Godmother.

Faeries are closely linked with Holda; she governs the well portals between worlds and was believed to ride out with the Wild Hunt from beneath a hollow hill – such places are often considered the haunt of faeries. In Germany she is perceived as a *Weisse Frauen* (*'White Faerie Woman'*), who lives in the mountains. These *Weisse Frauen* were also portents of death, though apparently not necessarily in a negative way (Knappert, 1887). In Scandinavia she is linked with the *Huldra* or *Ulda*, a kind of seductive woodland faerie, also known as the *Skogsrå* (*'Guardian of the Woods'*), who wears robes of green – the colour of nature and of faerie, and has a hollow back like a tree trunk. Jacob Grimm, in his *Teutonic Mythology* referred to Holda as *"queen of the mountain-sprites, who are called Huldrefolk ('Hidden People')"*, and they do appear to have been named for her (Grimm, 2004:I:271-2). Grimm also noted that Holda was often said to lead the procession of *Huldrefolk*, while dressed in grey and carrying a milk pail (2004:1:271) - milk being a favourite beverage of faeries. In Germany, Holda is said to be served by a class of very mischievous imps or gnomes known as *Hollen* after her (Altmann, 2006:212).

Holda is a Faerie Queen of the weather: snow is said to be created when she shakes out her goose-feather bedding, rain was Holda doing her washing, thunder was made as Holda reels her flax or shakes her keys and fog was smoke from Holda's chimney (Ellis Davidson, 1993:116). Winter was her season, with its cold, crisp, long nights. The twelve days of Yule were her sacred time, as indeed Halloween, also known as *Hollentide*, may have been. In some tales it was Holda, not Santa, who brought presents and she knew whether children had been naughty or nice that year (Siefker, 2007:163).

She is also sometimes equated with Mother Goose as their tales are similar. Several descriptions of Holda, as Perchta, mention her having a foot like that of a swan or goose and a long, bird-like nose. Grimm believed that her bird-like extremities indicated that Perchta was a Goddess with the ability to shape shift in to animal form (Grimm, 2004.I:280-1), while the association with swans clearly points to her faerie connections as swans are a faerie creature. Like faeries, Holda has a wild side. She is the Goddess of not only the domestic environment, but also of the mountain wilderness and wild woods. Holda is a protector of animals, and for that matter of souls, yet she is also their hunter (Motz, 1984:159). Her sacred animals were the hare, boar and the deer as well as cats, cattle and domesticated bees (Knappert, 1887). There is a dichotomy in the character of Holda; she is both a light and a dark Faerie Godmother, the bright faerie woman and the dark hag, and this is best shown through the followers of Perchta, for there are two types; the *Schönperchten* (*'beautiful Perchten'*) who bring luck and wealth, and the animalistic *Schiachperchten* (*'ugly Perchten'*) with their fangs and talons, who drive out demons and ghosts (Frazer, 2005:240-242.).

Holda is Goddess and Queen and of the Witches; her name appeared in several mediaeval documents, such as the *Canon Episcopi*, in association with witchcraft and the Wild Hunt (Ginzburg, 1990:94). The arts of spinning and magic are closely interwoven in folklore and we still *'weave'* spells. Witches were said to ride out with her in spirit form on their spinning distaffs, which closely resemble the classic witches' broom. In 16th century Germany, a woman was exiled for participating in the Wild Hunt with Holda (De Vries, 2008:57), so the belief continued for many years. In some areas witches or nocturnal spirits were known as *Hulde,* taking their name from Holda. Holda may also be the *seiðkona* - *'sorceress'* or *'witch'*, Huld, who appears in the *Ynglinga Saga*, which is allegedly a history of the Kings of Norway (Sturluson, 1991:13). In the saga, Huld kills a man using her witchcraft; she hag-rides him in the form of a type of goblin known as a mara - from which we get our word *'nightmare'*. Divination by water, or skrying, is another of Holda's arts; during Diel Breull's trial for witchcraft in 1630, he confessed that Holda had shown him *"the strangest things, reflected in a bowl of water"* (Ginzburg, 1992:12). Several of Holda's sacred wells, such as one on Schlossberg Hill in Freiburg im Breisgau, were used for divining the future (Knappert, 1887). Like Frigga and the Norns, Holda is associated with the idea of destiny, knowing the path that each soul will take, the length of our thread of life, or perhaps knowing what is written in our stars. She rules over both life and death and this was particularly evident during winter when, in times past, life and death hung in the balance.

Holda is also a Goddess of the stars; one Old Dutch name for the Milky Way was *Vroneldenstraet* meaning *'Frau Holda's Street'* (Grimm, 2004:I:266). Night, like winter, was when Holda walked abroad, with or without her entourage of faeries or witches. Holda's name can be found in several regional German names for specific days, all of which refer to night or evening: *Perchtennacht* (*'Perchta's Night'*) was the night before Epiphany in Steiermark, Saturdays were known as *Frauhollenabend* (*'Frau Holle's evening'*) in Rhöngebirge and *Hollenbend* (*'Holle's evening'*) was the Thursday before

Christmas in Westerwald (Waschnitius, 1913:18, 83 & 93). In the Netherlands, Germany, Austria and Scandinavia, Holda still lives on in place names, such as *Hollabrunn* (*'Holle's Well'*), *Holderberg* (*'Holda's Mountain'*) and *Holdenried* (*'Holda's Slope'*). Some even believe that *Holland* derived from *'Holle's Land'*, though generally *Holland* is said to have derived from *Hol Land* (*'Hollow Land'*) or *Holtland* (*'Wooded Land'*) (Room, 2006:265).

In Britain we know Holda as the Elder Mother - the guardian of the elder tree; this is a lingering memory of her as a Huldra. In Germany the elder tree is still called *Holunder* and in Denmark it is *hyldetræet*. The elder has a sinister reputation as a tree of evil magic, yet the elder offers a great deal of positive magic and its parts, if properly used, have beneficial properties (McGarry, 1995:193-195). The elder was also a faerie tree; in Danish lore if you stood beneath an elder on Midsummer's Eve you could witness a procession of Elves (Franklin, 2002:66) and in Scotland there was a similar belief, as long as you stood under the elder on Halloween (Mac Coitir, 2003:111).

It is still possible to connect with Holda at sacred places such as sacred wells, where elders grow, or during the types of weather she is connected with, or simply in dreams and meditation – focusing on the stillness of slumbering nature and the depths of the dark earth below the snow. Many who work with Holda see her as a white-robed, luminous Faerie Queen, or as a grey-robed, chthonic Faerie Witch, who is attended by *Huldrefolk* or *Hollen*. She is a powerful Faerie Queen who can teach us of the mysteries of magic, winter and spirit. We can turn to her to re-shape our fate or to reveal the mysteries of the hidden. She is a Goddess of transformation or crystallising and realising our wishes, but above all Holda is a Goddess of the ancient wisdom locked into myths and faerie tales.

## Bibliography

Altmann, Anna (2006) *The Seven Swabians & Other German Folktales*. Westport: Greenwood Publishing.

CIL -Corpus Inscriptionum Latinarum XIII. 8830. Latin inscription from Beetgum, Netherlands.

De Vries, Eric (2008) *Hedge-Rider: Witches and the Underworld*. Sunland, Pendraig Publishing.

Dronke, Ursula (1997) *Völuspá. The Poetic Edda, Volume II Mythological Poems*. Oxford: Clarendon/Oxford University.

Duden (1989) Das Herkunftswörterebuch: Etymologie der deutschen Sprache. Mannheim.

Ellis Davidson, Hilda. R. (1993) *Lost Beliefs of Northern Europe*. New York: Routledge.

Franklin, Anna (2002) *Midsummer: Magical Celebrations of the Summer Solstice*. St. Paul: Llewellyn Publications.

Frazer, Sir James. G. (2005) *'The Scapegoat'. The Golden Bough: A Study in Magic and Religion*. Oxford: Elibron Classics.

Geddes-Ward, Alicen & Neil (2006) *Faeriecraft*. London: Hay House.

Gimbutas, Maria (2001) *The Living Goddesses*. Berkeley: University of California Press.

Ginzburg, Carlo (1990) *Ecstasies: Deciphering the Witches' Sabbath*. London: Hutchinson Radius.

Ginzburg, Carlo (1992) *The Night Battles: Witchcraft and Agrarian Cults in the Sixteenth and Seventeenth Century: Witchcraft and Agrarian Cults in the Sixteenth and Seventeenth Centuries*. Baltimore: The Johns Hopkins University Press.

Grimm, Jacob (2004) *Teutonic Mythology*, Volumes I & III. Dover Phoenix Edition.

Grimm, Jacob & Wilhelm (2009) *The Complete Grimm's Fairy Tales*. Digireads.

Knappert, Laurentius (1887) *De Beteekenis van de Wetenschap van het Folklore voor de Godsdienstgeschiedenis Onderzocht en aan de Holda-Mythen Getoetst*. Amsterdam.

Mac Coitir, Niall (2003) *Irish Trees: Myth, Legend and Folklore*. Wilton: Collins Press.

McGarry, Gina (1995) *Brighid's Healing: Ireland's Celtic Medicine Traditions*. Strathe: Green Magic.

Motz, Lotte (1984) 'The Winter Goddess: Percht, Holda, and Related Figures'. In Folklore, 95:ii.

Radford, Dollie (2004) 'The Snow Queen'. *A Ballad of Victory and Other Poems*. Kessinger Publishing Co.

Room, Adrian (2006) *Placenames of the World: Origins and Meanings of the Names for 6,600 Countries, Cities, Territories, Natural Features and Historic Sites*. Jefferson: McFarland & Co Inc.

Schrijnen, J. (1977) *Nederlandsche Volkskunde*. Arnhem: Gysbers & Van Loon.

Siefker, Phyllis (2007) *Santa Claus, Last of the Wild Men: The Origins and Evolution of Saint Nicholas, Spanning 50,000 Years*. Jefferson: McFarland & Co Inc.

Sturluson, Snorri (1991) 'Ynglinga saga'. *Heimskringla*. Austin: University of Texas Press.

Waschnitius, Viktor (1913) 'Percht, Holda und Verwandte Gestalten'. Sitzungsberichte der Kaiserlichen Akademie der Wissenschaften, Vienna: Philosoph-Historisch Klasse, 174.

# The Skogsrå

## Queen of the Wild Woods of Sweden

## Helena Lundvik

*The Skogsrå*, or *Skogsfru* as she is also called, is one of the most famous nature spirits in Sweden. Many legends and myths about her can be found throughout Sweden as well as in Norway, Denmark, Finland, Estonia and other European countries.

My journey through the myths, folklore and legends about the Skogsrå has been amazing and it's far from over. The more I read about her, the deeper the rabbit hole goes. Some questions came up during the process of researching and writing this essay: How old is the ruler of the forest and the wild beasts? Is she really just a mischievous seductress or is she an ancient Scandinavian Goddess of the hunt?

The scholars don't agree whether the Skogsrå originates from the faeries, *de underjordiska*, or if she is a solitary female nature spirit. Gunnar Granberg has done extensive research about the myths and legends of the Skogsrå in the Nordic tradition, and his conclusion is that it is a regional matter. In Norway, and some parts of Sweden, the Skogsrå and *"the little people beneath the earth"* were described as faerie folk, but in most parts of Sweden they have become separated, and the Skogsrå is seen as a solitary nature spirit.[169]

In my opinion she is very much a Queen as she has dominion over many places: the forest, mountains, hills, lakes and mines. The stories about the Skogsrå are seldom told in modern times and nowadays people seem to be viewing nature as just trees, rocks and lakes rather than being alive with Spirit. Some scholars claim that the Skogsrå disappeared during the

---

[169] Granberg. *Skogsrået i yngre nordisk folktradition*, 1935

## The Faerie Queens

industrial revolution. The sightings of her simply stopped during the early parts of the 20th century.[170]

The Skogsrå was held in high esteem and everyone knew that you needed to treat her, the forest and the wild animals with respect and kindness, or you would have great misfortune. She was a powerful nature spirit who was both feared and turned to for help.

The animals of the forest were called the Skogsrå's cattle, especially elks, bears, wolves, foxes and capercaillies. She was often seen riding an elk. If you were kind and acted respectfully towards the Skogsrå and the creatures in the forest, you would be rewarded with gold or luck with hunting. But if you acted in a disrespectful way it was very likely that you would have an accident or be unable to ever kill an animal again. Beltane Eve, 30th April, was the Skogsrå's sacred day and nobody was allowed to hurt or kill an animal. If you did, you would have bad luck in hunting for the rest of your life.

THE SNOW QUEEN, LAURA DALIGAN, 2012

---

[170] Granberg. *Skogsrået i yngre nordisk folktradition*, 1935

There is a story about a man from Rödeby in Sweden who went hunting on the 30th April, despite warnings from the other villagers. He saw black grouse everywhere but when he tried to shoot them, he kept missing them. After a few hours of not being able to kill anything, the man realized that the Skogsrå must have had something to do with it. Since that day the man rarely managed to kill an animal again.[171]

In many myths the Skogsrå protects wolves and hides them from hunters by turning them into sheep. The saying *"det finns rå för alla djur"* implies that all animals are protected.[172]

It was the Skogsrå who decided whether a hunter would be able to kill any animals. There are many variations of this myth and this is one version:

The Skogsrå approached two hunters in the forest and took the rifle from one of the men. She blew down the barrel of the rifle and said, *this is a good rifle*, and returned it. She then took the other man's rifle, spat down the barrel of the rifle, and said, *this is a useless rifle*, and returned it. Before they met the Skogsrå the hunters had been equally good. But now the first hunter would never miss his target, whilst the other would never be able to kill an animal again.[173]

## Her features

The Skogsrå was mainly described as a young, beautiful and attractive woman with large breasts and she was known for taking mortals as lovers. Her hair was long and blonde, or red, and her eyes were green and penetrating. When she was running she threw her long, large breasts over her shoulders so that they wouldn't get in the way. The Skogsrå was described as clad in a white or green dress or dressed in beautiful, expensive clothes. From time to time she could appear as an old hag dressed in rags.[174]

The Skogsrå was a shape-shifter and sometimes transformed herself into an elk, a hare, a capercaillie or a grouse. When a hunter was unable to kill an animal it was usually because the Skogsrå had been disguising herself as the hunted animal, avoiding his bullets.[175]

In some folk-tales the Skogsrå was able to take on a non-physical form. Her famous laugh was very high-sounding and beautiful and people could often hear her sing or laugh without actually seeing her. A folk legend tells us about a coal miner who was working near the Norwegian border. He kept hearing someone calling his name night after night. Finally he swore and asked who it was. He heard laughter coming from the forest and in that instance his charcoal stack caught fire. When he tried to put out the fire he

---

[171] Duppils Krall, *Skogsråets samband med Freyja*, 2003
[172] Granberg. *Skogsrået i yngre nordisk folktradition*, 1935
[173] Schön. *Älvor, troll och talande träd*, 2000
[174] Schön. *Älvor, vättar och andra väsen*, 1986
[175] Granberg. *Skogsrået i yngre nordisk folktradition*, 1935

fell into it instead. His friends tried to rescue him, but he was already dead. That was his punishment for swearing at the Skogsrå.[176]

Even if the Skogsrå is always described as being very beautiful and lovely from the front, her back was a different matter. In some parts of Sweden you could clearly see her tail sticking out from beneath her dress. It was a fox's tail, a horse's tail or simply described as a *råa's tail*.[177] Twelve counties in the Middle and North of Sweden have myths about the Skogsrå with a tail, and in Norway she was seen with a cow's tail.[178]

In the South of Sweden and in Denmark instead of a tail the Skogsrå had a hole in her back that looked like *'an empty dough tray'* or a rotten piece of wood.[179] The tail and the hole were the most common descriptions of the Skogsrå's backside.

Understandably the Skogsrå was quite reluctant to show mortals her back; whether it was a hole or a tail she was trying to hide. But when she turned her back on you, you would know who this enchanting woman was that had crossed your path. Granberg's theory is that the attribute of the tail, or the hollow back or rump, is simply a way of telling people that the Skogsrå is not human, but an otherworldly being. [180]

## Both wicked and good

The Skogsrå was known for *'turning your sight'* and this would make you lose your way in the forest or be unable to find your cattle. It was common that people got lost in the vast forests or the mountain regions of Sweden and usually the Skogsrå was to blame. Luring travellers away was something she was famous for. It was called being *"skogstagen"* in Swedish, meaning being taken by the forest. If you were taken by the forest you had to perform certain tasks to break the Skogsrå's power over you. Saying a prayer to God or turning a piece of clothing inside out usually worked.

An ancient belief, that is very likely pre-Christian, is that water has magical and protective properties. The Skogsrå could not follow you across a stream or a river. Sometimes she would ask a man to help her across water and if he didn't, she would push him into the stream and laugh at him.[181]

Making a small bag of certain herbs and plants also provided sufficient protection against any wicked nature spirits. Some of the most common plants were garlic, mezereon, valerian and heath spotted-orchid. You would

---

[176] Granberg. *Skogsrået i yngre nordisk folktradition*, 1935
[177] Granberg. *Skogsrået i yngre nordisk folktradition*, 1935
[178] Schön. *Älvor, vättar och andra väsen*, 1986
[179] Granberg. *Skogsrået i yngre nordisk folktradition*, 1935
[180] Granberg. *Skogsrået i yngre nordisk folktradition*, 1935
[181] Granberg. *Skogsrået i yngre nordisk folktradition*, 1935

then carry the bag around your neck. The use of certain herbs for protection is another ancient practice.[182]

Other ways to ensure that the Skogsrå had no power over you were to carry a knife made of steel, or go hungry and unwashed into the forest. The Skogsrå was not very fond of unwashed hunters, and they were not able to kill her animals. There is a story about a hunter who encountered the Skogsrå in the forest one morning. She was accompanied by her elk who became frightened of the hunter. The Skogsrå calmed the animal with the words: *"Unwashed and unfed will not harm us."* The hunter then urinated in his shoe, washed himself with it and drank the rest. He then shot the elk, which fell dead to the ground. It was common knowledge that a hunter had to wash before he went out into the forest, otherwise the hunt would not go well. This is a myth that is exclusively told in Sweden.[183]

The Skogsrå could also be very helpful in keeping children safe if they got lost in the woods. However, if the children never returned from the woods the Skogsrå was to blame.

Often she watched over the coal-burners in the forest and if the charcoal stack caught fire during the night, she would wake the coal miner up before the fire had spread.

People used to give offerings to the Skogsrå in return for protection and prosperity. Hunters would offer her some meat and the coal miner some coal. The offerings were usually left on tree stumps. People would also give offerings to the Skogsrå when they needed help with retrieving lost animals, protection for both people and domestic animals, or if they needed to find their way through the forest. Offerings could consist of: pieces of cloth, salt, coins, food and tobacco. The tree stumps were also decorated with flowers and branches from the birch tree. Certain trees that looked a bit peculiar would also be seen as sacred to the Skogsrå and offerings were made there. It was important to keep the area around the tree nice and tidy.[184]

There is a folk story from the North of Sweden about a specific offering ritual. When the cows were let out for the summer, a coin was wrapped in a cloth which was then hung around the cows' necks, one by one. Meanwhile you had to whisper into the cow's ear the time you wished for it to return home. The coin then had to be placed inside the first tree stump you came across and the Skogsrå asked to send the cows home at the exact hour you asked for. This ritual always had a good effect. Also, if one

---

[182] Granberg. *Skogsrået i yngre nordisk folktradition*, 1935
[183] Granberg. *Skogsrået i yngre nordisk folktradition*, 1935
[184] Duppils Krall, *Skogsråets samband med Freyja*, 2003

of your cows did not come home, you had to place a coin into a tree stump and the cow would return.[185]

## The erotic myths

Only about 10 % of the stories about the Skogsrå mention her erotic side. However, these are the myths that are the most well-known. You can find erotic references to the Skogsrå all over Scandinavia.

There are plenty of folk stories about coal miners who have had contact with the Skogsrå in various ways. She was usually kind to them and watched their fires while they slept. The men who encountered her were the men that usually spent a lot of time on their own in the forest due to work. She was described by these men as sensual and forward, but at the same time you had to be careful as her power over a man was very hard to break.

The Skogsrå liked to take mortals as lovers and in many myths the man lived a double life. He had one life with the Skogsrå and their children in the forest and one with his ordinary family. It was common that men would spend the summer months in solitude in the forest, watching over the coal stacks. This was when they met the Skogsrå.[186]

If the Skogsrå favoured a man it was very difficult for him to get away. She was very attractive, but also very strong. Any mortal man who had an intimate relationship with the Skogsrå would later go insane or become withdrawn. In some cases he would have bad luck for the rest of his life, depending on the outcome of his relationship with the Skogsrå. If a man abandoned the Skogsrå he would sometimes die in mysterious circumstances.[187]

When the Skogsrå was after a mortal lover she could take the shape of his sweetheart and visit him at night. The man eventually noticed the hollow back/tail and realized that he had been duped. The Skogsrå then laughed and said: *"It was fun to trick Christian blood!"* The man replied: *"And it was fun to lie with the Devil just once"*. This is an exclusively Swedish myth and can be found in many parts of the country.[188]

A famous legend, called *the mezereon legend (tibastsägen)*, is told in various versions in all parts of Sweden. There was a farmer who the Skogsrå would not leave alone. As soon as the evening came he was unable to stay at home, but run outside into the forest, where he stayed all night. Once his wife happened upon the Skogsrå and the wife asked, *what should I do about the big bull that will not come home at night?* Well, the Skogsrå said, *you take mezereon and valeriana and moss from the roof on the north side of the chimney, and boil it and give to*

---

[185] Granberg., *Skogsrået i yngre nordisk folktradition*, 1935
[186] Granberg. *Skogsrået i yngre nordisk folktradition*, 1935
[187] Granberg. *Skogsrået i yngre nordisk folktradition*, 1935
[188] Granberg. *Skogsrået i yngre nordisk folktradition*, 1935

*him*. The wife did this and gave it to her husband and he never went to the forest at night again. The Skogsrå's cry could be heard all over the land: *Mezeron and valeriana, damned shall I be for teaching you healing!*[189]

To have a successful hunt the hunter had to give offerings to the Skogsrå in form of a small piece of meat. The hunter could also choose to offer himself to the Skogsrå. If a man usually caught many animals, people said that he had sexual contact with the Skogsrå. There is a strong connection between a successful hunt and myths about the Skogsrå and those are the most widespread. She was the ruler of the wild animals and if she approved of you, you would be able to kill them. [190]

There was a young man, who didn't really know his own age, but believed he was 19. He was charged with the crime of having had a sexual relationship with the Skogsrå. The year was 1737 and his name was Anders Månsson from Halmstad. The court asked Anders about his encounter with the Skogsrå and he told them how he kept meeting this tall, slim woman dressed in white. She was quite persistent and Anders finally went with her to her house. He made love to her a couple of times before he passed out. This happened on several occasions. The court was convinced that it must have been the Skogsrå, since decent women would not behave in this way. The poor boy was questioned for two days and had to reveal exactly how he had spent his time with the Skogsrå. Anders was lucky and didn't get a death sentence, but it was common that men were sentenced to death for having been intimate with the Skogsrå. It was believed, even amongst scholars, that the Skogsrå was a creature of flesh and blood and these encounters were fully possible. The erotic myths about the Skogsrå and mortal men survived into the early twentieth-century.[191]

## The origins of the Skogsrå

The Skogsrå is the ruler of the forest and wild places, guarding and protecting the animals, and this description is very similar to myths about an ancient hunting goddess of the North.

In North-western Europe hunting was very important to the inhabitants, even after they adopted a more settled way of life and became farmers. Many think that the earliest goddess worshipped during the Paleolithic Age was a hunting one. The goddess of hunters was a major power in early times in Northern Europe and worshipped mainly by men. She was hostile and unfriendly towards women and they were more or less forbidden to enter the forest during the hunt. The domain of the women

---

[189] "Tibast och vändelarot, tvi vale mig som lärde dig bot!" Schön. *Svenska sägner*, 2008
[190] Granberg. *Skogsrået i yngre nordisk folktradition*, 1935
[191] Schön. *Svenska sägner*, 2008

was the hearth and the home; however, there were some communities where women were skilled hunters and responsible for the fishing. [192]

The early Scandinavian hunting goddess would allow hunters to kill her animals if they kept to her rules. But if you offended her she could be a very dangerous enemy. It is also believed that the goddess of the hunt had a male equivalent, a co-ruler of the wild.[193] This might explain why the Skogsrå is seen as male in certain countries like Russia and Estonia.

Ebbe Schön, a Swedish folklorist, believes that the Skogsrå is a pre-Christian nature Spirit.[194] There is, however, no mention of the Skogsrå or other nature spirits in the Old Norse literature.[195] The only reference to the Skogsrå is in the myth called Odin's hunt where Odin hunts down the Skogsrå and kills her. The Skogsrå is described with long, flowing hair and large, long breasts. There are many versions of this myth and in an earlier version the hunted Skogsrå is none other than the Goddess Freyja.[196] Folk myths and legends were not recorded in Scandinavia until after Christianity had been introduced. After the important church meeting in Uppsala in 1593 a serious fight against the old beliefs and pagan traditions began.

A mediaeval belief in Sweden was that all nature spirits and otherworldly beings were Lucifer's angels that *"rained down upon the Earth for three days"*. Some of the beings ended up in the lake and became *Sjörå*, others landed in the forest and became *Skogsrå*, the ones in the mountains became *Bergrå* and the ones that fell on the roof tops turned into *tomtar* (gnomes/pixies).[197]

The religious text *Svebilius Katekes (catechism)* from 1714 had a huge impact on pagan beliefs in Sweden and people's relationship with nature spirits. In this text Svebilius asks the question: *"How and in what way is idolatry practiced?"* The answer is: *"In many different ways: worship of the sun / moon / and the heavenly host; Angels, fallen saints / skogsrå / sjörå / pixies / and more."*[198]

## Her names

The Skogsrå, which is the name I've chosen to use, has many names and most of them are honourable titles.

### Skogsrå, Skogsråda, Rånda, Råhanda, Råanda

*Skogsrå* is the most common name for her and it can be translated as ruler of the forest. The word *rå* comes from the word *råda* which means to

---

[192] Davidson. *Roles of the Northern Goddess*, 1998
[193] Davidson. *Roles of the Northern Goddess*, 1998
[194] Schön. *Älvor, vättar och andra väsen*, 1986
[195] Granberg. *Skogsrået i yngre nordisk folktradition*, 1935
[196] Duppils Krall. *Skogsråets samband med Freyja*, 2003
[197] Granberg. *Skogsrået i yngre nordisk folktradition*, 1935
[198] Duppils Krall, *Skogsråets samband med Freyja*, 2003

rule. In old Norse the word *ràu* means gods. *Skog* is the Swedish word for forest.

*Anda* translates as the female form of spirit.

Skogsfru, Skogsjungfru, Skogskäring

These names can be translated as the Lady or Virgin of the forest.

*Fru* = lady/wife

*Jungfru* = virgin/maiden

*Käring* = old lady

All of the above titles are honourable and respectful.

Skogsnuva, Skogstippa

Both of these names are belittling, referring to a slightly silly woman or a hen.

Torspjäska, Grankotte-Kari, Trasåsafröken, Talle-Maja,

Lomtjärnsfrun, Korumpa-Kersti, Skogela, Besta,

Landkäringen, Sigrid

Local names for Skosrået.

## Skogsrå myths around the world

The concept of the Mistress of the Wild is found in many parts of the world.

In Denmark the faeries were called *Ellefolk*. There were both male and female Skogsrå-like beings. The female, *Ellekvinnan* (faery woman), is described like the Swedish Skogsrå as an erotic nature spirit with a hole in her back like a rotten tree stump.

In Norway *Huldran* had a cow's tail, otherwise she was identical to the Swedish Skogsrå. *Huldrefolket* is the Norwegian name for the faeries, the ones who live beneath the earth. Lardal council in Norway has to this day a picture of a Huldra on their crest, tail and all![199]

In Caucasus the memory of a hunting-goddess still survives. The Ossetes had a main hunting deity, the male *Aefsati*, pictured as an old and bearded man that was sometimes blind or one-eyed. Aefsati had many beautiful daughters who were occasionally allowed to marry poor huntsmen. Male divinities like Aefsati were regarded as patrons of the hunt and rulers of the animals, but the Caucasian people also worshipped hunting-

---

[199] Granberg. *Skogsrået i yngre nordisk folktradition*, 1935

goddesses. One of these goddesses was *Dali*, in the mountainous regions of Georgia. The goddess Dali was the ruler of the hoofed and horned animals. Birds, fishes, wolves, bears and foxes were ruled by the male gods. Myths and poems tell us about Dali's relationship with the hunters. Dali was described as young and beautiful with long hair, either golden or black, and she inspired terror in those who met her. Sometimes Dali took on the form of one of her animals. Dali would accept a mortal hunter as her lover, but he was then forbidden to have sexual relations with mortal women, and his relationship with Dali could lead to his death. [200]

In Finland the myths tell us about the male forest spirit *Metsänhaltia*, seen as an old man with a long beard. In Estonia he was called *Metshaldj*. This forest man was also a shape-shifter. The myth about a female forest spirit was not so common; however, a certain forest wife, forest hostess, or forest maiden is mentioned in the poetic writings. She was called *Metsa-piiga* and was seen as an old woman sitting on a rock with her knitting, or as a young woman in a white dress. You could tell that it was her by the non-existing eyebrows or the hole in her back. Offerings for Metsa-piiga were placed in ant hills to ensure a successful hunt.[201]

The Finnish Lapps worshipped a goddess of the forest and also mentioned a female spirit with a tail. But unfortunately there isn't enough information about these myths.[202]

In Russia there was a male forest spirit with long hair and beard and a body covered with fur. They called him *Ljeski* (lijes = forest). He was sometimes described with horns and goat's feet. Ljeski was the ruler of the animals and was especially fond of wolves. The bear was his servant and friend and watched over Ljeski when he had been drinking too much vodka. People left offerings for Ljeski on tree stumps.

In Poland there was a myth about female wood spirits, *Dziwozony* (the wild women). These women were very tall, athletic and sensual with long hair and long breasts, which they threw over their shoulders when they were running. They moved around the woods in a large group and therefore young men avoided walking in the woods on their own, as they might encounter the Dziwozony.[203]

In Czech Republic there were the *Lesni panni* (forest maidens), who even features in Polish legends. Lesni panni are solitary beings, dressed in white and flowers weaved into their long blonde hair.[204]

In Germany the Skogsrå and her sisters was called *Holzfräulein* (woodwives), *Waldweibchen* (forest women), *Moosweibchen* (moss-women) and

---

[200] Davidson. *Roles of the Northern Goddess*, 1998
[201] Duppils Krall, *Skogsråets samband med Freyja*, 2003
[202] Granberg. *Skogsrået i yngre nordisk folktradition*, 1935
[203] Duppils Krall, *Skogsråets samband med Freyja*, 2003
[204] Duppils Krall, *Skogsråets samband med Freyja*, 2003

*Lohjungfren* (bush women). All of these forest spirits were dressed in green. They were mainly friendly and helpful.[205]

## The Sjörå – the Lady/ruler of the Lake

The Sjörå, the erotic creature of the waters, had many similarities to her sister the Skogsrå. A myth tells us about Harald, a young fisherman from Bohuslän County in Sweden. One beautiful summer's evening Harald was sitting in his boat waiting for the fish to bite. It was a fine, calm evening and to his surprise his boat was suddenly rocking violently, almost causing him fall into the lake. He was even more surprised to see a young naked woman climbing into his boat. She was only showing him her front, carefully hiding her back. Harald realized that this was the Sjörå, because he had heard many tales about her. Some people said that she had a hole in her back, or a tail. And some people even said that she had a fishtail. Her hair was long, black and wavy, but he knew that sometimes her hair could be golden, white or green. The Sjörå started touching and kissing the fisherman and he forgot all about who she was and enjoyed himself instead. Before the Sjörå left Harald she promised him good luck with his fishing, and that he would never die whilst at sea. And that was exactly what happened. However, Harald never wanted any other fisherman to accompany him when he was out in his boat. *"I get company anyway"*, he used to say…[206]

If you were kind to the Sjörå she would return the kindness and often warned her favourite fishermen if a storm was coming. However, if you offended her, she might drown you or make sure that you never caught a fish again. To ensure a good catch people gave offerings to the Sjörå in the form of silver coins, which were thrown into the lake.

The Sjörå, or *Havsfrun* (the lady of the sea) as she was called out at sea, was usually seen sitting on a rock or on top of the waves combing her long hair. If she showed you her back it was a sign that a storm was coming. Her voice was the most beautiful in the world and she loved singing and humming. [207]

*Den lille havsfrue* (the little mermaid) is a famous sculpture in Copenhagen, Denmark, and a reminder of the myths about the sensual Sjörå.

## The end of the Skogsrå?

In modern days we rarely here about people's encounters with the Skogsrå. The storytellers of old were all very convinced that they had seen her, spoken to her and given her offerings. We no longer depend on hunting

---

[205] Granberg, *Skogsrået i yngre nordisk folktradition*, 1935
[206] Schön. *Älvor, troll och talande träd*, 2000
[207] Schön. *Älvor, troll och talande träd*, 2000

which instead has become a popular sport. And we rather watch TV than gather around the fire telling stories. Electricity is everywhere and the dark forests have lost some of their magic and mystery. It is not just the Skogsrå that has disappeared from the Swedish forests, mountains and lakes but also the Sjörå, trolls, giants and faeries. The Skogsrå and her kin have, in other words, become extinct.

Some say that she has disappeared because her forests have been cut down, or because new roads and buildings have been built. Some blame the railway, electricity and Christianity. But there is no definite story about *why* she is gone.

The last wolves in the South of Sweden were killed in the 1860's, so perhaps she has departed further north, where her beloved animals are still safe...

## Bibliography

Davidson, Hilda Ellis (1998) *Roles of the Northern Goddess*. London: Routledge

Duppils Krall, Sara (2003) *Skogsråets samband med Freyja* (essay). Högskolan i Gävle

Granberg, Gunnar (1935) *Skogsrået i yngre nordisk folktradition*. Uppsala University

Schön, Ebbe (2000) *Älvor, troll och talande träd*. Semic

Schön, Ebbe (1986) *Älvor, vättar och andra väsen*. Rabén & Sjögren

Schön, Ebbe (2008) *Svenska sägner*. Bilda förlag

# Diana's Moon Rays

## By Sorita d'Este

> "there are certain women who do say that they have dealings with Diana the Queen of the fairies. There are others who say that the fairies are demons, and deny having any dealings with them..."
> [William Hay, 1564]

The Roman Diana was one of the most formidable goddesses of the ancient world. The moon, oak groves, lakes and the wilderness were all associated with her, and she was the protector of women in childbirth, young children and wild animals. Her cult predates that of Rome and found ways of adapting to the ever changing political and cultural landscapes it encountered as her worship spread to ever extensive regions, incorporating some of the practices and traditions it encountered - notably that of the Hellenic goddesses Artemis and Hekate. In this essay I present a small part of my research on this fascinating goddess, including examples that illustrate the way in which she was seen as both a *Faerie Queen* and a goddess in Scotland and in her home country, Italy.

With the dawn of new religious movements in Europe the older traditions often became amalgamated into the new, continuing earlier practices and beliefs in varied guises. It was a natural progression which continues today as different cultures and traditions continue to cross-fertilise one another. Christianity continued this approach, seeking to convert the followers of the older traditions by finding ways of integrating older traditions and practices into its Church. However, it is clear that some cults and customs simply did not lend themselves to comfortable conversion, with their adherents not allowing their deities to be demoted into positions of diminished power, and desiring to continue their practices as their ancestors had done for generations. This presented an obstacle for the Church which responded with increased efforts to remove the power and strongholds from these traditions —demonising the gods and practices of the older traditions. Through this process the good gods of the past became the evil devils and demons of the new religion. The spiritual practices of the older religions became the witchcraft of the new. Notwithstanding this, the older cults found ways to survive, they became more exclusive, elusive and secretive, developing methods of keeping their teachings alive until such times as circumstances no longer forced them to survive like fugitives on the margins of society.

### Invocation to Diana.
*Diana, beautiful Diana!*
*Who art indeed as good as beautiful,*
*By all the worship I have given thee,*
*And all the joy of love which thou hast known,*
*I do implore thee aid me in my love!*
*What thou wilt 'tis true*
 *Thou canst ever do:*
*And if the grace I seek thou'lt grant to me,*
*Then call, I pray, thy daughter Aradia,*
*And send her to the bedside of the girl,*
*And give that girl the likeness of a dog,*
*And make her then come to me in my room,*
*But when she once has entered it, I pray*
*That she may reassume her human form,*
*As beautiful as e'er she was before,*
*And may I then make love to her until*
*Our souls with joy are fully satisfied.*
*Then by the aid of the <u>great Fairy Queen</u>*
*And of her daughter, fair Aradia,*
*May she be turned into a dog again,*
*And then to human form as once before!*
*(Aradia, Leland, 1899)*

The book *Aradia- Gospel of the Witches* by Charles G. Leland (1899) has become one of the most significant books through which Diana became recognised and worshipped again as a goddess in the revivalist Pagan traditions of the 20th century. In *Aradia*, Leland presents Diana as the primary goddess of witches in Italy who worshipped her as a goddess of magic, witchcraft and of the Moon – all attributes which were linked to her in antiquity too, of course. The above spell from chapter VI of this book specifically names Diana as a *"great Faerie Queen"* highlighting that Leland and his informant Maddalena were familiar with Diana as both a Pagan goddess and as a Faerie Queen in the late 19th century. Speculations that the work presented by Leland might have been, as Prof. Hutton suggests in his *Triumph of the Moon*, "*to some extent the concoction of Leland himself*" and indeed that it is possible that the author was duped into believing he was being presented with authentic material by his informant Maddalena abound. The evidence suggests differently and the work Leland presented in *Aradia* fits neatly into a long tradition of the continued recorded and alleged worship of Diana in Italy, often also associated with folk magic, witchcraft and superstition.

Intriguingly, even though *Aradia* was a hugely influential text on the development of initiatory Wicca (a ceremonial tradition of witchcraft taught by Gerald Gardner), as well as modern Paganism, it is rarely credited as such. Yet, one of the best known ritual texts used in Wicca, *The Charge of the Goddess* clearly borrowed its opening lines from *Aradia*. *The Charge of the Goddess* is used not only by the initiatory branches of Wicca today, but also by various other traditions of modern Paganism and Goddess spirituality. I include an extract from Aradia (1899) for comparison with an extract from a published (public domain) version of Gerald Gardner's *Book of Shadows* (a book of rituals copied by initiates of the tradition) dated to 1949.

In *Aradia* the words below are spoken by Aradia, the daughter of Diana with her brother/lover Lucifer, after she was instructed to teach magic to the witches by her mother, Diana:

> *"When I shall have departed from this world,*
> *Whenever ye have need of anything,*
> *Once in the month, and when the moon is full,*
> *Ye shall assemble in some desert place,*
> *Or in a forest all together join*
> *To adore the potent spirit of your queen,*
> *My mother, great Diana. She who fain*
> *Would learn all sorcery yet has not won*
> *Its deepest secrets, them my mother will*
> *Teach her, in truth all things as yet unknown.*
> *And ye shall all be freed from slavery,*
> *And so ye shall be free in everything;*
> *And as the sign that ye are truly free,*
> *Ye shall be naked in your rites, both men*
> *And women also: this shall last until*
> *The last of your oppressors shall be dead..."*
> (Aradia, Leland, 1899)

In Wicca the words of *The Charge* are spoken by the High Priestess of a Coven as part of the ceremony of *Drawing Down the Moon* which is performed at most ceremonies:

> *"Whenever ye have need of anything, once in the month, and better it be when the moon is full, ye shall assemble in some secret place and adore the spirit of Me who am Queen of all Witcheries and magics. There ye shall assemble, ye who are fain to learn all sorcery, yet have not won its*

*deepest secrets. To these will I teach things that are yet unknown. And ye shall be free from slavery, and as a sign that ye be really free, ye shall be naked in your rites, both men and women, and ye shall dance, sing, feast, make music, and love, all in my praise. "*
(Charge of the Goddess, Book of Shadows, Gerald Gardner, 1949)

Numerous historians and writers recorded their beliefs and observations that Diana was associated with witchcraft and sorcery long before Leland published *Aradia*. For example, in the mid-18th century the Italian author Girolamo Tartarotti wrote that *"The identity of the Dianic cult with modern witchcraft is demonstrated and proven"* in his book *Del Congresso Notturno Delle Lammie*. Tartarotti's writings attacked the popular notions held by the Church about witchcraft as being anti-Christian, instead attributing magical practices of his day to the cult of the goddess Diana. A century before Tartarotti, Pietro Piperno in his 1647 essay *De Nuce Maga Beneventana & De Effectibus Magicis* mentions Diana in the context of witchcraft, and earlier still, in 1576, Bartolo Spina wrote saying that witches gathered at night to worship Diana, in his work *Quaestio de Strigus*.

There were many fascinating rituals, customs and festivals associated with Diana in antiquity. *The Nemoralia* was perhaps the most ancient as well as the most famous of the festivals dedicated to Diana, named after Lake Nemi in Aricia where the festival originated as a provincial cult, eventually spreading throughout Italy. Here Diana Nemorensis (Diana of the woodlands) was celebrated. Stratius wrote describing this, saying that:

> *"It is the season when the most scorching region of the heavens takes over the land and the keen dog-star Sirius, so often struck by Hyperion's sun, burns the gasping fields. Now is the day with Trivia's Arician grove, convenient for fugitive kings, grows smoky, and the lake, having guilty knowledge of Hippolytus, glitters with the reflection of a mu
> ltitude of torches; Diana herself garlands the deserving hunting dogs and polishes the arrowheads and allows the wild animals to go in safely, and at virtuous hearths all Italy celebrates the Hecatean Ides..."*[208]

Lake Nemi was also named *Speculum Dianae (*Mirror of Diana) by Virgil and was a wealthy centre where Diana was worshipped as a goddess for at least 1000 years. Here Diana was served by the *Rex Nemorensis* (King of the Woods) who was both Priest and guardian to the temple, fulfilling an important role of office, one which started and ended with bloodshed. The British historian Thomas Babington Macaulay (1800-1859) in his translation of *The Battle of Lake Regillus* poetically describes Lake Nemi and the cruel reality of its priest:

> *'From the still glassy lake that sleeps*
> *Beneath Aricia's trees--*

---

[208] Statius, Silvae 3.1.52-60, c. 93 CE.

> *Those trees in whose dim shadow*
> *The ghastly priest doth reign,*
> *The priest who slew the slayer,*
> *And shall himself be slain."*[209]

Strabo's *The Geography* provides us with further insights on the *Rex Nemorensis* telling us that the position of priest was held by a man who was a run-away slave, who having successfully attacked and killed his predecessor, took his place as King of the Woods. As a result the serving priest was always armed with a sword and on the look-out for would-be attackers in order to defend his life and his position. Thus the Priest-King of Diana was a hunter who was hunted in turn, a King who had to prove him-self to be the best against each challenger in order to maintain his position as servant and guardian to the goddess.

In her 2010 work *The Visions of Isobel Gowdie: Magic, Witchcraft and Dark Shamanism in Seventeenth-Century Scotland,* Emma Wilby writes that:

> *"Among contemporary scholars, the Scottish fairy queen and her train or host are generally agreed to represent a version of the 'European nocturnal goddess' commonly associated with these narratives. This link is also reflected by the fact that educated Scots linked the fairy queen with Diana, one of the deities identified with the female spirit-group leader as early as the first decade of the tenth century. James VI referred to 'That fourth kind of spirits, which by the gentiles was called Diana and her wandering court, and amongst us was called the fairy or 'our good neighbours'; while Scottish minister William Hay claimed, in 1564, that 'there are certain women who do say that they have dealings with Diana the queen of the fairies'."*[210]

This then provides us with a glimpse of Diana as the *Queen of the Faeries* in Scotland and raises the question of how an ancient Roman goddess came to be known as the Queen of the Faeries in Scotland. The Romans travelled far and wide throughout Europe, the Mediterranean and beyond, taking with them their household gods and goddesses. Likewise merchants and travellers often took the worship of their deities with them to other parts of the world and in this way the worship of Diana, as is the case for many other deities, became known in parts of the world which might not be immediately apparent. In Britain there are at least six known Roman inscriptions to Diana, and at least five engraved gems, all dating to the 2nd to 4th century CE. These gems were found in the south of England and the Welsh borders, two of which show just Diana's head, and three showing her as a huntress with bow and arrows.

---

[209] Thomas Babbington Macaulay, *The Battle of the Lake Regillus,* 1860:113.
[210] **Wilby,** *The Visions of Isobel Gowdie: Magic, Witchcraft and Dark Shamanism in Seventeenth-Century Scotland,* 2010:306.

*But how and when did Diana become a Faerie Queen?*

As we have seen from the quote by Wilby above, Diana was already equated to the Faerie Queen in 1564 in Scotland, enough for a Scottish minister to name her as such and indeed it seems to have been a widely held belief in the 16th and 17th centuries.

The poet Dryden (1639-1700) also identified the queen of the faeries with the goddess Diana, writing in his *The Flower and the Leaf*:

> "*Where we with Green adorn our Fairy Bow'rs,*
> *And even this Grove unseen before, is ours.*
> *Know farther; Ev'ry Lady cloath'd in White,*
> *And crown'd with Oak and Lawrel ev'ry Knight,*
> *Are Servants to the Leaf, by Liveries known*
> *Of Innocence; and I myself am one*
> *Saw you not Her so graceful to behold,*
> *In white Attire, and crown'd with Radiant Gold?*
> *The Soveraign Lady of our Land is She,*
> *Diana call'd, the Queen of Chastity...*"[211]

In 1590 and 1596 Spenser's famous *The Faerie Queene* was published, a beautifully written allegorical text which remains one of the longest poems written in the English language. In this text Spencer addresses many of the political issues of his day, making many poignant remarks about religion at a time when the religious landscape of England was changing fast at the hands of the Reformation. He praises the Tudor dynasty linking them to that of King Arthur and in it many of the prominent people of the political and social landscape of the time were represented as characters, all in an allegorical manner of course! Spenser's clever use of classical mythology to tell his story shows his familiarity with Diana:

> "*The woodborne people fall before her flat,*
> *And worship her as Goddesse of the wood;*
> *And old Sylvanus selfe be eems not, what*
> *To thinke of wight so faire, but gazing stood,*
> *In doubt to deeme her borne of earthly brood;*
> *Sometimes Dame Venus selfe he eems to see,*
> *But Venus never had so sober mood;*
> *Sometimes Diana he her takes to bee,*
> *But misseth bow, and shaftes, and buskins to her knee.*"

Spenser's work was highly influential, though it was not the first to merge Diana the goddess with that of the Faerie Queen, it would certainly have helped to perpetuate it. In a letter to Sir Walter Raleigh, in which he expounds on his intentions for writing his book, Spencer writes that:

---

[211] Dryden, *The Poems of John Dryden*, 1822:221

> "So have I laboured to do in the person of Arthure: whom I conceive, after his long education by Timon (to whom he was by Merlin delivered to be brought up, so soone as he was borne of the Lady Igrayne) to have seen in a dreame or vision the Faerie Queene, with whose excellent beautie ravished, hee awaking, resolved to seek her out: and so, being by Merlin armed, and by Timon throughly instructed, he went to seeke her forth in Faery land. In that Faery Queene I mean Glory in my generall intention: but in my particular I conceive the most excellent and glorious person of our soveraine the Queene, and her kingdome in Faery land. And yet, in some places else, I doe otherwise shadow her. For considering shee beareth two persons, the one of a most royall Queene or Empresse, the other of a most vertuous and beautifull lady, this latter part in some places I doe expresse in Belphoebe, fashioning her name according to your owne excellent conceipt of Cynthia, (Phoebe and Cynthia being both names of Diana)."[212]

But Spenser was just following an already established tradition of seeing Diana in the role of faerie queen. The writings of the Bishop of Exeter (1161-84), Bartholomew Iscanus, show that the association between Diana and faeries was already established in the twelfth century:

> "Whosoever, ensnared by the Devil's wiles, may believe and profess that they ride with countless multitudes of others in the train of her whom the foolishly vulgar call Herodias or Diana, and that they obey her behest. Whosoever has prepared a table with three knives for the service of the fairies, that they may predestinate good to such as are born in the house…" (MSS Cotton. Faust. A. viii, fol. 32)

Iscanus also provides us with a bridge between Diana's association with faeries and her association with the magical ability to fly through the air, which is a classical image of witchcraft and sorcery in Europe. He was however not the first to make this association, instead he was simply continuing an already established Christian tradition. In the ninth century *Canon Episcopi* similar associations are highlighted in association with Diana:

> "This also is not to be omitted, that certain wicked women, turned back toward Satan, seduced by demonic illusions and phantasms, believe of themselves and profess to ride upon certain beasts in the night time hours, with Diana, the Goddess of the Pagans, and an innumerable multitude of women, and to traverse great spaces of earth in the silence of the dead of night, and to be subject to her laws as of a Lady, and on fixed nights be called to her service."[213]

---

[212] Spenser, *The Works of Edmund Spenser: With Observations of his Life and Writings*, 1849:3.
[213] Thomsett, *Heresy in the Roman Catholic Church: A History*, 2011:131.

## The Faerie Queens

It is a theme which was persistent, centuries after the Bishop of Exeter and nearly a thousand years after the *Canon Episcopi*, similar accusations were still made of Diana. This example is from the 1834 text *The Darker Superstitions of Scotland: Illustrated from History and Practice*:

> *"Some wicked women, resigning themselves to Satan and to the illusion of demons, believe and declare that they ride forth on certain animals in the night, along with Diana the goddess of the Pagans, or with Herodias, accompanied by a numberless multitude of women : and summoned to serve on particular nights by the orders of her whom they obey as their mistress, they pass silently over many regions during a tempestuous season".[214]*

In his 1597 *Daemonologie,* King James wrote about Diana and her faerie court saying that:

> *"That fourth kind of spirits, which by the gentiles was called Diana and her wandering court, and amongst us was called the fairy or 'our good neighbours'."[215]*

This further emphasises that Diana was viewed as having a court of faeries who accompanied her, or that women seeking knowledge of sorcery would follow her. The origins of this motif can be found in classical mythology where Diana is accompanied by a group of nymphs or virgin priestesses on her travels, who often feature as key figures in the recorded myths. Conversely translators writing in the 1560s such as Phaer and Golding believed that it was not the Roman goddess who developed into Diana the Faerie Queen, but rather that it was the other way around and that the Faerie Queen developed into the goddess. Bennett notes:

> *"The Renaissance notion that the English fairies were the equivalents of Diana and her band of nymphs. Such important translators as Phaer and Golding treated 'fairies' as the nearest English equivalent to the classical wood deities, the 'nymphs' of Vergil and Ovid. Diana, as chief of the nymphs, was identified with the fairy queen."[216]*

Another major theme which needs investigating further within the context of Diana as the faerie queen is her association with witchcraft and sorcery. An examination of the history of the Roman Diana shows that she has close associations with the Hellenic goddesses Hekate and Artemis. Hekate in particular has a very long history of being associated with witchcraft and sorcery, as well as with the spirits of the dead and practices such as necromancy. Furthermore, as early as the fifth century BCE the goddess Hekate was conflated with the virgin huntress Artemis, who in turn is considered to be the Greek Diana. The histories, myths and cults of these

---

[214] Dalyell, *The Darker Superstitions of Scotland: Illustrated from History and Practice*, 1834:537.
[215] King James VI, *Daemonologie*, 1597 Book 3.57
[216] Bennett, *The Evolution of "The Fairie Queene"*, 1942:8.

three goddesses are at times exceedingly tangled and so it is a tangible argument that Hekate's magic would become that of Diana. This is a consideration supported by the 19th century writer Walter Scott, who also links Hekate and Diana to other powerful and divine female figures from Scottish mythology, who could also be considered to be faerie queens in their own right:

> *"Like Diana, who in one capacity was denominated Hecate, the Fairy Queen is identified in popular tradition with the Gyre-Carline, Gay Carline, or mother witch, of the Scottish peasantry ... She is sometimes termed Nicneven"*[217]

The connection between the Greek Hekate and the Scottish faerie queen tradition is explored a little by the author David Rankine in his essay *Hekate Wears Tartan* which was published in the anthology *Hekate Her Sacred Fires* (2010). In it Rankine discusses the connection between the Greek Hekate and the Scottish Faerie Queens in the context of the practice of Flyting, he asserts that:

> *"The reference to Nicneven and her nymphs comes from an earlier 1585 work, The Flyting of Montgomery and Polwart. Flyting was a verbal contest of insults, often given in verse, between two poets in medieval Scotland. This tradition has an ancient history, and may be found in many cultures around the world. Interestingly it was often used as a prelude to physical battle between warriors, including in ancient Greece, where we find Hekate."*[218]

Here we should note that Nicneven which means the daughter of Nevis and the traditional Queen of the Faeries who has a hall in the otherworld under the earth, believed to be under Ben Nevis, the highest mountain in Scotland. Rankine provides an extract from one such flyting from Scotland in which Hekate is named:

> *"On ane thre headit hecate in haist pair they cryit:"*
> (On a three-headed Hecate in haste there they cried)[219]

In the tradition of conflating Hekate with Diana and giving these two goddesses the same attributes and shared myths, Scottish folklore does not disappoint. In his epic work *Albion's England* (1586) William Warner describes Hekate as the queen of hell, or possibly the otherworld and links her with faeries and elves who act as her servants, which seems to imply that they are her servants and therefore that she might also be considered to be a faerie queen in this context:

> *"Saw Hecat new canonized the Sourantisse of hell,*

---

[217] Scot, *Minstrelsy of the Scottish Border*, 1869:449.
[218] Rankine, in *Hekate Her Sacred Fires*, 2010:257.
[219] Rankine, in *Hekate Her Sacred Fires*, 2010:257.

*And Pluto had it holiday for all which there did dwell ...*
*The Elves, and Fairies, taking fists, did hop a merrie Round."* [220]

The Italian historian Carlo Ginzburg suggested that the Scottish fairy queen has her origins in the night goddesses of Europe and explores this theme in his work *The Night Battles* in which he examines the evidence and trial records of the Benandanti of 16th and 17th century Italy. Claims of night-time excursions, flying through the air on the back of animals or by other means and obeying their female leader, who is sometimes named as Diana, seems to be similar – if not identical – to the claims made of Diana in Scottish lore. In the 10th century this notion of women flying out at night with Diana was already established enough to cause the French cleric Reginon de Prum to speak to priests regarding such women saying that:

> *"One cannot allow that certain wicked women, perverted and seduced by Satan's illusions and mirages, believe and say that they go out at night with the goddess Diana, or with Herodias, and a great crowd of women, riding astride certain animals, covering large amounts of ground in the night silence and obeying Diana like a mistress"* advising them to preach *"...to the men of their parishes that all this is absolutely false and that such fantasised in the minds of the faithful come not from the spirit of God but from Evil..."*.[221]

Perhaps it was not so much a transformation of *Diana the Roman Goddess* into *Diana the Faerie Queen*, but rather that Diana gained the additional role of Faerie Queen whilst also retaining her place as a goddess. This process allowed her traditions and myths to be kept burning brightly, for a minority this beckoned them towards desiring knowledge and understanding of her mysteries – whilst others feared and continued to demonise it and her followers.

> *"We are moon-rays, the children of Diana,"* replied one:--
> *"We are children of the Moon;*
> *We are born of shining light;*
> *When the Moon shoots forth a ray,*
> *Then it takes a fairy's form."*
> *(The Aradia, Leland, 1899)*

## Bibliography

Bennett, J.W. (1942) *The Evolution of "The Fairie Queene"*. New York: Burt Franklin

Dalyell, J.G. (1834) *The Darker Superstitions of Scotland: Illustrated from History and Practice*. Edinburgh: Waugh & Innes

---

[220] Chalmers & Johnson, *The Works of the English Poets from Chaucer to Cowper*, 1810 Vol 4.548.
[221] Wilby, *The Visions of Isobel Gowdie: Magic, Witchcraft and Dark Shamanism in Seventeenth-Century Scotland*, 2010:304.

Dyer, T.F.T. (1884) *Folklore of Shakespeare*. London: Harpers

D'Este, Sorita (ed) (2010) *Hekate Her Sacred Fires*. London: Avalonia

D'Este, Sorita and Rankine, David. (2007) *Wicca Magickal Beginnings*. London: Avalonia

D'Este, Sorita and Rankine, David. (2008) *The Isles of the Many Gods*. London: Avalonia

D'Este, Sorita. (2005). *Artemis: Virgin Goddess of the Sun & Moon*. London: Avalonia

Green, C.M.C. (2007) *Roman Religion and the Cult of Diana at Aricia*. Cambridge: Cambridge University Press

Leland, Charles G. (1899) *Aradia or the Gospel of the Witches*. London: David Nutt

Paton, Lucy Allen (1960) *Studies in the Fairy Mythology of Arthurian Romance*. New York: Burt Franklin

Schlam, Carl C. (1984) *Diana and Actaeon: Metamorphosis of a Myth*. In *Classical Antiquity* Vol 3.1:82-110.

Scot, Reginald (1886, first edition 1584) *Discoverie of Witchcraft*. London: Elliot Stock

Scott, Walter (1869) *Minstrelsy of the Scottish Border*. London: Alex Murray & Son

Thomsett: M.C. (2011) *Heresy in the Roman Catholic Church: A History*. North Carolina: McFarland & Co. Inc.

Wilby, Emma (2010) *The Visions of Isobel Gowdie: Magic, Witchcraft and Dark Shamanism in Seventeenth-Century Scotland*. Eastbourne: Sussex Academic Press

Internet:

http://www.sacred-texts.com/pag/gbos/gbos02.htm, accessed March 2013-07-01

# THE VALKYRIES

## Norse Fairie Queens?

## VALERIE KARLSON

> *"High under helmets
> across the field of heaven,
> their breastplates all
> were blotched with blood,
> and from their spear points
> sparks flashed forth."*[222]

The name Valkyries means *"choosers of the slain"*,[223] which doesn't fill the listener with confidence. It is clear that the further back in time we go, the more primal and ferocious the Valkyries become, thus Branston notes:

> *"In Old English, the word waelcyrge, the exact equivalent of Old Icelandic valkyrja, seems to have been applied to female demons who were connected with war and viewed with sensations of horror. The word is used to gloss Erinyes, Tisiphone, Allecto, and Bellona."*[224]

By contrast, in the later texts the Valkyries seem to have been reduced to glorified mead-bearers for the huge number of warriors feasting and fighting until the final conflict of Ragnarok. Between these two ends of the spectrum, from bloody roots to warrior waitresses, we find the more recognisable figure of the Valkyrie with her faerie queen qualities.

Some Valkyries share the faerie queens' passion for human lovers. The most famous of these tragic love affairs is that between Brynhildr and Sigurd, the dragon-slayer, which was immortalised in Wagner's operatic *'Ring'* Cycle. Brynhildr had been punished by the god Odin for not

---

[222] *Volsungakvida 16*.
[223] From the Old Norse *val* meaning *"battlefield carnage"* and *kjósa* meaning *"to choose"*.
[224] Donahue, 1941:3.

following his instructions and causing a battle to be won that he had wanted lost. This is interesting, as it shows the power of the Valkyries, even though in this instance Brynhildr was punished for her choice. Sigurd rescued Brynhildr from the enchanted tower she slept in surrounded by a ring of fire, and they pledged their love, only for Sigurd to be enchanted and caused to love a sorceress' daughter. The resulting tragedy played out with everyone dying, and Brynhildr and Sigurd being reunited in death.

Another example of this passion for human lovers is found in the *Volundarkvida*, with three Valkyries, referred to as swan maidens due to their alternate form. Volundr (Wayland Smith) and his two brothers found three maidens by a lake shore and stole their swan cloaks. The three couples lived happily for seven years, but then the swan maiden Valkyries disappeared never to be seen again. The swan maidens leave after regaining their cloaks and thus the ability to transform and be free from what was effectively enforced servitude, a theme seen in other tales of shape-shifting faerie women associated with water, e.g. seal maidens. Both the bird form and the disappearance of the female lover after a period of time are themes also seen in fairie queen romances.

The assumption of a bird form is common amongst both fairies and gods, and indeed even links the human to the divine, with witches and shamans wearing cloaks and skins to shift into the animal world. Noted Norse scholar Ellis Davidson refers to this phenomena, writing:

> *"An episode in one of the Fornaldarsogur where a witch called Lara hovers over the head of her lover in battle in the form of a swan, chanting spells with such powerful magic that the enemy could not defend themselves, suggests a memory of the valkyrie tradition"*[225]

As already mentioned, Valkyries had the ability to predict the outcome of a battle, i.e. to prophesy the future. In this context it is significant that one of the Valkyries is Skuld, the youngest of the three Norns, the Norse weavers of fate. She is described in this role in more than one text, thus in the *Prose Edda* we see:

> *"These are called Valkyrs: them Odin sends to every battle; they determine men's feyness and award victory. Gudr and Róta and the youngest Norn, she who is called Skuld, ride ever to take the slain and decide fights."*[226]

There are several magical charms from across Europe associated with Valkyries. The 10th-11th century CE Anglo-Saxon *Lacnunga* includes a charm which has also been suggested as referring to Valkyries. This charm, *Wid Faerstice* (Against a Sudden Stitch), also mentions the barrow or burial mound, which is also particularly associated with the faerie:

---

[225] Davidson, 1973:26-27
[226] *Gylfaginning 36*, in Brodeur, 1916:48

> *'Loud were they, lo! Loud as they rode over the barrow ... where the mighty women declared their might and yelling they sent spears'*[227]

An interesting example of calling on the Valkyries is given in a jealousy spell from Norway. This is the *'Valkyrie'* spell recorded from a witchcraft trial in Bergen in the year 1324, which the witch Ragnhild Tregagas used to dissolve the marriage of her former lover, Bard:

> *I send out from me the spirits of (the valkyrie) Gondul.*
> *May the first bite you in the back.*
> *May the second bite you in the breast.*
> *May the third turn hate and envy upon you.'*[228]

A later Norwegian charm also mentions Valkyries, associated with other supernatural creatures. This is the 14th century protective *'Valkyrie stick'* found amongst the Bryggen runes, for protection:

> *'I cut runes of help, I cut runes of protection, once against the elves, twice against the trolls, thrice against the ogres.... Against the harmful 'skag'-valkyrie, the evil woman, so that she never shall, though she ever would, injure your life....'*[229]

Another example, the first Merseburg Charm from the 9th-10th century CE, seems to specifically refer to the ability of valkyries to influence battles:

> *"The Old High German Merseburg Charm tells of "noble ladies" (idisi) who "bound fetters" and "hindered the army." In the Grimnismdl a valkyrie called Herfjotur is mentioned. The word means literally "army-fetter," "war-fetter." As a common noun it means a terrifying weakness that comes over the warrior, hindering his ability and presaging his death. This weakness was apparently thought of as the work of the valkyrie. The noble ladies of the Germanic charm seem to correspond to the Scandinavian valkyries."*[230]

The juxtaposition of Valkyrie and witch is also found in the 11th century Icelandic *Volsungakvida*; verse 40 refers to the death of Gollveir, which has been suggested as one of the causes for the divine war between the Aesir and the Vanir:

> *"Thou wast a Valkyrie*
> *thou loathsome witch*
> *evil and base*
> *in Allfather's hall;*
> *the Champions all*

---

[227] Pollington 2003:229.
[228] MacLeod & Mees, 2006:37
[229] Liestol, 1966:55.
[230] Donahue, 1941:4.

> *were forced to fight
> for thy sake
> thou subtle woman.'*[231]

The use of the term *'subtle woman'* is interesting here, as it is not one that you would associate with battle maidens. This is further reinforces when you look at the earlier text this seems to have been drawn from, the *Voluspa*. In the earlier *Voluspa* (stanzas 20-25), the volva says:

> *"I mind the folk war,
> the first in the world
> when they pierced Gollveig
> with their pointed spears,
> and her they burnt
> in the High One's hall;
> she was three times burnt
> and three times born,
> over and over
> yet ever she lives.
> They call her Heidr
> who came to their home,
> a far-seeing witch
> cunning in sorcery. . . ."*[232]

Branston notes that this indicates an equation of the two characters as being the same, a point which is substantiated by the similarity of the meanings of their names as well as the circumstances of the death: *"It appears then that Gollveig (Gold Might) otherwise called Heidr (Shining)"*[233] The triplicities in her death and birth are also suggestive, as the number three is commonly associated with faerie queens as well as the Valkyries.

Different texts give varying numbers of Valkyries, often multiples of three such as nine or twenty-seven. One of these texts gives a very different role for the Valkyries, as pointed out by Branston:

> *"There is another remembrance of Valkyries in one of the hero lays from the Verse Edda, in Helgakvida Hjorvardssonar 17. But here the maidens have nothing to do with the choosing of the slain; instead they fulfil the role of guardian angels at sea by bringing Helgi's ships safely to harbour:
> There were three nines in ranks;
> one maid rode ahead
> with a helmet and all in white;*

---

[231] Branston, 1955:174-175.
[232] Branston, 1955:174.
[233] Branston, 1955:174.

> *when their horses reared*
> *there rippled from their manes*
> *dews into the deep dales,*
> *hail into the high woods,*
> *whence men their harvests have."*[234]

The Valkyries riding claiming souls with Odin are a form of the Wild Hunt, which was associated with different gods and goddesses across Europe. Significantly however the Irish battle goddess the Morrigan also leads the wild hunt and is a faerie queen, so a clear parallel can be found in this psychopompic role.

That the Valkyries ride horses also reminds us of the faerie queens. The image seen in paintings over the last two centuries is predominantly of them riding white horses (like some of the faerie queens), but this seems to be an artistic impression which has become popular, rather than a specific reference to the old Norse sagas and myths. Nevertheless, it seems clear that the Valkyries, with their wide range of roles and qualities, are reminiscent in many ways of European faerie queens, and as such are worthy of a place in their company.

## Valkyrie Names in the Norse Sagas

| *Name* | *Meaning* | *Text References* |
| --- | --- | --- |
| *Brynhildr* | *Armour-battle* | *Helreið Brynhildar, Skáldskaparmál* |
| *Eir* | *Help, Mercy* | *Nafnaþulur* |
| *Geirahöð* | *Spear-battle (alternate version of Geironul)* | *Grímnismál* |
| *Geiravör* | *Spear-goddess* | *Nafnaþulur* |
| *Geirdriful* | *Spear-flinger* | *Nafnaþulur* |
| *Geironul* | *Spear-bearer* | *Grímnismál, Nafnaþulur* |
| *Geirskogul* | *Spear-raging* | *Hákonarmál, Völuspá, Nafnaþulur* |
| *Goll* | *Screaming* | *Grímnismál, Nafnaþulur* |
| *Gondul* | *Wand-wielder* | *Völuspá, Nafnaþulur* |

---

[234] Branston, 1955:189.

| | | |
|---|---|---|
| Gunnr | War | Darraðarljóð, Gylfaginning, Nafnaþulur Völuspá |
| Herfjötur | Host-fetter | Grímnismál, Nafnaþulur |
| Herja | Devastate | Nafnaþulur |
| Hervör alvitr | Devastating strange-creature (?) | Völundarkviða |
| Hildr | Warrior, Battle | Darraðarljóð, Grímnismál, Nafnaþulur, Völuspá |
| Hjalmþrimul | Helmet-clatterer | Nafnaþulur |
| Hjörþrimul | Sword-warrioress | Darraðarljóð, Nafnaþulur |
| Hlaðguðr svanhvít | Hlaðguðr swan-white | Völundarkviða |
| Hlökk | Shrieking | Grímnismál, Nafnaþulur |
| Hrist | Shaker | Grímnismál, Nafnaþulur |
| Hrund | Pricker | Nafnaþulur |
| Kára | Wild stormy one | Helgakviða Hundingsbana II |
| Mist | Mist | Grímnismál, Nafnaþulur |
| Ölrún | Ale-rune | Völundarkviða |
| Prúðr | Strength | Grímnismál |
| Raðgrior | Plan-destroyer | Grímnismál, Nafnaþulur |
| Randgriðr | Shield-bearer | Grímnismál, Nafnaþulur |
| Reginleif | Gods' kin | Grímnismál, Nafnaþulur |
| Róta | Sleet and storm | Gylfaginning |
| Sanngriðr | Very violent | Darraðarljóð |
| Sigrdrífa | Victory-urger | Sigrdrífumál |

| | | |
|---|---|---|
| *Sigrún* | Victory rune | *Helgakviða Hundingsbana I, Helgakviða Hundingsbana II* |
| *Skalmöld* | Sword-time | *Nafnaþulur* |
| *Skeggjöld* | Axe-time | *Grímnismál, Nafnaþulur* |
| *Skögul* | Raging | *Grímnismál, Hákonarmál, Nafnaþulur, Völuspá* |
| *Skuld* | Shall be (the youngest Norn) | *Gylfaginning, Nafnaþulur, Völuspá* |
| *Sveið* | Noise | *Nafnaþulur* |
| *Svipul* | Changeable | *Darraðarljóð, Nafnaþulur* |
| *Þrima* | Fight | *Nafnaþulur* |
| *Þrúðr* | Strength | *Grímnismál, Nafnaþulur* |
| *Þögn* | Silence | *Nafnaþulur* |

# Bibliography

Branston, Brian (1955) *Gods of the North.* London: Thames & Hudson

Brodeur, A.G. (trans) (1916) *The Prose Edda of Snorri Sturluson.* New York: American-Scandinavian Foundation

Davidson, H.R. Ellis (1988) *Myths and Symbols in Pagan Europe: Early Scandinavian and Celtic Religions.* Manchester: Manchester University Press.

Davidson, H.R. Ellis (1973) *Hostile Magic in the Icelandic Sagas*, in *The Witch Figure*, ed. Newell, V. (1973) London: Routledge & Kegan Paul

Donahue, Charles (1941) *The Valkyries and the Irish War-Goddess*, in *PMLA* Vol. 56.1:1-12

Fee. C.R. with Leeming, D.A. (2001) *Gods, Heroes, & Kings: The Battle for Mythic Britain.* Oxford: Oxford University Press

Liestol, A (1966) *The Runes of Bergen: Voices from the Middle Ages*, in Minnesota History Summer 66.49:58

MacLeod, Mindy & Mees, Bernard (2006) *Runic Amulets and Magic Objects.* Woodbridge: Boydell Press

McMahon, James V. (1994) *Valkyries, Midwives, Weavers, and Shape-Changers: Atli's Mother the Snake*, in Scandinavian Studies 66.4:475-487

Pollington, Stephen (2003) *Leechcraft: Early English Charms Plantlore and Healing.* Norfolk: Anglo-Saxon Books

Raudvere, Catharina (1996) *Now you see her, now you don't: some notes on the conception of female shape-shifters in Scandinavian traditions*, in *The Concept of the Goddess* (ed.) Billington, S. & Green, M. London: Routledge

# MORVEREN

The Sea Queen

## DOROTHY ABRAMS

Morveren of Zennor, like many Queens in Faery, means to challenge our assumptions about love and the twilight vision of our intuitive nature. Humans typically misunderstand her approach. Our understanding is distorted by fear or superstition. We are taught a mermaid is a seductress intending to drown her lovers. She comes to land to marry a human and gain a soul for herself. She would sink a ship as readily as save it. These misrepresentations of Morveren appear in several Cornish folk tales, *The Mermaid of Zennor* and *Lutey and the Mermaid* among them. More recently but following the same theme, she has surfaced in pop culture through the *Pirates of the Caribbean* films and a lovely hypnotic song called *Morveren's Lullaby* recorded by Isobel Anderson in *Cold Water Songs*. Each of these appearances gives us a brief encounter with the Lady. But who is Morveren, Faery Queen beneath the Sea? Beyond the illusion of predatory female, what is her teaching for ordinary humans?

Mike O'Connor re-tells the classic story of *Lutey and the Mermaid*[235] in *Cornish Folk Tales*. There Morverna, an alternate spelling for our Faery Queen, calls to the old fisherman Lutey for help. She is stuck in a shallow pool left by the retreating tide. Lutey carries her to the sea in exchange for three rewards for his compassion: he will have healing ability, wise advice for those seeking help and prosperity for his family. When they reach the deeper water, Morverna clings to Lutey and invites him to join her beneath the waves. She is very beautiful. She is desirable. She promises a life of riches, sunshine and merriment beneath the sea. Her kiss nearly seals the bargain. Then on the shore Lutey's dog calls him back from the enchantment of a mermaid. Nevertheless, Lutey learns he will be claimed in

---

[235] O'Connor, *Cornish Folk Tales*, 2010:17.

nine years. He struggles to the beach and falls asleep in a cave, fortified by his smuggled brandy cache.

Lutey's wife finds him in time for breakfast the next day. Unable to keep his adventure a secret, Lutey tells his wife and she tells the entire village. For the next nine years he heals and helps the villagers. His family prospers. Morverna is true to her word in all things. She finds him at the end of nine years when Lutey walks out of his boat into her embrace and is never seen again. The gifts of the mermaid do not end with Lutey. Prosperity, healing and service to their village continues in his family though at a cost of one family member lost at sea just short of each decade.

O'Connor's telling of Morverna's story has many elements in common with Faery Queens around Europe. The sprite is beautiful. She seeks a human lover. She grants his wishes. Her seduction is otherworldly. She releases him but her will is done at the end of things. The human lover's family prospers and is blessed in the exchange. These are traits we ascribe to a Faery Queen. There is also the implication of trickery.

From the first encounter, Morverna pretends to be stranded in the shallows unable to return to her family. She claims her husband will eat her children if she is not there to fix supper. Like Lutey we accept her at face value because such a thing mirrors the human condition of female helplessness, gender roles and male dominance. It is unlikely to be true. Those who populate the Faery world are shapeshifters. They can appear as they wish in size, species, and body configuration. Morverna could have shifted into a woman's form, as mermaids are known to do, and walked into the sea herself. She did not because she sought out the encounter with Lutey.

Her claims about her husband are also questionable. Although mermen have an ugly reputation as creatures who might actually eat their children instead of cooking supper themselves,[236] encounters with Manannan, Llyr, or Dylan indicate this is another distortion. In fact merfolk of both genders are described as particularly attractive and passionate beings who *"embody and guard treasures of empathy, sensuality and love that the human race has yet to discover."*[237] The love offered by mermen to human women who are sometimes faithless is recognized in English poetry of the Romantic Era. Matthew Arnold's *The Forsaken Merman* ends with the lament for the lost human lover:

> *"There dwells a loved one,*
> *But cruel is she!*
> *She left lonely for ever*

---

[236] Littleton, *Gods, Goddesses and Mythology*, volume 11, 2005:1273.
[237] Mistele, *Undines: Lessons from the Realm of the Water Spirits*, 2010, e-book location 103.

*The kings of the sea.'*[238]

Aggrieved though the merfolk may be, their interaction with humans teaches deep emotional and physical merger beyond the ordinary capacity of a human to love. This deeper experience is a sign of our encounters with the world of Faery. Were the mermen as ill-tempered as Morverna claims in her appeal to Lutey, faithless women would find themselves imprisoned with no means to return to land when they are once claimed by the sea spirits. Upon escape they would be stalked and hunted down.

The themes we see in *Lutey and the Mermaid* are typical of the legends about the sea spirits. In the *Mermaid of Zennor*, the story is turned about to reflect more completely what I understand the Sea Queen of Faery to be about. Known as a mermaid, Morveren hears the beautiful singing voice of Matthew Trewella up at St. Senara's Church near Zennor. She is drawn to it and against the advice of her father the Sea God Llyr, she shapeshifts into a female form and slides into the back of the church. People notice this extraordinarily beautiful visitor but she slips out and avoids them each time she attends. Matthew decides he will discover her origin and follows, some say after he has heard her sing. Wishing to make beautiful music together, he catches her before she dives into the sea and goes with her since she will not stay ashore.

Mathew's family and friends mourn his loss presuming him drowned but he is heard of once more when a sea captain drops anchor near the harbour. A lovely mermaid asks him move the anchor from her doorway for she needs to return to her husband Matthew and their children. The sea captain quickly complies, knowing it is unwise to cross a mermaid. When he tells his story to the people of Zennor, they understand their Matthew is alive and well, living in the realm of Faery with his beloved Morveren.[239]

In this story Morveren remains true to her own realm. Rather than go ashore and live as a human woman in search of love and a human soul, Morveren takes her lover to sea. This story is a contrast to Christian versions of Faery tales. Those stories claim mermaids come ashore to seek out human males in order to lose their elemental nature and take on a human soul.[240] Presumably humans were compliant in this endeavour because the mermaids made good wives and mothers as long as the human kept her comb or mirror.[241] In *The Faery Teachings*, Orion Foxwood views the matter of soul differently. He indicates the world of Faery is the origin of all souls, including humans.[242] His understanding of the soul ties it to the

---

[238] Arnold, "The Forsaken Merman", Arthur Quiller-Couch, ed., *The Oxford Book of English Verse: 1250–1900*, 1919.
[239] "The Mermaid of Zennor and other Cornish Mermaids", *Cornwall Guide*, http://www.cornwalls.co.uk/myths-legends/mermaids.htm
[240] Mistele, *Undines: Lessons from the Realm of the Water Spirits*, 2010, e-book location
[241] Littleton, *Gods, Goddesses and Mythology*, volume 11, 2005:2173.
[242] Foxwood, *The Faery Teachings*, 2007:33.

expression of chi or life force (*toradh* in Gaelic indicating the fruit or results of life). For him, a soul moves through all levels of the earth, especially the Faery underworld, and that *"all beings have a soul."*[243]

What makes humans in ordinary reality or the surface world question the relative soulfulness or soullessness of the merfolk is their wisdom. Merfolk see the larger picture and as a result often act in ways that are judged cruel or selfish by the humans who feel victimized by their tricks or taxes. The merfolk's concern is to bring their humans, since they each relate specifically to a specific number of individuals, into greater consciousness as guides and teachers. Sometimes that requires tough love. Evaluated from a dispassionate distance, the complaints people level at the Faery Queens are more apt to be typical of their own human actions. We call this projection in human psychology.

A simple example is seen in the love story of Morveren and Matthew. The old women in Zennor warned repeatedly *"no good will come of this."*[244] For his family ashore, that was true. The beautiful seductress enchanted Matthew away from his hearth and home to live in a foreign place beneath the waves. Criticism of Morveren as a selfish conniving sea witch was only a small leap for them. On the other hand, by all accounts Matthew lived happily ever after with his beautiful Queen. He chose to enter her domain since she would not stay in his. Morveren neither demanded nor coaxed his compliance. Some say it was love at first sight. She was as smitten as he was. So who was it whose souls were shrunken and small? Not Morveren and Matthew.

The shift in setting from land to sea is an important clue in seeking out Morveren's identity. From the sea we see that the merfolk have souls. They interact with humans for our good and theirs, as a loving exchange of energy. The cost of this to the human ego can be shattering. It may be equally transformative for the merman or maid. Humans are rewarded for their connection to Faery.

In some versions of this story, Matthew or his beloved sends warnings of sea storms to the village. The Land of Lyonesse is a legendary land off the coast of Cornwall near the Scilly Islands. According to Tennyson, Lyonesse was the battle field for the final war between King Arthur and Mordred.[245] Its demise beneath the sea occurs sometime thereafter. In the mermaid stories of Zennor, a lone church bell chimed from beneath the waters to warn of approaching storms, rung by Matthew who had done the same ashore to call the faithful to worship before he met Morveren. The problem with this, of course, is that the siting of Lyonesse is to the west southwest of Land's End, 40 miles or better away from Zennor. Would

---

[243] Foxwood, *The Faery Teachings*, 2007:131.
[244] Connor, *Cornish Folk Tales*, 2010:xx.
[245] Tennyson, *Idylls of the King*

they hear an underwater warning over that distance? Nevertheless, geography as well as time is malleable in the land of Faery so the patronage of Matthew to his people stands.

But is Morveren more than a mermaid in love? Is she a Faery Queen? Orion indicates that there are many types of Fair Folk, some solitary and some in clans or hives. The greater the Fae population in a given location, the more likely they are to have a gentry class though that may be mostly for our benefit as humans. Further he explains because the Fae work together in collectives *"easily translated by human consciousness, [t]he kings and queens are more like focal points where numerous thousands even, of Fay coalesce into a colonial type of being with a central and extremely powerful intelligence."*[246]

Certainly Morveren holds the power and compassion to fit that description since her word is true and obeyed. In addition she offers great passionate love to Matthew and transition to the Underworld at the end of life for Lutey. These clearly are characteristics typical of the Fae. Her lineage is royal in that she is the sister of the God of the Isle of Man known as Manannan and the daughter of the Sea God Llyr. Further investigation of the lineage reveals Manannan's wife is the Faery Queen Fand[247] and their daughter is Naimh the Moon Goddess who also rules crops and cattle, typical responsibilities of the Fae.[248]

If that is not convincing enough, we should remember than Morveren's image appears in St. Senara's church in Zennor carved on the chancel seat with a plaque above attesting to the connection of mermaids and Sea Goddesses. Arthur Quiller-Couch in the *Oxford Book of Verse* concludes that St. Senara binds the mermaids, saints and pagan princesses together with the Sea Goddesses.[249] The saint's legend is as magical as any of the stories about Morveren.

As Quiller-Couch records her history, Senara was a pagan princess in Brittany, set asea in a barrel perhaps because she was pregnant. She floats all the way to Ireland, miraculously survives and returns triumphant with her child. However, before returning to Brittany, she converts to Christianity. Her journey home passes through Zennor where she founds the church named for her. Quiller-Couch suggests that Senara is one example of the transformation of a Sea Goddess into a Christian saint. Faery Queens, Goddesses, and mermaids are all inhabitants of the world of Faery. This shifting and merging of races and kin in the Otherworld may disturb the linear mind which walks the surface of the earth with a science text held tight against the heart. Nevertheless, the flexibility of form and identity among the Fae is one of their key characteristics. A familiar chant reminds

---

[246] Foxwood, *The Faery Teachings*, 2007:21.
[247] Evans-Wentz, *The Fairy-Faith in Celtic Countries*, 1911:346.
[248] Gregory, *Gods and Fighting Men, Part II Book IX Oisin's Story*, 1904.
[249] Quiller-Couch, ed. *The Oxford Book of English Verse: 1250–1900*. 1919:198.

us *"one thing becomes another, in the Mother, in the Mother."* And so it does. Morveren is mermaid, Faery queen and Sea Goddess. She is also an undine.

Undines are generally understood to be merfolk. They are also the element of water itself. Like a wave they break apart and re-form. Their humanoid appearance is a convention assumed to connect with humans. Friedrich de la Motte Fouque in his fairy tale *Undine* depicts the changeable nature of the water elementals. The fair maiden Undine who appears as a beautiful damsel marries the knight Huldbrand. Her uncle Kuhleborn is a merman of interior waters, both pleased and wary of his niece's choice of a husband. When she tried to dismiss her uncle once she had a human husband:

> *'Kuhleborn seemed to become angry at this; his countenance assumed a frightful expression, and he grinned fiercely at Undine, who screamed aloud and called upon her husband for assistance. As quick as lightening, the knight sprang to the other side of the horse, and aimed his sharp sword at Kuhleborn's head. But the sword cut through a waterfall which was rushing down near them from a lofty crag; and with a splash, which almost sounded like a burst of laughter, it poured over them and wet them through to the skin.'*[250]

Thus there is a sense in which the elemental undine is water itself. Orion cites W. B. Yeats classification of the Fae which includes elementals.[251] Orion indicates elementals are linked with the more traditional folklore spirits in that the elementals create and the Fae sustain the creation. Clearly it takes a multitude of the Faefolk to balance and preserve the Earth in the face of the thoughtless mucking about of their human charges.

In that line of thought, William Mistele indicates that some problems like replacing war with peace and ending the use of weapons of mass destruction might be among the issues only a partnership between the Fae and humans can resolve. The undines offer *"heart-to-heart connection…on earth"*[252] that these planet-rescuing changes might occur. The four types of elementals referenced in western mysticism to which Yeats refers are undines of the water, gnomes of the earth, sylphs or the winged fairies of the air and salamanders or dragons of the fire. Each has different responsibilities in creation. For the undines, the world of water, emotional realities, love, passion and death are primary.

Both William Mistele and Friedrich de la Motte Fouque make the ultimate mission of the merfolk clear. They are among us to teach us love. Science texts set aside, the merfolk uncover our hearts and draw us in to the depths of emotional chaos and upheaval found in loving, passionate, sensual

---

[250] de la Motte Foque, *Undine*, 2010 :32.
[251] Foxwood, *The Faery Teachings*, 2007:73.
[252] Mistele, *Undines: Lessons from the Realm of the Water Spirits*, 2010: e-book location 88.

relationships. They visit to convince us it is acceptable to love without reason. They offer us love, foolish and unworthy as we may be. From their example, we need not be so frightened of the merger of souls brought about by a deep spiritual merger in sexual passion. Mistele documents his meditations with a variety of undines who are nothing short of spirit lovers. Christian theology warns human souls to flee from these creatures and fight against their natural elemental passions. The Church even pronounces our biological and spiritual urges as sinful. The merfolk come to say it isn't so.

Though she has no relationship to Mistele, Morveren is such a spirit lover or succubus. She is set up as an opponent of the sailors in *Pirates of the Caribbean* because of her seductive ways. Never mind the humans are pirates, thus less likely to be capable of selfless passion and veneration of the beloved. Never mind they capture and ravish women unless, like Elizabeth Swann, the women are as fierce as they are. The pirates are human and that is sufficient for the film makers and audience to make them the hero in any contest with Morveren and her sisters. The merfolk take away the human will and create a mushy enchanted puppet, if you believe the stories. Like the sirens in the Mediterranean world, Morveren sings her song. Men who do not stop their ears are drawn away from human striving and fall to enchantment.

Now what exactly is wrong with that, I'd like to know? Less striving and more passion might truly transform this world and protect the environment. Make love not war! I remember that slogan. It was a good idea. Isobel Anderson exactly captures that seductive otherworldly tone in *'Morveren's Lullaby'*. The song is hypnotic. Irresistible. Morveren calls Matthew to her with the promise of play, and that he will never forget her: *"A memory that lingers in your dreams/A melody that lingers in your thoughts."*[253] The song is a seduction. *"Just let me play with you boy,"* she asks, not telling him he will live and love with her forever in a state of forgetfulness, that he will appear to have drowned. In exchange for his human life she gives him a crown and exquisite love.[254] The song is a lullaby which puts to sleep his cares and inhibitions. Love does that.

Because we are rarely ready for immortal love, the Fae are infamous in our stories about their affairs with humans. Men like Lutey drown. Matthew disappears to live in the sea. Other unsuspecting men are drawn into Faery mounds and kept for seven years. Orion says this is an initiation of consciousness which gives the human a healthy, pain-free, physical body, psychic sight and magic, as in the *Ballad of Tamlane*.[255] Furthermore, humans are told to be fearful of the cost of a love affair with the Fae. There is some truth in that. The secrets of Morveren or any other resident of the underworld cannot be stolen or taken away without a price or Ordeal. The

---

[253] Anderson, "Morveren's Lullabye" *Cold Water Songs*, 2010.
[254] Anderson, "Morveren's Lullabye" *Cold Water Songs*, 2010.
[255] Motherwell, ed., *Early Scottish Ballads*, Scott, "The Young Tamlane", 1864:58

Ordeals faced in learning the skills of the Fae and in being released to one's home include facing one's fears and illusions. Humans rarely enjoy such confrontation with their shadows. However, if we succeed as humans in that Ordeal, we gain a new vision of reality. Because of the love of the Fae the initiated human can travel from the Underworld to the Surface world and remember both. S/he sees both worlds at once and, like Morveren, is committed to a mission outside of the self to redeem the ignorant from their follies.

The failure to love unselfishly is one of those follies. Seduction by Morveren is pure pleasure unhampered by guilt and outside of time and space. The human is meant to imitate the Fae in their sensual giving without reservation. The Fae open our hearts without fear. We are asked to live with an open heart and draw others to do the same. The Fae expand human awareness of all connected beings both in and out of Faery. We are asked to share that awareness with our families and lovers. Morveren teaches love by being Love, but the love of the Fae is not the same as that with humans. Their love is not monogamous. The Fae expect their seduction to work. They are impatient with delay and excuses. They are eager to create the ecstatic epiphany with their human partners. The only game to play is theirs. Generally speaking humans are not skilled in this kind of love.

Human love tends to idealize unconditional love with a single soul mate. Couples pretend that is what they feel as they seek marriage. The truth surfaces quickly when personal desires are thwarted, the beloved strays or hard times hit hard. Divorce rates attest to that. Economic pressures have ended otherwise solid marriages at an increasing pace. *"Overall, the rate of divorce in Britain has been creeping up over the past 40 years. ONS indicated that fully one-third of marriages that commenced in 1995 had ruptured by what would have become their 15th anniversary. For marriages that started in 1970, the figure was one-fifth."*[256] Clearly there were conditions on their love which were poorly understood by these couples.

In contrast, love which is truly unconditional love is a spiritual love. It finds fulfilment in generosity and forgiveness. Behaviour and emotional commitment are disconnected. If the Fae are impatient with our human excuses, they readily accept our contrition and agree to start anew. Humans hold grudges and keep score and take advantage of the other. They forgive but never forget. Human love has all kinds of conditions.

Between humans, unconditional love requires maturity from both parties. Loving despite the actions of the partner cannot be seen as a license to act out adolescent fantasies. An immature partner will conclude since

---

[256] Ghosh, "Divorces Rate in UK Rose in 2010 for First Time in 8 Years," *World Business Times*, December 8, 2011, http://www.ibtimes.com/articles/263879/20111208/divorce-rate-recession-marriage-england-wales.htm.

compassion and forgiveness are offered, love means never having to say *'sorry'*, as in Eric Segal's *Love Story*.[257] Such is not the case in love between humans or with a Faery Queen. Being aware and care full of the lover's heart means the opposite: a ready and sincere apology for the inadvertent offense, and intention to guard and nurture the beloved, and a commitment to the best and highest good of the other. Such love is rare.

For Morveren and others like her, such rarity is exactly the point. Her love story with Matthew is told from a human perspective since that is all the story tellers had to work with. William Mistele suggests there is more available if we seek it. He writes that these Queens give the essence of a feminine energy that is *"all-embracing love…so receptive, so giving, so empty so free of ego and [formless]"*[258] that it shelters the human soul, inspires it and essentially re-creates it. The good news is that humans can learn to reproduce this energy themselves. For her humans, Morveren is able to assist in that reformation.

Mistele says that undines have the beauty and wisdom humans are meant to reach. One of his undine queens told him *"All that I am in my being you have the power to create in yourself…."*[259] Although the spirit lover connection with the Fae is sensual it exists outside of ego. Mistele's purpose extends beyond storytelling and into the transformation of humanity's future. He means for us to be the sort of human who can negotiate with the Fae and return to teach others to do the same. This is not a work of the imagination, nor is it a wet dream. It is a quantum shift in human compassion and intelligence.

A few years ago I attended a seminar on the Outer Banks of North Carolina in the U.S. called *'Teach at the Beach'*. It was organized by my friends Espeth and Nybor of the Haven Community. Sharing the seminar sessions were shamanic teachers Bekki ShiningBearHeart and Crow SwimsAway of the Church of Earth Healing. The shamanic sessions were focused on identifying and building a relationship with a Spirit Lover from the sea, not at all a difficult thing to imagine sitting on an island off the coast of the Atlantic. Through a series of shamanic journeys under the influence of the drum and rattle, I re-connected with a long time spirit friend Manannan. I acknowledged the magical turns and twists of synchronicity in our relationship going all the way back to my teenage years and music about the Isle of Man.[260] Little did I know it would continue with his sister Morveren.

Some time later in my own drum journeys I met a sea witch who lived beneath the lagoon where I typically alight in underworld journeys. She

---

[257] Segal, *Love Story*, re-printed 2005:91.
[258] Mistele, *Undines: Lessons from the Realm of the Water Spirits*, 2010:e-book location 193.
[259] Mistele, *Undines: Lessons from the Realm of the Water Spirits*, 2010:e-book location 215.
[260] Wood, *Mannin Veen*, England, 1933.

became a faithful friend and guide in times of stress. She reminded me of Susan Cooper's stories *Under Sea, Under Stone* and *The Greenwitch*, both of which took place in Cornwall. A little research revealed the sea witch and mermaid of my shamanic workings was associated with Zennor. She was Morveren, sister to my spirit lover Manannan. These connections together with the fact Morveren took on an appearance very much like my human friend Ditchwitch triggered me to the importance of all this happenstance. Clearly something significant was going on.

In *The Greenwitch*, Cooper builds her story around a folk custom in the fictional village of Trewissisck based on either of two existing villages: Trevissick or Mevagissey, Cornwall. Perhaps Cooper combined these with other villages. In these tales, Cooper describes an old folklore custom which the girl child Jane Drew is allowed to join with the village women. They create a larger than life simulacrum of magical woods—rowan, hazel and hawthorn--weighted with stones and offered to the sea on summer solstice. Unlike most of the village women who are up all night building the effigy as a lark, Jane feels the isolation and sadness of the Greenwitch. She wishes the figure would find happiness[261]. The wooden weaving is thrown into the sea on schedule to find the sea Goddess Tethys. When the Old Ones Merriman Lyon and Will Stanton approach Tethys to intervene for them with the Greenwitch they are told their concern is none of hers, *"the Greenwitch is mine."*[262] Eventually Jane speaks in a dream state with the Greenwitch to retrieve the lost talisman. She is magically granted her wish because of her compassion for the woven figure at its making. Her caring was offered without a thought for herself and it is the selflessness that carries her through her quest.

Compassion, love, and friendship are lessons from the Fae and/or the Divine. There is no real difference. For some reason our human ability to accept the lessons and learn the benefits of these soul-preserving emotions is stunted. We tell terrible tales of the very sprites that would trip us into unconditional love. Our resistance to them grows out of our ego-based fears. I am no different. Morveren aligns herself with the unconditional love aspect of the Fae when she points out deficits in my loving. Withholding forgiveness while wisely refraining from criticism is not enough growth, in her view. I thought life had taught me that in the realm of human relationships there is a complex tapestry of responses. None of them are right or wrong - they just are. As a result, what works for me may not be effective for my friends and family. With that understanding I learned to refrain from judgment, though not without keen observation of someone's acts against me.

I was pleased with my tolerance learned late in life. After expending a great deal of youthful energy in trying to convince people that my ways were

---

[261] Cooper, *The Greenwitch*, 1974:34.
[262] Cooper, *The Greenwitch*, 1974:81.

best, I retreated. I learned each person does the best they can with the information available to them. What I might judge a mistake is their learning experience. As a mentor, I point this out to people making strategical errors in their life, but anyone insistent on a course of action is free to go it alone. I have no intention of climbing fool's hill with them, but I will welcome them home with the Light on when they return, sadder but wiser. Under Morveren's tutelage, I hear my smugness.

*"Not good enough,"* says Morveren who loves more completely. She climbs the hill with the foolish, offering food and water and snuggles on the way. She kisses the stubbed toe and makes it all better. She seduces the climber into the shade when the sun is hot. She calls on the winds to blow against the climber headed in the wrong direction so he decides to turn back, though he may curse the weather. She points out the strengths gained from the experience. When the climber bemoans his failure, she disagrees saying the experience is enough to justify the effort. She is the true mentor.

Our frame of reference is different, Morveren and I. Humanly I reach out to save the individual pain. I want to avert disaster. I rescue and repair the situation. At times I also am resented instead of loved for being the rescuer. There is a triangular relationship among people involved in a crisis: victim-rescuer-persecutor. Frequently, as the victim is being rescued, s/he shifts the relationship to become the persecutor and goes after the rescuer, forcing the well intentioned cop or social worker into victim status.

The roles we play around that triangle are malleable. We take them on out of fear. Thus the victim complains about an inattentive lover. The rescuer points out solutions to the problem: counselling, confrontation, or separation. The victim acts on the recommendation and dislikes the outcome. Then the victim heaps criticism on the rescuer for ruining a perfectly good relationship. Shocked the rescuer is drawn into a debate and loses the argument. The rescuer feels persecuted and victimized, misunderstood and abused. The rescuer is the new victim. The old victim finds personal power restored through the attack on the would-be rescuer.

Morveren is too smart to be drawn into that dynamic. She knows how fickle humans can be. She shares the dreamer's dream, manipulates the environment and creates wisdom out of the disaster. All the while the victim clings to the illusion of free will. When Morveren croons *"come let me play with you boy"*, we are reassured this is a game which we can quit at will. It is not. When we join with a spirit lover from Faery, we experience the ecstasy of an out of the body love affair. We also experience inner transformation which turns us into someone we were not before.

Orion says clearly the merger with the Fae is a symbiotic relationship. Both partners benefit and are transformed. As we see into the world of Faery, Morveren sees into the surface world of ordinary reality. As we humans learn the lessons of spiritual work beyond the boundaries of the senses, Morveren learns the limitations of a physical body. Both of us deepen our experience with body, soul and spirit. This deepening comes within the context of love and sensuality if not sexuality.

The stories about merfolk seeking out human lovers to receive a soul are misinterpretations of this experience of unconditional love. Similarly, the stories of merfolk seeking human lovers in order to destroy them are a misrepresentation of the human joining the world of the Fae in the Underworld for partnership and merger. The sea sprite learns and experiences lessons about a human soul. Their own Faery souls expand as they understand the realities of the surface world: time, geography, union, separation, death, grieving, physical sex and child birth. The Fae learn longing and deferred gratification. Their innocence becomes experience.

On the other hand, the human learns lessons about the Faery soul. The human learns to stretch beyond perceived limitations of the body/mind. Humans time travel, join and merge with Spirit, and approach the Gods as a co-worker. Desires become manifest. Thoughts are shown as things. Sexual passion enters a spiritual ecstasy in ways no one ever discussed in church. Right and wrong, good and evil, human and Fae, male and female, merge into the One. Such distinctions are no longer necessary. Morveren is an aspect of The One. So are her human soul mates.

With these experiences integrated into one's life, the human and the Fae lovers are forever changed. Orion points out this level of connection with the Fae is rare. When it occurs, the partners bridge the worlds and create connections between the Underworld of the Fae and Ancestors below the middle world of human endeavour on the surface. In that context Morveren keeps calling, *"Just let me play with you, boy."* Sometime brave human souls step up to the game.

## Bibliography

Anderson, Isobel (2010) *Morveren's Lullabye* on *Cold Water Songs*

Cooper, Susan (1974) *The Greenwitch*. London: Chatto & Windus

Cornwall Guide (accessed 2012) *The Mermaid of Zennor and other Cornish Mermaids*, at http://www.cornwalls.co.uk/myths-legends/mermaids.htm

Evans-Wentz, Walter Y. (1911) *The Fairy-Faith in Celtic Countries*. London: H. Frowde

Foxwood, Orion (2007) *The Faery Teachings*. R.J. Stewart Books

Ghosh, Pasha R. (accessed 2012) *"Divorces Rate in UK Rose in 2010 for First Time in 8 Years,"* World Business Times, December 8, 2011,

http://www.ibtimes.com/articles/263879/20111208/divorce-rate-recession-marriage-england-wales.htm.

Gregory, Lady Augusta (1904) *Gods and Fighting Men, Part II Book IX Oisin's Story*. London: J. Fowler

Littleton, C. Scott (2005) *Gods, Goddesses and Mythology*, volume 11. London: Marshall Cavendish

Mistele, William R. (2010) *Undines: Lessons from the Realm of the Water Spirits.* North Atlantic Books

de la Motte Foque, Friedrich & Paul Turner (trans.) (2010) *Undine.* Surrey: Alma Classics

O'Connor, Mike (2010) *Cornish Folk Tales.* Stroud: The History Press

Quiller-Couch, Arthur (ed.) (1919) *The Oxford Book of English Verse: 1250–1900.* Oxford: Clarendon

Scott, Sir Walter (1864) *The Young Tamlane in Motherwell,* in William (ed.) *Early Scottish Ballads.* London: Charles Griffin & Co.

Segal, Eric (2005) *Love Story.* London: Harper Collins

Tennyson, Alfred (accessed 2012) *Idylls of the King* at http://www.gutenberg.org/catalog/world/readfile?fk_files=1442999

Wood, Haydn (1933) *Mannin Veen.* England

# THE TRANSFORMING ILLUSION OF MORGAN LE FAY

## FRANCES BILLINGHURST

> *"No-one knows the real story of the great King Arthur of Camelot. Most of what you think you know about Camelot, Gwenhwyfar, Lancelot and the evil sorceress known as Morgaine le Fay, is nothing but lies. I should know, for I am Morgaine le Fay, priestess of the Isle of Avalon, where the ancient religion of the Mother Goddess was born."*

(Morgaine, *Mists of Avalon*, Turner Network Television)

I cannot recall when my interest in the Arthurian legend commenced, or indeed how. All I know is that I had been fascinated with the trials and tribulations of King Arthur, his magical adviser Merlin, and the various knights for a number of years prior to reading Marion Zimmer Bradley's *The Mists of Avalon* in the late 1980s. Until then, Guenever (Guinevere) was merely some flimsy aspect of femininity whose true love was that of a man other than the one she was married to; the Lady of the Lake, who presented Arthur with the famous Excalibur, was a surreal apparition; and of course, there was the evil sorceress, Morgan le Fay, the bane of Arthur's very existence.

This description of Morgan is one that is still commonly used today within modern adaptations of the Arthurian legend, such as the recent BBC produced television series *Merlin*. It can be accredited to Sir Thomas Malory and what has been hailed as the greatest piece of English literature to have emerged from the medieval era, his *Le Morte d'Arthur*. Whilst Malory was believed to have finished his version of the Arthurian legend during the *"ninth year of Edward IV"*[263] (1469-70), his masterpiece was not widely published until after his death by William Caxton in 1485, who was responsible for splitting the 21 *'books'* into the chapter headings we are familiar with today.

In order to gain a more accurate understanding of who Morgan le Fay actually is, I consider it is important to detail her appearance within Malory's classic, as well as noting how she has evolved since the early Middle Ages. In doing this, we are also able to gain a deeper insight into the woman described as the *'Arthurian Queen of the Faeries'* and *'priestess of Avalon'*.

Due to the constant change in the spelling of the various character names, I have attempted to retain Malory's spelling as the source of truth, except when referring directly to a particular text. Further, where Malory's spelling differs from modern day common usage, I have also attempted to note this.

*Queen Morgan le Fay, Beatrice Clay, 1911*

---

[263] Malory, *Le Morte d'Arthur: King Arthur and of his Noble Knights of the Round Table*

*Le Morte d'Arthur* commences with a meeting having taken place between Uther Pendragon, the king of all Britain, and the Duke of Tintagil (Tintagel), who was accompanied by his wife, the beautiful Igraine. When the king's desire for Igraine became apparent, the Duke returned to Cornwall, placed his wife at Tintagil castle and himself at castle Terrabil, and proceeded to battle Uther. Because of the king's *'sickness'* for Igraine, Merlin used his magic to give Uther the disguise of the Duke, and Arthur, the future king, was conceived. It is here that Morgan is first briefly mentioned as being one of three sisters:

> *"... And the third sister Morgan le Fay was put to school in a nunnery, and there she learned so much that she was a great clerk of necromancy. And after she was wedded to King Uriens of the land of Gore,[264] that was Sir Ewain's le Blanchemain's father."[265]*

The other two sisters mentioned were Margawse, who married King Lot of Lothian and of Orkney (the mother of a number of Arthur's knights), and Elaine, who married King Nentres of the land of Garlot (who does not seem to appear anywhere else in the story).

Morgan and Arthur do not actually meet until towards the end of Book 1 when Igraine was summoned to verify Arthur's true bloodline, and where she *"came and brought with her Morgan le Fay, her daughter"*.[266]

In Book 2, Morgan appears again, this time as the wife of King Uriens (the father of Sir Ewaine, now spelt with an *'e'*). It is here that Arthur *"betoke the scabbard of Excalibur to Morgan le Fay, his sister"*[267] which prevented him from losing any blood while he had it upon his person during battle. The reason as to why Arthur gave Morgan the enchanted scabbard was never explained; however Morgan's true feelings towards both her brother and her husband were revealed:

> *"... and she loved another knight better than her husband King Uriens or King Arthur, and she would have had Arthur her brother slain, and therefore she let make another scabbard like it by enchantment, and gave the scabbard Excalibur to her love; and the knight's name was called Accolon, that after had near slain King Arthur."*[268]

The reasoning as to why Morgan hated Arthur and produced a replica scabbard is found in Book 4 where, following a battle against five kings who opposed his rule, Arthur, together with King Uriens and Sir Accolon, went hunting, which resulted in them dining upon a boat with a number of damosels (damsels), after which they fell into a drug-induced sleep. Uriens

---

[264] Gore is believed to be a part of modern day Cornwall, England
[265] Malory, *Le Morte d'Arthur: King Arthur and of his Noble Knights of the Round Table*
[266] ibid
[267] ibid
[268] ibid

woke to find himself having been transported back to Camelot; both Arthur and Accolon however found themselves caught up in a feud between two warring brothers. Arthur, having woken up in prison, was convinced to represent the *'evil'* Sir Damas in a battle to resolve the feud; meanwhile Accolon, awoke beside a well near the *'good'* Sir Ontzlake's manor. Excalibur and the magical scabbard were presented to Accolon by a dwarf who was sent by Morgan, whereas copies were given to Arthur.

Had it not been for the intervention of Nimue, the Lady of the Lake, Morgan may have succeeded in killing Arthur after his fake sword snapped off at the handle. However, with the aid of Nimue's enchantment, Arthur managed to knock Excalibur from Accolon's hands and gained the upper hand. On the verge of killing his opponent, Arthur asked his name, wherein Accolon confessed his relationship with Morgan, and that the reasoning behind the brothers' feud was her scheme to have Arthur replaced:

> *"Now, sir, said Accolon, I will tell you; this sword hath been in my keeping the most part of this twelvemonth; and Morgan le Fay, King Uriens' wife, sent it me yesterday by a dwarf, to this intent, that I should slay King Arthur, her brother. For ye shall understand King Arthur is the man in the world that she most hateth, because he is most of worship and of prowess of any of her blood; also she loveth me out of measure as paramour, and I her again; and if she might bring about to slay Arthur by her crafts, she would slay her husband King Uriens lightly, and then had she me devised to be king in this land, and so to reign, and she to be my queen ...".*[269]

Arthur decided to spare Accolon's life, however after the knight died from his wounds, Arthur sent the body back to Morgan as a *'present'*, before taking refuge in a nunnery to recover from the wounds he had received.

Unaware of the outcome of the battle, Morgan, confident that Accolon would kill Arthur, was about to kill Uriens when Uwaine (the spelling of Ewain having changed again) intervened. After blaming her actions on being tempted by the devil, Morgan rode to the nunnery where Arthur was recovering. Here she managed to steal the scabbard, only to be chased by Arthur. But Morgan had time to cast the magical scabbard into a lake before she *"shaped herself, horse and man, by enchantment unto a great marble stone"*,[270] eluding capture.

Despite this hatred, Malory managed to make the reader feel some sympathy towards Morgan, towards the end of Book 4, where, whilst on route to her castle in Gore, she encountered a bound knight about to be drowned for adultery. This knight was Manassen, a cousin of her deceased lover Accolon, who swore his innocence to having any affair. Morgan

---

[269] ibid
[270] ibid

released him, allowing him to drown his accuser, and news of her good deed was received back at Camelot where Arthur referred to her as a *"kind sister"*. That was until a *'damosel'* arrived bearing *"the richest mantle that ever was seen in that court, for it was set as full of precious stones ... and there were the richest stones that ever the king saw"*.[271] The sender of this wonderful gift was revealed to be Morgan. However, the Lady of the Lake once again intervened by insisting that the damsel put on the mantle, revealing the truth - the garment appeared to have been laced with poison, as the damosel *"fell down dead, and never more spake word after and burnt to coals"*.[272]

As *Le Morte d'Arthur* focused on the adventures of the various knights of the Round Table, it was not until Book 9 that Morgan made another appearance, this time turning her attention to Guenever, Arthur's queen, and exposing her as an adulterer, in respect to her long running affair with Sir Launcelot du Lake. Morgan provided Sir Tristram de Liones with a shield to be delivered to King Arthur at a tournament.

> *"Then the shield was brought forth, and the field was goldish, with a king and a queen therein painted, and a knight standing above them, [one foot] upon the king's head, and the other upon the queen's."*[273]

When Sir Tristram asked for the image to be interpreted, Morgan explained that it *"... signifieth King Arthur and Queen Guenever, and a knight who holdeth them both in bondage and in servage"*.[274] The knight was Sir Launcelot. Malory explained that Morgan's reasoning for the shield which was not actually directed at King Arthur but toward Launcelot, who:

> *"... Queen Morgan loved Sir Launcelot best, and ever she desired him, and he would never love her nor do nothing at her request, and therefore she held many knights together for to have taken him by strength. And because she deemed that Sir Launcelot loved Queen Guenever paramour, and she him again, therefore Queen Morgan le Fay ordained that shield to put Sir Launcelot to a rebuke, to that intent that King Arthur might understand the love between them."*[275]

Once again, Morgan's plans failed, as upon the presentation of the shield, Arthur appeared to be oblivious of what it was supposed to represent and asked Tristram to explain its meaning. Tristram denied any knowledge. Guenever, on her part, was fully aware of the meaning.

In Book 10 Morgan was mentioned again as being one of two sorceresses in a letter by King Mark. The other sorceress was the Queen of Northgalis (North Wales). Later in this book, another knight, Sir Alisander

---

[271] ibid
[272] ibid
[273] ibid
[274] ibid
[275] ibid

le Orphelin, found himself at Morgan's castle, La Beale Regard, where she applied ointment to his wounds, the first of which provided him with great pain while the second provided relief. When Sir Alisander is advised that Morgan is keeping him there as a prisoner *"to do her pleasure with"*, he manages to escape with the aid of an unnamed damosel, and La Beale Regard is burnt in a fire.

Morgan then disappeared from the story until after the battle of Camlann where, in the last book, Book 21, Arthur received the mortal wound from his son, Mordred, and was taken to the magical isle of Avalon:

> *"... he led away in a ship wherein were three queens; that one was King Arthur's sister, Queen Morgan le Fay; the other was the Queen of Northgalis; the third was the Queen of the Waste Lands. Also there was Nimue, the chief lady of the lake, that had wedded Pelleas the good knight."*[276]

In studying Malory's *Le Morte d'Arthur* in detail, particularly concerning references made of Morgan, I note that there appear to be a number of differences when compared to the modern interpretation of the story. The first is the modern perception that Morgan was the mother of Mordred, conceived from an incestuous liaison with Arthur. Whilst Malory did record the conception of Mordred within Book 1 of his classic, it detailed Arthur being paid a visit by the wife of King Lot of Orkney (mother of four sons, Gawaine, Gaheris, Agravine and Gareth, all of whom were knights of Arthur's Round Table):

> *"... she was a passing fair lady, therefore the king cast great love unto her, and desired to lie by her; so they were agreed, and he begat upon her Mordred, and she was his sister, on his mother's side, Igraine."*

Unbeknown to Arthur at the time, King Lot's wife was, in fact, his sister, Margawse. This incident was mentioned again in Book 2, in that King Lot held against Arthur the fact that he slept with Lot's wife and got her with child. In later adaptations, including John Boorman's 1981 movie *Excalibur* and Marion Zimmer Bradley's 1987 novel, *The Mists of Avalon*, it was Morgan who appeared to be the mother of Mordred. Boorman portrayed the liaison as part of a sinister plan Morgan (played by Helen Mirren) hatches in order to rule; whereas Bradley depicts it being part of an ancient Bealtaine fertility rite, where the *'Virgin Huntress'* (a role enacted by Morgan) couples with the *'Stag King'* (Arthur), and the child of that union is considered sacred.

The second point of interest was how far Morgan had actually evolved from her first appearance in the Arthurian legend and accredited to Geoffrey of Monmouth's *Vita Merlini* (*The Life of Merlin*) in c.1150 CE. In

---

[276] ibid

this work, Morgan barely got a mention, except that she was one of nine sisters who dwelt on the magical island located in the sea which was referred to as the island of apples, or *'the Fortunate Isle'*, Avalon:

> *"She who is first of them is more skilled in the healing art, and excels her sisters in the beauty of her person. Morgen[277] is her name, and she has learned what useful properties all the herbs contain, so that she can cure sick bodies. She also knows an art by which to change her shape, and to cleave the air on new wings like Daedalus ..."*[278]

Geoffrey also refers to Morgan as being one of the three queens who received Arthur after the battle of Camlann, in more poetic fashion than Malory:

> *"... and Morgan received is with fitting honour, and in her chamber she placed the king on a golden bed and with [h]er own hand she uncovered his honourable wound and gazed at it for a long time. At length she said that health could be restored to him if he stayed with her for a long time and made use of her healing art. Rejoicing, therefore, we entrusted the king to her ..."*[279]

Appearing in such a manner could allude to Otherworldly connections; however it may seem that Morgan's fairy associations stem from the origins of her name. Lynne Woods suggests that Morgan, meaning *'women (or woman) of the sea'* may have originally referred to a title as opposed to an actual name. She also indicates that *"in both Wales and Brittany ... the name 'Morgwen' means 'born of the sea', from Muir gena, 'sea born'."*[280] Indeed it is believed that in the original recordings of the story, Morgan was an *'offspring of the sea'*, an Aphrodite like character, who devoted herself to the study of magic.[281]

Leila Norako, in her paper *Morgan le Fay* (that formed part of the Camelot Project at the University of Rochester), also indicates Morgan having possibly originated from Brittany, as local folklore contains fairy sprites, the *'mari-morgan'*. Evans-Wentz[282] describes *"the 'Île Molène' (the Morgan) who is depicted as a fairy eternally young, a virgin seductress whose passion, never satisfied, drives her to despair"*. Living beneath the sea, and accompanied by other fairies, when the Île Molène rises to the surface, her beauty is revealed. *"By day she slumbers amid the coolness of grottoes and woe to him who troubles her sleep"*. Very much a creature of the night, *"she sings in a harmonious voice a plaintive melody whose charm is irresistible."*[283]

---

[277] Geoffrey's spelling of Morgan with an "e"" is considered to be the feminine version whereas the modern spelling with an "a" being the masculine version.
[278] Geoffrey of Monmouth, *Vita Merlini (The Life of Merlin)*
[279] ibid
[280] Sinclair-Wood, *Creating Form from the Mist: Wisdom of Women in Celtic Myth and Mythology*
[281] Forbush, *The Queens of Avalon*
[282] Evans-Wentz, *The Fairy-Faith in Celtic Countries*
[283] ibid

Evans-Wentz records a tale where Morgan was referred to as Dahut, the daughter of King Gradlon, the ruler of the city of Is. Dahut stole the key for the sea-dike flood gates that her father had tied around his neck, and gave it to the Black Prince, who may have been the devil, whose spell she had fallen under. As the Black Prince opened the flood gates, and the sea began to flood the city, St Guenole woke the king, allowing everyone to flee. As the waters gained on them, St Guenole advised the king to throw into the water *"the demon you have behind you"*, which was the king's own daughter Dahut. King Gradlon did what he was told and both he and St Guenole were saved. Today the local fishermen declare that when the sea is rough and the moonlight clear, Dahut (known as *'mari morgan'* in Breton) can be found sitting on the rock where her father flung her.

Morgan's own origins have caused a lot of debate amongst analysts and Arthurian experts. Caitlin Mathews records a link between Morgan being a *"Queen of the Underworld"* in the Arthurian legend to that found within the Breton tradition, similar to the one mentioned above. Here Morgan Fay is the giver of gifts, the haunter of wells and springs and is related to the *'nine Korrigans'* or prophetic fairy sisters, who live off the coast of Brittany, a similar account to Geoffrey of Monmouth's description of Morgan in *Vita Merlini*.[284]

John Mathews, on the other hand, suggests that Geoffrey recognised Morgan as a *'tutelary spirit'* or a Goddess of Avalon, the Otherworld, and that her animosity towards Arthur is an aspect of the challenging and testing role that such figures eternally offer in order to discover who among her followers is actually worthy of favour.[285] This point seems to be strengthened by the 14th century tale of *Gawain and the Green Knight*, where Morgan tests warriors for their courage.

John Mathews also indicates that Morgan has become *"... known by the epithet 'le Fay' (the fairy) retained many of her Goddess qualities even in the Medieval tales"* as well as being *"portrayed as an enchantress and shapeshifter who constantly opposed Arthur"*.[286] However, despite this animosity, Morgan's contradiction in taking Arthur to Avalon indicates to Mathews that the Morgan is not actually a mere mortal, but in fact a Goddess.[287]

From a priestess of Avalon skilled in healing arts, the next distinct change in Morgan's character occurred in the 12th century when French poet, Chrétien de Troyes, translated Geoffrey's work from Latin into French. In *Erec et Enide*, Morgan was mentioned briefly as a guest who attended the wedding of Erec and being *"a friend of Guigomar, Lord of the Isle of Avalon"* as well as being King Arthur's sister when the king *"had a plaster*

---

[284] Matthews, *King Arthur and the Goddess of the Land: Divine Feminine in the Mabinogion*
[285] Matthews, *King Arthur: Dark Age Warrior and Mythic Hero*
[286] ibid
[287] ibid

brought which Morgan, his sister has made" when Erec's wounds were being attended to. In another poem, *Yvain, the Knight of the Lion*, Morgan's healing ability is further noted when the hero is returned to his senses after taking a potion that *'Morgan the Wise'* has made.

Up to the end of the 12th century Morgan was described as being one of great beauty with magical healing powers. From the 13th century, this seemed to have changed with the publication of a collection of prose known as the *Vulgate Cycle*, which was believed to have formed the basis of Malory's *Le Morte d'Arthur*.

The longest prose within the *Vulgate Cycle* is the *Lancelot Propre*, where Morgan was given very human characteristics, with her being described as the youngest daughter of Gorlois, the Duke of Cornwall, and the Lady Igraine. When her father was killed by Uther Pendragon who married her mother, Morgan was sent to a convent where she commenced her studies in the magical arts until Uther married her to the aging Uriens, the King of Rheged in northern Wales. Unhappy with being married off to a man older than her own father, Morgan took many lovers, one of them being Guenever's nephew Giomar. After Guenever put an end to the romance, Morgan sought revenge by attempting to expose the affair between Guinevere and Lancelot, and whilst unsuccessful, she ended up becoming infatuated with the queen's champion herself which resulted in her imprisoning him a number of times. In *Estoire de Merlin*, Morgan was described as being the sister of King Arthur, " ... *gay and playful, wonderfully seductive ... most sensual woman in all Britain ..*".[288]

The *Vulgate Cycle* places Morgan in a castle as opposed to Avalon, and her use of her magical powers for manipulative or evil purposes, as opposed to healing. Likewise, her appearance in *Le Morte d'Arthur* appears to be mainly to capture knights.

Within the later *Post Vulgate Cycle* can be found the prose *Suite du Merlin* where Morgan was described as being married to King Uriens by whom she had a son, Yvain.[289] Morgan is said to take many lovers, one of whom is Merlin, who, after she learned his magic, she threatens with death should he come near her again. This inclusion of Yvain may shed additional light onto the origins of Morgan unbeknown to the writers at the time. Caitlin Matthews indicated that within early Welsh literature, in particular the tale of *The Dream of Rhonabwy*, the wife of Uriens and mother of Owein, was Modron, (whose name means *'divine mother'*), who was also referred to as the daughter of Afallach in Geoffrey of Monmouth's *Historia Regum Britanniae* (History of the Kings of Britain). Afallach himself was, according to myth, the ruler of Ynys Afallach, or Geoffrey's *'Insula Avalonis'*, the Island of Avalon. In the 6th century CE Cumbria was ruled by Urien Rheged who

---

[288] Mathews, C & J, *Ladies of the Lake*
[289] The spelling being Ewain or Ewaine in *Le Morte d'Arthur*.

was said to have presided over a loose coalition of various kings. One ally, Morcant Bulc, plotted to assassinate him. Historians believe that this may have given Malory inspiration as how to develop Morgan's alleged hatred towards her brother, Arthur, in his *Le Mort d'Arthur*.[290]

In her dissertation of the character of Morgan within *Le Morte d'Arthur*, Mary Lynn Soul brings to our attention the fact that from the outset of the myth, Morgan does not appear to fit the characteristics and mannerisms of the *"'conventionally passive woman' of the Middle Ages, in that she kidnaps Lancelot, orders knights to pursue or destroy Lancelot or Tristram, attempts to expose the adultery of Guenevere ...".*[291] Morgan is also portrayed as a woman in command as she has her own castle that she can defend and spares no mercy for her husband. Instead of being subservient and demure, blending totally into the background, it is her rebellious nature that comes to light, right from her initial recorded action where she manipulates a battle between her lover Accolon and Arthur, in order to rule the country herself.

Lynn raises the point that Malory, writing in the 14th century, manages to construct a rather complex character in that of Morgan le Fay, more so that any of the other male characters found within *Le Morte d'Arthur*, which begs the question, why? Likewise amongst the stories of courtly love of Lancelot and Guenever as well as Tristram and Isolde, his focus tends to be on the battles which, according to Lynn, are described in much detail. This, in itself, leads to the question of what is a character such as Morgan le Fay doing in Malory's rather masculine book, especially where in earlier sources, in particularly Geoffrey of Monmouth's *Vita Merlin*, she is barely mentioned at all.

Saul also refers to the work of Geraldine Heng, *Enchanted Ground: The Feminine Subtext in Malory*[292] indicating that there is a positive to Morgan's 'evil' in that *"in the final analysis, however Morgan's impact is not as destructive as it might superficially seem. The trials she provides Arthur's knights serve to increase their abilities and reputations with successful endurance."* Saul agrees to a certain extent, however she indicates that Morgan *"frequently does intend to cause great destruction"*, and that *"Morgan is not a fit agent for reform and that her testing is not usually positive".*

Saul refers to the characterisation of Morgan as an expression of masculine fear of women's power because she is not controlled by any man, and thus uses her power to harm men. Morgan has more power over men than medieval male readers could accept, and such power would identify her as a witch. Malory was writing at a time when there were increasing restrictions on women healers and whilst Morgan does not show any satanic

---

[290] Taylor, *Morgan le Fay*
[291] Soul, *A Rebel and a Witch: The Historical and Ideological Function of Morgan Le Fay in Malory's Le Morte d'Arthur*
[292] Heng, *"Enchanted Ground: The Feminine Subtext in Malory"* in *Courtly Literature: Culture and Context* edited by Keith Busby and Erik Kooper (John Benjamins Publishing Company, 1990)

associations, it is her own rebellion against the social norms of the time that casts her under great suspicion.

It was not until the 1980s that another attempt to rewrite the character of Morgan came to light, that being in the neo-Pagan and feminist-inspired *The Mists of Avalon* by Marion Zimmer Bradley. Here, Morgaine (as Morgan was called), was described as being *"a fairy child, one of the fellows of the hollow hills"*[293] by her father, Gorlois, prior to her fostering in Avalon where her aunt, Viviane, ruled as Lady of the Lake. All throughout the book, reference was made to Morgaine being of the fairy folk, with Lancelet (Launcelot) referring to her as *"Morgaine of the fairies"*[294] and being beautiful, yet it was with the arrival of Gwenharyfar (the Welsh spelling of Guenever), herself described as being *"an exquisite creature"*, that Morgaine's true perception of herself is exposed, *"... little and ugly like one of the fairy folk, Morgaine of the Fairies ... so they had taunted her since childhood"*,[295] especially in the light of the developing love Lancelet has for Gwenharyfar.

According to Bradley's version, it is Morgaine who conceives Mordred during the Bealtaine rites whereby she played the role of the Virgin Huntress of Arthur's King Stag as *"the royal line of Avalon must not be contaminated by commoner blood"*. Shortly after she becomes aware of who the father of her child is, Morgaine meets one of the dark people who addresses her as *"Morgaine of the fairies"*.[296] It is only later in the story that Viviane, the Lady of the Lake, clarifies what all this means; that Morgaine bears the royal blood line of the Old People, and that *"in the ancient days long before the wisdom and the religion of the Druids came here from the sunken temples in the western continent, the fairy people, of who we are both born, you and I my Morgaine, lived here on the shores of the inland sea ..."*[297] (which is Avalon).

Despite writing what has been termed as a *'feminist inspired'* book, Bradley's depiction of Morgaine tends to be of a rather confused and unhappy person, which is emphasised in the 2001 television miniseries of the same name, where Morgaine was played by Julianna Margulies. Instead of truly embracing her role as being Viviane's successor to inherit the role of Lady of the Lake, their relationship soured after the Bealtaine rites as Morgan headed to Scotland to be with her aunt Morgause (Margawse) where she gave birth to Mordred. After leaving her child to be brought up in King Lot's court, Morgaine then returns to Arthur's court at Camelot instead of her own castle, Tintagel, to be a maid in waiting to Gwenharyfar. It is at Camelot that, after a number of failed attempts to win Lancelot's love from Gwenharyfar, she is tricked into marrying the older King Uriens, instead of his son, Accolon.

---

[293] Bradley, *The Mists of Avalon*
[294] ibid
[295] ibid
[296] ibid
[297] ibid

It is not until after Accolon's death and her failed attempt to murder her husband, that Morgaine eventually withdraws to Tintagel before finally returning to Avalon. Here she was visited by Lancelot, who had been made mad from the grail quest, which Morgaine apparently inspired in an attempt to keep the sacred vessels of the Goddess out of Christian hands. Morgaine realised that she had not seen the Queen of the fairyland who appeared at Bealtaine because *"... I am the queen now. There is no goddess but this, and I am she. And yet beyond this, she is, as she is in Igraine and Viviane and Morgause, and Nimue and the queen. And they live in me too and She, and within Avalon they live forever."*[298]

In *The Mists of Avalon*, Morgaine's goal appears not to be to usurp Arthur from his throne, but to bring people back to the worship of the Goddess as opposed to the new religion of Christianity. She is still depicted as a flawed character, in particular in her inability to find happiness and peace. This however does not appear to prevent Morgan from today being ironically described as *"a role model for women (and men) who wish to 'take their power' in this world"*.[299] It is also interesting to note that despite the malicious or confused depiction of Morgan, modern writers such as Kathy Jones refer to her being *"... a great healer who can heal us of our deepest wounds"*.[300] Jones also describes Morgan as the *"mother of time and space, the weaver of the web, of the matrix of life itself"*.[301] This is interesting in itself, considering Morgan's disassociation with life and her unacceptance of her role of Lady of the Lake and High Priestess of Avalon, as depicted in *The Mists of Avalon*, as well as how she is portrayed in other interpretations, including Malory's *Le Morte d'Arthur*.

Maybe the continuation of the subtle alluring nature that Morgan seems to cast over authors and readers alike, regardless of how her character has evolved, is a remnant of her fairy past, and thus, the final point of difference in the evolution of Morgan's character to look at.

From her first appearance within what has become the Arthurian legend, that being Geoffrey of Monmouth's *Historia Regum Britanniae (History of the Kings of Britain)*, Morgan has transformed from a *"loving fairy with the ability to heal Arthur"* to a seemingly schizophrenic character as depicted in Malory's *Le Morte d'Arthur*. Marianne Bul suggests that this has been a result of the change in the relationship between Arthur and Morgan, transforming from patient and Otherworldly healer to that of brother and sister. This is because once seen as siblings, Morgan's fae-like heritage would naturally also impact upon that of the *"once and future king"*.[302]

In the French romance verses of de Troyes, Morgan is briefly mentioned as a rather benevolent and powerful fairy whose power wanes

---

[298] ibid
[299] Black, *Morgan le Fay* (http://doirebhrighid.net/uploads/DB/pdf/articles/morgan.pdf)
[300] Jones, *Priestess of Avalon, Priestess of the Goddess*
[301] ibid
[302] Bul, *Morgan's Revenge: A Dissertation on Morgan's attempts to Destroy Arthur and the Origin of this Motif*

during the *Vulgate Cycle* prose, resulting in her being reduced to the physical appearance of a rather mortal, disenchanted woman. By the time of Malory, Bul notes that Morgan no longer had innate magical abilities, or even the healing skills that she originally was mentioned as having in Geoffrey's *Vita Merlini*. All the skills she possessed were taught to her by Merlin, and were used to preserve her youthful appearance, which would have naturally occurred had she remained a fairy.

Bul refers to a dissertation by Ilse Stokker in which Stokker indicated that this was largely due to the religious perception of women at the time, in that *"by making Merlin Morgan's teacher, the monks downplayed the powerful character of Morgan, a woman who knows what she wants and has the power to make things happen"*.[303] When looking at the evolution of Morgan, Stokker's assertion appears to be accurate, as in the older Arthurian texts, as Bul points out, Morgan appears as a rather *"benevolent fairy who takes care of Arthur in his time of need"*. However, over the centuries, she changes into a malevolent sister, with the various authors disagreeing as to what were the underlying motives for her hatred towards Arthur, as first depicted in the *Post-Vulgate Cycle*. Contrary to this evolution, Morgan still retained her fae-like abilities and undying love for her brother and in both the *Vulgate* and *Post-Vulgate Cycle*, as well as in *Le Morte d'Arthur*, she was still depicted as being on the barge that took the wounded Arthur to Avalon, the Otherworld, the land of the fairy.

Carolyne Larrington attempted to draw a possible Greek as opposed to Celtic connection, saying that the names of the nine sisters Geoffrey of Monmouth records as residing in Avalon are similar to those of the nine muses of Apollo, and to the fact that they have Greek sounding names. Larrington also drew comparisons between Morgan and Circe with the capturing of men (although Morgan did not turn any knight into an animal). As with the stories within the *Vulgate Cycle*, where Sebile and Morgan both appear as practitioners of evil magic, Larrington finds a similar comparison with the role of a sibyl found within classical myths who were *"prophetesses able to foretell the future"*, as well as also having the ability to destroy men; similar actions to that of the Celtic fae.[304] Bul, however, somewhat dismisses Larrington's evidence as being somewhat weak in comparison to the evidence contained within Celtic sources. She confirms her belief that whilst there may be similarities, Morgan has definitely evolved from Celtic traditions, in particular those where fairies who are scorned by their human lovers, take revenge.

In the early versions of the Arthurian legend, there is an indication, according to Bul, that Morgan and Arthur were lovers. This could explain Morgan's dislike for Arthur in the *Post-Vulgate Cycle* as her actions are similar to those of a rejected fairy. For this reason, Bul asserts that *"the balance of*

---

[303] ibid
[304] Larrington, *King Arthur's Enchantresses: Morgan and her Sisters in Arthurian Tradition*

benevolence and malevolence points towards the Morrighan and Modron as models for Morgan's character". Bul concludes that *"the Celtic motif of the scorned fairy ... predates the earliest written source"*[305] and this explains Morgan's evolution *"from lover to sister and from revenge to plain spite"*.[306]

Bul also examines another fae-like character in the Arthurian legend, the Lady of the Lake who has also evolved over the centuries in spite of being a later addition to the original story. Bul indicates that the character of Morgan appears to have been split into two separate characters by the authors of the *Vulgate* and *Post-Vulgate Cycle*, in that by the 12th century resulting in *"... two separate types of fairies"*[307] to merge.

In doing so, it is the Lady of the Lake (the good fairy) who is associated with the positive attributes that Morgan (now the bad fairy) once had. This dual role is clearly found within *Le Morte d'Arthur* where on the two occasions that Morgan nearly succeeds in killing her brother, he is saved through the intervention of the Lady of the Lake. Andrea Whyland also comments on this contrast between Morgan and the Lady of the Lake, indicating that Malory adds *"more of an evil element"*.[308] Whyland also refers to the works of Myra Olstead who commented that the *"opposition between Morgan and the Lady of the Lake and their actions within the plot make the reader more interested in the individual character and create suspense within the episodes"*.[309]

Whyland notes that up until the end of the 12th century Morgan was *"considered a fay and lives in an Otherworld called Avalon. She is Arthur's sister, retains a mystical power and possesses great beauty"*. This is not echoed in the 1998 television movie *Merlin* where Morgan (played by Helena Bonham Carter) appears rather ditzy and facially disfigured. This Morgan recognises Uther when he disguises himself as the Duke of Cornwall to lie with her mother Igraine, but she appears more as a pawn to the whims of the villainess, Queen Mab (played by Miranda Richardson).

In the earlier 1981 movie *Excalibur* (directed by John Boorman) the character of Morgan (called Morgana and played by Helen Mirren) appears to be a combination of Morgan as well as Nimue (one of Malory's Ladies of the Lake, but Viviane's successor in *The Mists of Avalon*) in her seduction of Merlin. Basing his story on Malory's *Le Morte d'Arthur*, Boorman applies some poetic licence in directing the source of Morgan's hatred towards Arthur; implying it is a consequence of Merlin's involvement in Uther's somewhat forceful sexual liaison (or rape of) with Igraine. Morgan entraps

---

[305] Bul, *Morgan's Revenge: A Dissertation on Morgan's attempts to Destroy Arthur and the Origin of this Motif*
[306] ibid
[307] Bul refers to Laurence Harf-Lancner's article *"Fairy Godmothers and Fairy Lovers"* found within *Arthurian Women: A Casebook* edited by Thelma Fenster (Garland Publishing Inc, 1996)
[308] Whyland, *Morgan le Fay: Origins and Evolution* http://vault.hanover.edu/~battles/arthur/morgan.htm (2000)
[309] Whyland refers to Myra Olstead's article. *"Morgan le Fay in Malory's Morte D'Arthur"* that appears in the *Bibliographical Bulletin* 19 (1967)

Merlin by using the same sorcery he used to deceive Igraine, that is through the use of the Charm of Making. Morgan then sets forth to *"find a man and give birth to a god"*, resulting in the incestuous encounter with Arthur.

In each evolution of the myth, Morgan tends to have moved further and further away from her original fae-like character and associations. Even in *Mists of Avalon*, save for the island of Avalon being Otherworldly, Morgaine appears far from her original roots, as well as completely devoid of any association with powerful ancient Celtic Goddesses, such as the Morrighan. Yet despite this modern depiction, Morgan is still referred as being *'inspirational'* to women by feminist writers, and within the Goddess spiritual movement. A rather flawed character filled with contradictions, who continues to entice despite her now human depiction, maybe this is the alluring aspect of Morgan. Despite how she is described, once a fairy queen, Morgan le Fay will always be a fairy queen.

# Bibliography

Black, Susa Morgan, *Morgan le Fay*, at

http://doirebhrighid.net/uploads/DB/pdf/articles/ morgan.pdf

Bradley, Marion Zimmer (1987) *The Mists of Avalon.* New York: Ballantine Books

Bul, Marianne (2010) *Morgan's Revenge: A Dissertation on Morgan's attempts to destroy Arthur and the Origin of this Motif*, at http://scripties.let.eldoc.ub.rug.nl/

De Troyes, Chretien, *Erec et Enide*, at

http://www.gutenberg.org/cache/epub/831/pg831.txt

Evans-Wentz, W.Y. (2002) *The Fairy Faith in Celtic Countries.* London: Dover Publications

*Excalibur* (1981) Warner Bros Pictures

Forbush, William Byron, *The Queens of Avalon*, at http://www.lib.rochester.edu/camelot/qaavalon.htm

Geoffrey of Monmouth (2010) *Vita Merlini (The Live of Merlin).* Dhaka: Classic Books International

Jones, Kathy, (2007) *Priestess of Avalon, Priestess of the Goddess: A Renewed Spiritual Path for the 21st Century.* Somerset: Green Magic

Larrington, Carolyne (2006) *King Arthur's Enchantresses: Morgan and Her Sisters in Arthurian Tradition.* London: I.B. Tauris

Malory, Thomas & Aubrey Beardsley (illus) (1893) *Le Morte d'Arthur.* London: J.M. Dent & Co

Matthews, Caitlin (2002) *King Arthur and the Goddess of the Land: Divine Feminine in the Mabinogion.* Vermont: Inner Traditions

Matthews, Caitlin & John (1992) *Ladies of the Lake.* London: Thorsons

Matthews, John (2004) *King Arthur: Dark Age Warrior and Mythic Hero.* London: Gramercy

Norako, Leila R., *Morgan le Fay*, at

http://www.lin.rochester.edu/camelot/morgmenu.html

Soul, Mary Lynn (1994) *A Rebel and a Witch: The Historical and Ideological Function of Morgan Le Fay in Malory's Le Morte d'Arthur.* Ohio: Ohio State University

Taylor, Patrick, *Morgan le Fay*, at http://www.arthurian-legend.com/more-about/more-about-arthur-8.ph

Telyndru, Jhenah (2005) *Avalon Within: Inner Sovereignty and Personal Transformation through the Avalonian Mysteries.* Booksurge Publications

*The Mists of Avalon* (2001) Turner Network Television

Whyland, Andrea, *Morgan le Fay: Origins and Evolution*, at http://vault.hanover.edu/~battles/arthur/morgan.htm

Wood, Lynne Sinclair (2001) *Creating Form from the Mists: Women in Celtic Mythology.* Chievely: Capall Bann Publishers

# NIMUE

## Ambiguous Enchantress

### Aili Mirage

The rediscovery of European pagan-originating folklore brought a great interest in the Arthurian legend, usually focusing on the pivotal half-heroine/half-villainess Morgan le Fay, Arthur's famous half-sister. The most popular piece of modern Arthurian fiction, Marion Zimmer Bradley's *The Mists of Avalon*, portrays Morgan (spelled Morgaine in the book) as the leading heroine, while the Lady of the Lake is presented in the form of three different women – Nimue, Viviane and Niniane – supporting characters who all meet a tragic end. However, digging deep into the Arthurian lore reveals a much more complex image. Not only is this ambiguous enchantress essential to the story, but also she expresses traits of a true archetypical Fairy Queen, a giver and taker of power.

Let's explore her part of the story.

### Origins

In many early Arthurian stories, fairy folk and their magical homeland play an important role. They often serve as some kind of natural force, sometimes benevolent, sometimes not, but always superior in some way. One may call it *'a hand of fate'* and quite literally so, as the very origin of the word *'fairy'* is the Latin *'fata'*, as in *'that which is ordained, destiny, fate'*. In Celtic mythology, which greatly influenced British folklore, a lot of stories contained an element of an otherworldly race (mostly of the Tuatha De Danann legacy) who often took an interest in human affairs. One of the strongest archetypes surviving was that of a fairy woman taking interest in a mortal man, taking him to her homeland, often called a Fairy Queen, and it's no surprise that it found a place in the most prominent British legend.

The Isle of Apples (more widely known as Avalon), and the nine fairy sisters that inhabit it, appears as early as in 12th century literature, in

Geoffrey of Monmouth's works *Historia Regum Britanniae* and *Vita Merlini* where Morgen (probably the first written version of Morgan le Fay) heals a gravely wounded Arthur. Further research shows that Monmouth based the magical part of his stories on earlier legends, like the one of Arthur raiding Annwn, the Welsh Otherworld (probably the origin of Avalon), so it's safe to assume that other characters and places are likely to be inspired in a similar manner.

Nimue's written story begins with the widely known Arthurian source – the *Vulgate Cycle* – and with a less known medieval romance *Lanzelet* by a Swiss cleric Ulrich von Zatzikhoven, both dated to late 12$^{th}$ or early 13$^{th}$ century. She appears in two different incarnations – as a guardian/mother figure to Lancelot (called originally in French *La Dame du Lac,* hence the Lady of the Lake) and as a beguiler of her lover Merlin (called Niniane/Niviene/Viviane in different versions). At first these two characters appear to be separate in their function: the Lady of the Lake being just the benevolent spirit to Lancelot, a wise mermaid queen who raised him in a fairyland, and Niniane being a dangerous woman who outsmarted the lustful Merlin, they seem to have nothing in common at all. Yet, there is this one thing – Niniane, just like Lancelot's Lady of the Lake, is of fairy descent, and additionally - at some point - she is granted the status of a spiritual descendant of the Roman deity Diana, popular in Late Medieval/Renaissance European folklore as a Fairy Queen and as a patroness of a sacred lake in Lazio, Italy. That started a long process of intertwining these two characters.

## Diana

In further renditions of the story the Lake *of La Dame du Lac* gets to be called *Lac de Dyane*, the Lake of Diana (allegedly located in the Forest of Briosque) and it's the same lake where Merlin and Nimue first met. It is hard to establish the exact moment of that event, as the sources have been rewritten and could have been compromised, but it is enough to compare several versions to notice Diana's increasing influence.

First of all, one needs to understand the reality of Arthurian romances' authors. Some of the really influential writers were not British – Robert de Boron and Chrétien de Troyes were French, Ulrich von Zatzikhoven was Swiss – and the stories were circulating widely in European courts, among people who were not very familiar with Celtic mythology. On the contrary, Roman and Greek myths were quite popular, especially on the verge of the Renaissance.

Roman mythology seems to have provided a common language for European courts and post-Roman Britain. Not only was the myth of Diana widely known, but also her cult was wide-spread in provinces of the late Roman Empire, so linking Nimue to Diana gave her a very strong, archetypical background and allowed the merging of two characters under a well understood banner.

One of the best known centres for the Roman goddess was in Aricia, where she was famous for her sanctuary on the shore of the aforementioned Lake Nemi. The sanctuary was guarded by a priest, who obtained his position in battle against the serving priest, showing himself to be strong and worthy. Diana here acquired some traits from other Roman goddesses, honoured as a goddess of wildlife and hunting, a patroness of pregnant women and childbirth, in a similar way to Juno Lucina. Another tale tells that Diana also falls in love with the beautiful Endymion, the man entrapped in eternal sleep for her pleasure.

From the examples above, we can note the comparisons between Diana's priests and her human lover, as well as the stories of mortals entering into relationships with the Fay Folk. We have a man (or a knight in a medieval setting) who is somehow special (the priest who proves himself to be strong enough; and Endymion for his beauty) and it makes him worthy of the attention of the goddess. But this very attention comes with a price - the man will often somehow be enslave or dedicated to the other realm. In the archetypical British fairy story of *Thomas the Rhymer*, the Elfland Queen made the hero disappear for seven years from the face of the Earth. This knowledge explains the emphasis on Diana becoming a way through which the British story was translated into a more universal, post-Roman Europe. The Diana myth was an echo of a magical pagan past, alluring yet dangerous. It was fitting to make her a guardian to the treacherous Lancelot du Lac who stole the heart of Arthur's wife, and to make her the only power to enchant the greatest wizard of all times.

However, it is important to notice that the Diana theme is not presented in a strictly villainous way. Nimue is presented as a free spirit, sometimes a virgin who doesn't want to succumb to Merlin (*Estoire de Merlin*):

> *"And she greeted him the most joyfully she knew how, and they ate and drank and lay together in the same bed. She knew enough about his doings so that, when she understood that he wished to lie with her, she knew how to cast a spell and bring forth a pillow, which she put in his arms, and then Merlin went to sleep."*
> Estoire de Merlin, translated by Rupert T. Pickens

Or indeed, the Damoiselle Cacheresse (Lady Huntress, the name given to Nimue in Post-Vulgate *Suite de Merlin*) who gets enchanted by stepping into Diana's footsteps.

Merlin is blamed for desiring her and the later course of events is a natural consequence of his lustful lack of reason. She is presented as an example, that some things are better left alone - a supernatural punishment for Merlin's pride. One can assume that her role is consistent with an archetypical goddess of magic and nature, she is a dangerous force that cannot be tamed.

The evolution of Merlin's entrapment also provides a good insight on Diana's influence. There are several versions of Merlin's eternal prison, but the oldest versions depict a castle with walls of mist or a cave. Lucy Allen Paton in her work *Studies in the fairy mythology of Arthurian Romance* concludes that in the versions where Nimue's connection to Diana is closer, the cave appears. It suggests that it is an echo of the cave of Endymion, while the misty castle suggests a more local, Celtic source.

So, let's try to dig a little deeper, into more native sources.

There are several stories with similar themes in Celtic mythology, and although none of them are as directly referenced as Roman Diana, they most probably provide an earlier inspiration for Nimue's story. The most likely inspirations from Celtic lore are the stories of Níamh and Oisín, Rhiannon and Pwyll, Ganieda, the sister of Merlin, the Welsh queen Nyfain and Nemain and Nicnevin.

## Níamh and Oisín

Oisín was a great poet and a warrior of the *fianna* who one day was visited by a fairy woman. She introduced herself as Níamh of the Golden Hair, the daughter of the King of *Tir na nÓg*, the Land of Youth. She asked Oisín to come with her to her father's land and he agreed. She took him away across the sea, on her milk white steed, to the land as fair as Paradise. There he forgot time and home, and three hundred years passed. But one day Oisín started to long for his home and a reluctant Niamh let him go, giving him her horse and warning him to not alight from it. Oisín disobeys and as a result turns into a very old man, with only a little time left during which he learns how much time has passed and tells his story.

Clearly this story shares a similar theme with that of Nimue and Merlin, a fairy woman meets an exceptional man, whom she entraps in a mystical place. It is interesting here to note that Oisín was a famous bard, just like Myrddin Wyllt, a historical prototype for the character of Merlin. Also, the fairy name sounds similar enough that it might have been turned into Nimue's early name – Niniane.

## Rhiannon and Pwyll

The story of Rhiannon and Pwyll is not similar at all to that of Nimue and Merlin, but it bears slight similarities to another romance of the Lady of the Lake and with Pelleas, a Knight of the Round Table. In Thomas Malory's *Le Morte d'Arthur*, Nimue hears the story of his unhappy love towards Ettarde, a high-born maiden. The Lady of the Lake takes revenge on Ettarde by making her fall in love with Pelleas, but at same time she makes Pelleas hate Ettarde, who subsequently dies of sorrow, enabling Nimue and Pelleas to marry.

Rhiannon and Pwyll's story differs as it is in short about Rhiannon getting away from an unwanted marriage in order to marry Pwyll, and later about their lost child. Noteworthy in both stories, that of Nimue and Rhiannon, are that both woman come up with a resourceful plan to get the man they want. This theory was introduced by Sir John Rhŷs, who argued that Rhiannon seemed to have some characteristics in common with a water fairy. He quotes an episode in which Rhiannon plays a part similar to that of the lake-lady Liban, and also emphasises that Rhiannon owns magical birds whose song is heard on land, while they are in fact singing somewhere far above the sea.

The names Rhiannon and Pwyll could easily have evolved into Niniane and Pelleas, a theory which was supported by the American medievalist, Roger Sherman Loomis.

## Ganieda

In the Welsh legends, Myrddin (Merlin) had a sister Gwenddydd, whose name means *'bright day'* in Welsh and was romanized into Ganieda by Geoffrey of Monmouth in *Vita Merlini*. It is one of the oldest sources and one that does not contain any references to Nimue nor Lady of the Lake in any form. In this story Ganieda acquires the power of prophecy while drinking from the same healing spring as her brother, to whom her powers were superior. Later she inherits Merlin's position as a prophet, reminding of Nimue's gaining of Merlin's power and taking on the role of King Arthur's advisor. It is possible that the motif of Merlin being entrapped in a magic place may have been inspired by the fact that Ganieda built a house for her brother. It is possible that introducing Nimue to the story rendered Ganieda superfluous, but the elements of her story became a part of the Lady of the Lake myth.

Modern Arthurian scholar August Hunt makes some interesting hypotheses about Ganieda suggesting that her light-related name might be a possible epithet for a goddess, suggesting Nemain and Diana. Hunt quotes Carin M.C. Green's *Roman Religion and the Cult of Diana at Aricea* who suggest that Diana's name could have been derived from the same root found in the Latin word *dies* (day). Additionally Diana, like Juno and Hekate, was given the epithet Lucina (the light-bringing one). Whilst this is a speculative theory, it still gives fair basis for further cross referencing Celtic and Roman mythology, looking for the influences which may have come earlier in the Vulgate Circle period.

## Nyfain

Nyfain was a queen from the 6th century, daughter to Brychan and wife to king of Rheged (northern England and southern Scotland) Cynfarch Oer and mother to Urien, the hero of Taliesin's songs. I managed to confirm four different variations of her name through *The Academy of St. Gabriel*, a medieval researchers group, but little is known of her.

August Hunt argues that she may be a historical inspiration, noting some interesting similarities. According to a tract called *"Mothers of Irish Saints"*, Brychan had a wife Dina, who may be an explanation of the very origin of Vulgate's Niniane. Additionally this family is linked with Arthurian mythos through Nyfain's son, Urien, who was said to be married to Morgan le Fay herself. There is also a geographical link, her kingdom, Rheged, is located on the western side of Hadrian's wall and two very important places linked to Arthur are found there: the City of Carlisle and the Roman fort Aballava. The latter is suggested as a possible original location for Avalon as its original name Avalana literally means *'the place of apples'*. Additionally, a dedication to the goddess Latis is found there, who is specifically a goddess of water which could be taken as a clear suggestion that the concept of *'the Lady of the Lake'* was an original part of local legends (even if not recorded in the earliest texts), rather than a later addition.

## Nemain and Nicnevin

This is a very circumstantial link which was suggested by August Hunt. Nemain is a Celtic goddess of battle frenzy, part of the Morrígan trio. At first glance nothing, besides the similar sound of her name, links her to Nimue, as there are no references to lakes. However, in the story of Merlin by Geoffrey of Monmouth, we find an account of the madness of Merlin in which he loses his senses following the death of three of his comrades in battle, and runs away to live in the woods. In the process he gains his prophetic gift. The madness might be a direct reference to Nemain's powers, even if she's not called by her name. Also, when comparing the later story of Nimue enchanting Merlin to eternal sleep in a cave, it might be a reference to the earlier story of Merlin's madness.

We can also see a clear evolution from a war goddess to a fairy in the character of Nicnevin, a Scottish Fairy Queen in John Koch's *Celtic Culture*:

> *"The Queen of the Fairies in Scotland, sometimes known as the queen of the witches, was Neven or NicNeven, a name Henderson and Cowan derive from Neamhain, OIr Nemain, a war goddess... variations on this name are found all over Scotland..."*

- and Sir Walter Scott's *Letters on Demonology and Witchcraft (1831)* –

> "...a gigantic and malignant female, the Hecate of this mythology, who rode on the storm and marshalled the rambling host of wanderers under her grim banner. This hag (in all respects the reverse of the Mab or Titania of the Celtic creed) was called Nicneven in that later system which blended the faith of the Celts and of the Goths on this subject. The great Scottish poet Dunbar has made a spirited description of this Hecate riding at the head of witches and good neighbours (fairies, namely), sorceresses and elves, indifferently, upon the ghostly eve of All-Hallow Mass. In Italy we hear of the hags arraying themselves under the orders of Diana (in her triple character of Hecate, doubtless) and Herodias, who were the joint leaders of their choir, But we return to the more simple fairy belief, as entertained by the Celts before they were conquered by the Saxons."

Considering the northern Avalon hypothesis, it is likely that Scottish fairy lore could have been general knowledge at the time of shaping of Arthurian legend, and might have influenced it.

In Sir Thomas Malory's *Le Morte d'Arthur* Nimue is mentioned by name 'Nymue', and is described as being on a boat with Morgan le Fay and two other women taking Arthur to Avalon. In Malory's version her role as Lancelot's guardian is shifted into that of replacing Merlin as Arthur's guardian. Her wild nature resurfaces with her love affair with Pelleas.

## Evolution

Nimue's origins are in fairy lore, but her evolution mirrors that of the faeries. She starts as a supernatural force of nature, wild and untamed and then is glorified when she lets herself be bound into the role of the courtly wife of a knight, finally becoming a temptress who is completely villainized in a puritan society. The social views on fairies follow a similar evolution, in medieval times belief in them was still alive and their power was similar to that of old pagan gods, morally ambiguous. The stories had to accommodate the new religion becoming more moralistic and educational. Characters were depicted as living examples of what's good and what's bad. After the Reformation and the rise of the Puritan movement, almost all references to non-Christian elements became evil, and were considered savage, backwards and uncivilized. Proper corset-clad English society maintained their longing for naughty liberties, and thus the *"romantic villains"* never lost their allure.

> "Then, in one moment, she put forth the charm
> Of woven paces and of waving hands,
> And in the hollow oak he lay as dead,
> And lost to life and use and name and fame.
> Then crying 'I have made his glory mine,'

*And shrieking out 'O fool!' the harlot leapt
Adown the forest, and the thicket closed
Behind her, and the forest echoed 'fool.'"*
~ *Idylls of the King*, Lord Alfred Tennyson

## Bibliography

Chandler, Erin (accessed 2012) *The Huntress and the Harlot: The Taming of Nymue, the Lady of the Lake* at http://vault.hanover.edu/~battles/arthur/ladyoflake.htm

Harper, Douglas (accessed 2012) *Online Etymology Dictionary* at http://www.etymonline.com/

Hunt, August. various works.

Keats, John (accessed 2012) *La Belle Dame sans Merci*, at http://englishhistory.net/keats/poetry/labelledamesansmerci.html

Koch, John (2006) Celtic Culture: A Historical Encyclopedia. Oxford: ABC-Clio Ltd

Larrington, Carolyne (2006) King Arthur's enchantresses: Morgan and her sisters in Arthurian tradition. London: I.B. Tauris

Malory, Thomas (1999) *Le Morte d'Arthur*. New York: Random House

Monmouth, Geoffrey of (accessed 2012) Historia Regum Britanniae at http://www.lib.rochester.edu/camelot/geofhkb.htm

Monmouth, Geoffrey of (accessed 2012) *Vita Merlini* at http://www.lib.rochester.edu/camelot/GMArthur.htm

Norris, Lacy (ed) (2010) *The Story of Merlin*. Cambridge: D.S. Brewer

Paton, Lucy Allen (1903) Studies in the fairy mythology of Arthurian romance. Boston: Ginn & Co.

Rolleston, T. W. (1994) *Celtic Myths and Legends*. London: Senate.

Scott, Walter (2005) Letters on Demonology and Witchcraft. South Dakota: Nuvision (originally 1830)

Tennyson, Alfred (accessed 2012) *Idylls of the King* at http://www.gutenberg.org/catalog/world/readfile?fk_files=1442999

Trigg, Jim (accessed 2012) *The Academy of Saint Gabriel* at http://www.s-gabriel.org/.

Unknown (accessed 2012) *The Spoils of Annwfn* at http://www.lib.rochester.edu/camelot/annwn.htm

Unknown, translated by Lloyd-Evans, Dyfed (accessed 2012) *The Tale of Taliesin* at http://www.celtnet.org.uk/texts/cronicl_wech_oesoedd/ystoria-taliesin-eng.php

# CLIODHNA

## Faerie Queen and Potent Banshee

## PAMELA NORRIE

> *I would like to dedicate this essay to the Yarrow Witches of Dundee and especially to Lesley-Anne Brewster for her patience, guidance and support.*

There is much mystery surrounding Cliodhna. Who is she, where is she from, and what connects her to the Faerie realm? Her name pronounced Cleena and spelled also as Cliona, Cleena, Cliodhna, amongst many other variations, is one I have seen in passing, but there is not a lot of information about her in the open, unless you happen to do a fair bit of digging. Partly one of the reasons why I have chosen to write about her is that she is so little known and I want to shed some light upon her. This essay aims to look at some of her myths and legends which connect her to the Faerie realm.

Cliodhna has been described as a Faerie Queen, a Goddess of the Tuatha De Danann, a banshee, and some tales even portray her as a beautiful yet tragic mortal maiden. One such quote described Cliodhna as a Faerie Queen of Munster under the High King and Queen of the Faeries, Finvarra and Oonagh:

> "....the present king of the Irish fairies is Finvarra, the same Fionbharr to whom the Dagda allotted the sidh[310] of Meadha after the Tuatha De Danann by the Milesians, and who takes a prominent part in the Fenian stories. So great is the persistence of tradition in Ireland that this hill of Meadha, now spelt Knockma, is still considered to be the abode of him and his queen, Onagh.

---

[310] Sidh in older texts refers specifically to *"the palaces, courts, halls or residences"* of the ghostly beings that, according to Gaedhelic mythology, inhabit them. O'Curry, E., *Lectures on Manuscript Materials*, Dublin 1861:504, quoted by Evans-Wentz 1966:291.

> *Finvarra rules day to day over a wide realm of fairy folk. Many of these, again, have their own vassal chieftains, forming a tribal hierarchy such as must have existed in the Celtic days of Ireland. Finvarra and Onagh are high king and queen, but, under them, Cliodhna is tributary queen of Munster, and rules from a sidh near Mallow in County Cork, while, under her again, are Aoibhinn,[311] queen of the fairies of North Munster, and Áine, queen of the fairies of South Munster.*"[312]

From this we can see there is a trinity between Cliodhna, Aoibhinn and Áine - the three Faerie Queens of Munster - and the Faerie realm runs upon a hierarchical system much as mortal monarchy would.

Another quote describes Cliodhna as a banshee and ruler of South Munster:

> *"Cleena is the potent banshee that rules as queen over the fairies of South Munster. In the Dinnsenchus there is an ancient and pathetic story about her, wherein it is related that she was a foreigner from Fairyland, who, coming to Ireland, was drowned while sleeping on the strand at the harbour of Glandore in South Cork. In this harbour the sea, at certain times, utters a very peculiar, deep, hollow, and melancholy roar, among the caverns of the cliffs, which was formerly believed to foretell the death of a king of the south of Ireland. This surge has been from time immemorial called Tonn-Cleena, 'Cleena's wave.' Cleena lived on, however, as a fairy. She had her palace in the heart of a pile of rocks, five miles from Mallow, which is still well known by the name of Carrig-Cleena: and numerous legends about her are told among the Munster peasantry."*[313]

The above quote connects Cliodhna as a *'potent banshee'*, a faerie creature with connections to the sea and realm of the faerie.

Interestingly, the sounds of the Tonn-Cleena can still be heard by people of today,

> *'In the vicinity of the entrance to Glandore Harbour the ocean wave produces a keening sound at times. This wave is known in Gaelic as "Tonn Chliodhna" i.e. "Cliona's Wave". Legend has it that in the distant past a love-sick young beauty was tragically drowned here and the intermittent keening of the wave is her ghostly lament. A more prosaic explanation is that, in certain conditions of wind and tide, the keening sound is produced by the wind echoing in the crevices and little caves hewn by the waves in the cliffs. But why accept a prosaic solution when*

---

[311] Pronounced Evin.
[312] Squire: *Celtic Myth, Legend, Poetry & Romance*, 1905:243-4.
[313] Joyce, *A Smaller Social History Of Ancient Ireland*, 1906:111.

*the other is more romantic and more in tune with alleged belief in banshees, leprechauns and other goblins."*[314]

Generally most of the legends attributed to Cliodhna agree, with slight variations, that she was a faerie maiden, who ran off with her lover. Some hint she was linked to the court of Manannan, the Land of Youth and that she did not drown, but simply was forced to return home,

> *"...The story about Cleena exists in several versions which do not agree with each other except insofar as she seems to have been a Danann maiden once living in Mananan's*[315] *country the land of youth beyond the sea. Escaping thence with a mortal lover, as one of the versions tells, she landed on the southern coast of Ireland, and her lover Keevan of the curling locks went off to hunt in the woods. Cleena who remained on the beach, was lulled to sleep by fairy music played by a minstrel of Mananan when a giant wave of the sea swept up and carried her back to Fairyland, leaving her lover desolate. Hence the place was called the Strand of Cleena's Wave."*[316]

She has been described as an Irish goddess of love, beauty and lust with connections to the sea and the four winds. Her sacred creatures were her three magical birds which healed the sick with their songs, thus also making her a goddess of healing. As she also had magical birds for companions, it can be said that the Goddess Rhiannon was a Welsh counterpart. Cliodhna was additionally considered to have the attributes of a Goddess of death and the afterlife,

> *"[Cliodhna] Goddess of Beauty. Bird Goddess of the afterlife who can take the form of a sea-wave or wren. The White Shee, or fairy queen of South Munster, is said to reside within her invisible palace at Carrig Cleena, near Fermoy, County Cork, Ireland. She rules as queen over the sheoques: fairy women of the hills of South Munster, or Desmond.... She has fair hair crowned with the Ferroniere of Allurement and is escorted by birds, one blue with a crimson head, one crimson with a green head and one speckled with a gold head, which eat from magic apples and heal the sick with their sweet songs."*[317]

As queen over the sheoques, she is a Queen of the Banshees. It is quite possible Cliodhna was a daughter of Manannan, or simply one who served in his court, but either way she was a noble of the faerie realm,

> *"She lives in Tír Tairngaire: the Land of Promise at Manannan's city and has a white marble palace; with floors of silver, doors of gold, and*

---

[314] West Cork Travel Information, www.westcorktravel.com.
[315] Manannán mac Lir an Irish sea deity, often seen as a psychopomp with connections to the Otherworld.
[316] T.W Rolleston, *Myths and Legends of the Celtic Race*, 1911:126.
[317] http://www.tartanplace.com/faery/goddess/cliodna.html.

*crystal-gemmed walls. It's portal is at Loch Dearg: Lake of the Red Eye, County Donegal, Northern Ireland. [In] Adventures of Tadg She gives him [Tadg] her emerald cup that will turn water into wine that is guarded from humans. She and her 2 sisters Aife: Radiant and Etain: Emerald Goddess with 150 young women went to Ireland with Ciabhan [Keevan] and the kings of India and Greece. She was lulled to sleep by the music of the Son of the Sea who sent a great wave to take her back. Where she drowned is Tonn Cliodna"*[318]

There is a further legend suggesting that Cliodhna could move between the Otherworld and the land of the living at will, and went in pursuit of a new lover, linking her as a Goddess of love and lust:

*"Despite this report of her watery demise, Clidna managed to live on to have more romantic adventures. She fell in love with a man named John Fitzjames, who already had a human lover named Caitileen Og; this girl followed Clidna into the Otherworld, angrily demanding the return of her man. Although she came close to persuading Clidna to let her sweetheart go, even the witty tongue of Caitileen Og was ultimately ineffective against Clidna's desires."*[319]

Generally she is a Goddess linked to nobility and had little to do with peasant families,

*"Clidna is connected with several important Irish families; she had affairs with Earl Gerald Fitzgerald of the Desmond Geraldines (son of the fairy queen Áine) and with Caomh, ancestor of the O'Keeffes. Clidna served as banshee to the MacCarthy's to whom she told the secret of the Blarney Stone that touching it with the lips would make anyone eloquent - a superstition that lasts to this day. Her connections with nobility suggest that Clidna was Goddess of the sovereignty of sea-lapped Munster."*[320]

*"Cliodna is loved and cherished by the people of Co. Cork, where a number of place names are associated with her. She is the guardian goddess of the O'Keefes, and said to be the eldest daughter of the last druid of Ireland."*[321]

In conclusion, Cliodhna is a Goddess of multiple backgrounds and many purposes. Her link to the sea and the Tonn Cleena connect her as a Goddess of the sea, the otherworld and the afterlife. She has been described as a Queen of the banshees, and one who reveals mysteries to others such as

---

[318] http://www.tartanplace.com/faery/goddess/cliodna.html.
[319] Monaghan. *The Encyclopedia of Celtic Mythology and Folklore*, 2004.
[320] Monaghan. *The Encyclopedia of Celtic Mythology and Folklore*, 2004.
[321] Macdonald. *Celtic Folklore: The people of the Mounds, Articles on the Sidhe*. 1993.

the magic of the Blarney Stone to a noble mortal family. She is a Goddess of love, lust and beauty bewitching mortal lovers. She is a queen in her own right as ruler of Munster alongside Áine and Aoibhinn forming a trinity. Other legends have connected her with Manannan Mac Lir, residing in the Land of Youth. She has links to the Welsh Rhiannon as she has three magical birds that heal illness and sing sweet songs. She is a goddess of the afterlife, continuing her existence in Manannan's realm after drowning. Overall, Cliodhna is a powerful and inspiring Faerie Queen.

## Bibliography

Joyce. P.W. (1906) A Smaller Social History Of Ancient Ireland. London: Longmans

Macdonald, L. (1993) Celtic Folklore: The people of the Mounds, Articles on the Sidhe, in Dalriada Magazine, Arran

Monaghan, Patricia (2004) *The Encyclopedia of Celtic Mythology and Folklore*. New York: Infobase Publishing

Rolleston T.W. (1911) *Myths and Legends of the Celtic Race*. London: George G Harrap & Co Ltd.

Squire, Charles (1905) *Celtic Myth, Legend, Poetry & Romance*. London: Gresham Publishing Co. Ltd

## Websites

http://www.tartanplace.com/faery/goddess/cliodna.html

www.westcorktravel.com

# RHIANNON

## Faerie Queen, Mortal Throne, Divine Equine

## HALO QUIN

> *"Neither man nor woman of these left Rhiannon without being given a memorable gift, either a brooch or a ring or a precious stone. They ruled the land prosperously that year and the next."*[322]

In the land of Wales, many years ago, a collection of tales were written down, grouped into four branches. These tales spoke of life as it had been when Wales was divided into kingdoms and filled with magical events. The collection is known as *Y Mabinogi* and in the first branch we find the stories of Pwyll, Prince of Dyfed and his adventures as he learns to rule with honour and compassion alongside his Queen from another world, Rhiannon. Historically Rhiannon has a strong connection with the Gaulish horse goddess Epona,[323] who also came to Ireland as Macha. All three embody the archetype of the Mare who has a long history of being linked with the land, worship of the earth and the Great Mother Goddess[324] and as such Rhiannon continues on the tradition of caring for the people of the land. The ubiquitous evidence of worship of the divine mother as the mare across Europe[325] indicates that Rhiannon is a divine mother in the Welsh mythologies the way Epona is in the Gaulish ones. Her exact nature in *Y Mabinogi* is ambiguous and, though described as a Goddess rather than a Faerie Queen in most modern interpretations of her role, I believe that Rhiannon embodies the connection between the Welsh otherworld of Faerie and the marriage to the magic of the land through the power of the horse in the tradition of Epona. This position is one which I shall demonstrate

---

[322] Anon, *The Mabinogian*, Translated by Jones and Jones, 1949:17.
[323] Green, *The Gods of the Celts*, 2004:82.
[324] Anon, *The Mabinogian*, 1949:92.
[325] *Ibid, 1949*:86-87.

through an exploration of her story and characteristics and this process highlights some key elements of the nature of Faerie Queens in general. Rhiannon is unusual in that she comes to sit upon a mortal throne; she is the Faerie Queen in a mortal realm which simultaneously loves and fears her magic and so the story of Rhiannon is one which discloses the links between land and horse and faerie queenship whilst illustrating the tumultuous relationship between mortal and faerie beings.

Two other well-known tales in which we find horse-riding Faerie Queens who cross from their world to ours can be found in two of the so-called *Border Ballads*; *Thomas the Rhymer*[326] and *Tam Lin*.[327] These grew out of the border between England and Scotland, which has a history of fierce fighting. Thomas the Rhymer has been dated to around the time of the Wars of Scottish Independence and Tam Lin was first recorded in *The Complaynt of Scotland*,[328] a political attack on the continued English attempts to unite with Scotland. The similarities between these tales demonstrate why I identify Rhiannon as a Faerie Queen, whilst the differences between them illuminate the nature of Faerie Queens in Britain. [329]

Rhiannon's story is also interesting in that, unlike the Faerie Queens in the *Border Ballads*, she enters our world to stay. The horse which carries her tells us who and what she is – as I shall demonstrate – but does not carry her lover away from his people. In common with the other two stories her beauty reveals the seductive nature of Faerie Queens whilst she is also clever in her counsel and, where her lover is childlike in his naivety, she uses her magic in wise and compassionate ways to solve problems and escape the fate she wished to avoid.

Here, then, we shall explore these relationships and the elements of her story which reveal Rhiannon as Faerie Queen. We will also come to understand the reasons for the differences between Rhiannon's story in Wales and Tam Lin and Thomas' stories in Scotland. As we shall see, the Faerie Queens are intimately linked to their lands as expressions of the magic within the wilds of the places they originate in. As such the thread which holds together this essay is the illustration of the way in which the different aspects of Rhiannon, as a Faerie Queen upon a Mortal Throne embodying the archetype of Divine Equine, connect to the land which she is rooted in.

Let us follow our fair lady upon her white horse to discover the philosophy underlying the nature of faerie-human inter-relations, investigating the differences and similarities between her story and those of other mystical riders of white horses as well as the root of contradiction

---

[326] Anon, "Thomas the Rhymer", *A Book of Narrative Verse*, 1930.
[327] Stewart, "Young Tam Lin", *The Living World of Faery*, 1995.
[328] Wedderburn, *The Complaynt of Scotland*, 1979.
[329] For the purpose of this essay I am assuming a familiarity with the story of Rhiannon and other similar folk stories, especially these two particular tales.

between the human reactions of love and fear to the otherworldly power which gives life to the human realm.

This tale of Rhiannon begins when Pwyll, prince of Dyfed (and, notably friend to Arawn, Lord of the Otherworld known as Annwn), becomes curious about a local mound:

> *"He sat upon the mound. And as they were sitting down, they could see a lady on a big fine pale white horse, with a garment of shining gold brocaded silk upon her, coming along the highway that led past the mound."*[330]

The mound upon which Pwyll sits echoes the mounds throughout the tales of faerie whereby mortals reach the Otherlands and Fae beings emerge into ours and so it makes perfect sense that Rhiannon should first appear, a vision of unearthly beauty, beside such a gateway to another world. Before we even meet her, the appearance of something Other, something Fae, is thus announced by the very structures of the land itself. The pure white colour of the horse and her shining gold garment tell the viewer clearly that here is a being of light, representing her origin in something other than matter. Even more peculiar is how the horse seems to have *'a slow and even pace'* and yet none of the men can catch her:

> *"One arose, but when he came on to the road to meet her, she had gone past. He followed her as fast as he could on foot, but the greater was his speed, all the further was she from him."*[331]

This chase is repeated on horseback and again the next day. The power of the horse to outstrip the fastest followers whilst appearing to move with little speed also indicates that magic is present here. The Lady is thus otherworldly from this first encounter and yet, unlike many faerie stories, she does not seek to lead the mortals from their realm, instead she seeks to permanently enter theirs. In this way Rhiannon brings the magic of the otherworlds into the human realm, rather than using a human intermediary she herself carries the gifts she offers. As such in her story, where she sits as a Faerie Queen on a mortal throne, we can see the results of integrating the magic which she embodies into our human realm. This is the story of the land offering its power to the people who reside upon it and the wisdom of the otherworlds becoming available to them directly rather than through an intermediary. When a Queen sits upon a throne she brings her power into the realm which she rules and so Rhiannon willingly brings Faerie power into a mortal realm. This model of human-fae interactions illustrates one way of building relationships between the two aspects of reality; integration of a magical world-view, wisdom beyond day-to-day thought and the power inherent in the wilderness into a structured society and rational way of

---

[330] Anon, *The Mabinogian*, 1949:9.
[331] *Ibid*, 1949:9.

working allows for greater happiness and productivity, as we shall see from the benevolence of Rhiannon's rule. The way in which this integration can come about is manifested in Pwyll's final attempt to reach her, she has escaped capture several times when eventually Pwyll himself calls out to her:

> *'Maiden,' said he, 'for his sake whom thou lovest best, stay for me.' 'I will, gladly,' said she, 'and it had been better for the horse hadst thou asked this long since.'*[332]

The surrender to the impossibility of overcoming magic through force is realised and Rhiannon deigns to answer the man whom she has come to find, responding to a call which invokes love, for it transpires that she intends to claim Pwyll as her husband in place of the man whom she is betrothed to. So even as a woman tied to an arranged marriage she demonstrates her sovereignty by rejecting the man she does not love and choosing one for herself. We can see in this pattern the way in which the land can offer its greatest blessings to humanity and how humanity can respond in order to enter into a fruitful partnership, this can be understood further when compared to the tales of other Faerie Queens as the role Rhiannon plays in this tale marks her as kin to the Ladies of the *Border Ballads*.

The otherworldly aspects - the mound and the white horse – coupled with her personal sovereignty mark Rhiannon as a Faerie Queen. Just as the Faerie Queens in the tales of *Tam Lin* and *Thomas the Rhymer* are depicted on horseback, Rhiannon first appears on a magical steed and then continues to be connected with the equine world through the journey of her son and the form of her punishment when accused of his murder.

> *"The penance imposed upon her was to remain in that court at Arberth till the end of seven years, and to sit every day near a horse block that was outside the gate, and to relate the whole story to everyone who should come there whom she might suppose not to know it; and to those who would permit her to carry them, to offer guest and stranger to carry him on her back to the court."*[333]

The behaviour and motifs of other Faerie Queens both mirror and contrast with Rhiannon's story. Thomas, sleeping under a Hawthorn tree, was also in a Fae place.[334] The Queen appears to him, shining and beautiful on a horse to carry him away, returning him after seven years in Faerieland where he was challenged to remain silent. Janet, in Tam Lin's tale, finds Tam Lin at a place known to be haunted, rescues him at a crossroads and encounters the Queen as the leader of the Wild Hunt – on a horse. All three tales feature specific locations known for their connections with the other

---

[332] *Ibid*, 1949:11.
[333] *Ibid*, 1949:19.
[334] Andrews, *Faeries and Folklore of the British Isles*, 2006:56.

world and a Faerie Queen who has power illustrated by the fact of her riding.

Traditionally the horse is a being of power, whose compliance has allowed humans to do much more than we would have been capable of without them. As such, horses have always been valuable and both a symbol of wealth and power as well as representing the power of the land itself, which is also embodied in the Queen. So the combination of both Queen and horse is a substantial statement. When Rhiannon's child is stolen away he is discovered, unbeknown to her, in stables far away where foals had been vanishing each spring. When she is accused of the crime of eating her child she is forced to take the place of a horse as punishment. In these ways Rhiannon does not simply ride a magical horse, she serves the same function as one. Both by taking on the role of a horse and giving birth to a child who is left in the foal stables she embodies the power that is contained within Horse. The connection to Epona is evident in these details and reinforces Rhiannon's status as divine. Epona is known to have long been worshipped across Europe as the Divine Mare, the connection between her and the mother horse is so great she may even have occasionally been depicted by a mare and a foal without any anthropomorphic elements, which is very unusual in Gaulish imagery.[335]

Rhiannon, as an expression of the archetypal Mare, is the sovereignty-power of the land as the Mother of all bounty and the land, chooses Pwyll who accepts her as a wiser, greater power and treats her with honour. Again we can see how a healthy relationship to the land can come about. Unlike in the tales of Thomas and Tam Lin, Pwyll's Faerie Queen comes to dwell with him instead of stealing him away

The nature of the lands from which these stories sprang is expressed through the behaviour of the Faerie Queens, who *are* the magic of those lands. Both *Tam Lin* and *Thomas the Rhymer* are tales from the borderlands of Scotland, where the land is harsher and wilder than in Dyfed, Wales. On the borders the land (and the fighting that raged upon it) could steal you away, whereas in Wales the land was gentler and more willing to work with the humans that inhabited it, even when humanity could be as violent. When Rhiannon chooses Pwyll and leaves behind her home she brings the magic of the otherworld into the human realm. Earlier in his story Pwyll had undergone a series of trials, one of which was in the underworld where he took the place of its king, Arawn, for a year. Pwyll behaved honourably in this role and thus earned his worth, his actions forging a friendship which strengthened the bridges between the worlds. Rhiannon, in travelling the other direction, demonstrates this interconnectivity again, blessing the people of Pwyll's realm with her wisdom and benevolence. The land recognises the honour of Pwyll and the initiatory journey he has made in

---

[335] Green, *The Gods of the Celts*, 2004:163.

forging a relationship with the otherworld powers and responds by offering a partnership. The borderland Queens, however, steal the men away and offer them challenges to overcome in order to prove their worth as it hasn't already been established. Thomas earns his freedom through keeping the challenge of silence, Tam Lin through rebelling against the terms and finding a mortal girl to save him.

In *Y Mabinogi* Rhiannon's wisdom and compassion is demonstrated in the reports of how fairly she ruled over Dyfed. Where Thomas is gifted with the tongue that cannot lie, which is in turn then given to the people of the land, the Welsh Faerie Queen brings her gifts into the world herself and bestows them on her people directly. Despite this, there is an obvious fear of her Fae nature, plus she is, and always will be, an outsider. So when she is accused of infanticide the people accept, almost without question, that the mother could have eaten her child. Beloved of her people and yet not of them she brings blessings from the otherworld to enliven the human realms despite their mistrust of her. Just as agricultural humans live in an uneasy relationship with the land, knowing that a bad harvest means a hungry year ahead and we are powerless to control nature, so humanity has ever been uneasy around the otherworld. Rhiannon brings blessings to her people but they know that if she chose to turn on them they would be powerless to stop her. The gratitude towards the earth that gives life and the embodiments of the magic which fills the land is always tempered by the knowledge that humanity is dependent upon the land's blessings and so the people never wholly trust in their benefactor. The human-land relationship in Wales was one, more often than not, in which the land could be generous but temperamental. In Scotland, particularly on the borderlands where fighting raged over land, not only was the land harsher, wilder, than in Wales but so was the social setting. As such, the way magic is personified in the different lands reflects this.

So far we have seen a strong link between the notion of the otherworld and the non-human parts of nature. If we accept that the *'world'* for humanity is where we live, our network of relationships and daily human interactions,[336] then we can see where this correlation comes from; our world is the human world, the *'other'* world is that which is not part of our day-to-day human interactions. As such the otherworld contains both non-human *'magical beings'* such as faeries and the wildness of the land which is as outside our daily life as the faerie realm. Also outside of our general daily life is our existence beyond death. Once we die it is assumed that we pass beyond daily life, so, unsurprisingly, the Fae have also always been intimately connected to the dead. The mounds which serve as entry points for our dead into the earth were often gateways for the Fae to emerge. Historically the Fae have been known to take children and women in childbirth, folk

---

[336] This particular position can be found in a more complex form in Heidegger's *Being and Time*.

close to the entry-point of souls to this world.[337] Both entering and leaving the human realm creates gateways between the worlds where the Fae can travel through. We see this with Rhiannon when she first appears to Pwyll who is sat upon a mound which was described as though it were haunted:

> "Lord," said one of the court, "it is the peculiarity of the mound that whatever high-born man sits upon it will not go thence without one of two things: wounds or blows, or else his seeing a wonder."[338]

Pwyll did indeed see a wonder for he saw Rhiannon, who is Fae and so carries the thread of those that reside in the otherworlds, including the human dead. The magic of a place, as embodied by the Faerie Queen, comes from that which belongs to that land; the marriage of Pwyll and Rhiannon is therefore a linking of the non-human powers of the area and those who have laid down the foundation of human society in that space to the current society. In carrying the wisdom of the dead back to the people of the land, Rhiannon also reminds her subjects of their own mortality, thus providing another reason to fear her. In another example of how she carries power not available to mere mortals, Rhiannon saves herself from an unwanted marriage a second time. During the feast thrown to celebrate their betrothal Pwyll, through his naivety, accidentally promises Rhiannon to the very man she chose to reject. It is only through her quick wit and magic that she is able to avert disaster, guiding Pwyll in how to solve the problem he has created:

> "Pwyll was dumb, for there was no answer he might have given. "Be dumb as long as thou wilt," said Rhiannon. ... "That is the man to whom they would have given me against my will," said she. "... and because thou hast spoken the word thou hast, bestow me upon him lest dishonour come upon thee.... and I will bring it about that he shall never have me." "How will that be?" asked Pwyll. "I shall give into thy hand a small bag," said she. "and keep that with thee safe and he will ask for the banquet and the feast and the preparation; but these things are not at thy command... And as for me ... I will make a tryst with him a year from to-night, to sleep with me. And at the end of the year... be thou, and this bag with thee, one of a hundred horsemen in the orchard up yonder."[339]

By her words she protects the feast she has thrown for her guests, by her wits she creates a plan to save herself from the fate she wishes to avoid – thus demonstrating her sovereignty over herself again – and by her magic she produces an impossible item which can be used to trap the unsuitable suitor. Rhiannon's demand of Pwyll to be silent (dumb) is a reminder that he holds less wisdom than she, though he has proved himself honourable in

---

[337] Purkiss, *Fairies and Fairy Stories A History*, 2007:117.
[338] Anon, *The Mabinogian*, 1949:9.
[339] *Ibid*, 1949:13-14.

earlier stories and she has clearly decided that he is worth marrying despite his naivety, perhaps because she has enough wit for the pair of them. The call to silence and the insistence that he uphold his word is also reminiscent of Thomas' challenge and the careful use of words common in faerie tales, perhaps indicating that the eloquence of Rhiannon is a faerie trait.

It is possible to read into the pattern here a story of faerie and Human relations where the Fae always have much wisdom or power which could benefit humanity if the relationship is entered into with honour. Thomas keeps silent, honouring the geas placed upon him, while Pwyll defers to the greater wit of his wife-to-be, accepting that she knows better than he. This lack of arrogance reflects upon the relationship one must have to the land if one is to forge a living from her dark soil; a lesson to be learned by our current society perhaps?

> *"In the middle of the night she heard the bridle ring*
> *She heeded what he did say and young Tam Lin did win*
> *Then up spoke the Faerie Queen, an angry queen was she*
> *Woe betide her ill-fard face, an ill death may she die*
> *"Oh, had I known, Tam Lin," she said, "what this night I did see I'd*
> *have looked him in the eyes and turned him to a tree."*[340]

Where Pwyll and Thomas show respect to the Queens who come to them, Tam Lin seeks to escape. Tam Lin ends his story with a lover and a curse from the Queen he cheated, where Thomas has gifts of truth beyond normal understanding and Pwyll has a partner who can rule at his side better than he can rule alone. Understanding these patterns allows us to see that, in the relationship with the land that supports us and the spirits which live there, we must have respect for those powers greater than ourselves. We may escape the hand of nature and build a family but, in the end, we all return to the earth and are all subject to her laws of death, decay and rebirth. In placing a Faerie Queen upon a mortal throne the wisdom of the non-human world becomes integrated with human understanding. While the people may mistrust the gifts of understanding which carry the promise of eventual dissolution and return to the earth, without that relationship all benefits are not given but forcefully taken – as Janet fights for her lover Tam Lin – and will eventually incur the curse of the Queen herself. Rhiannon, even when saddled as a horse, is never cast aside by her husband who keeps his marital vows and so she returns to his side when the truth is revealed.

It is telling that her unjust punishment cast her in the role of a horse for as we saw earlier, Rhiannon is connected with horses even more than the border Queens and it shows as much about her nature as it does about her magic and wit. Throughout the ages the horse has been more than a mere

---

[340] Fairport convention, "Tam Lin", *Liege and Lief,* 1969.

resource, more than a partner, more than a mortal animal. From Odin's eight-legged steed Sleipnir to the Greek Pegasus and beyond we have tales of magical horses which move between the worlds. In the Hindu ritual of Ashvamedha, the kingship rites of Ireland and the worship of Frey horses were often sacrificed. In these rites the interaction between the ritual participants and the horse could include a sexual element, perhaps indicating a marriage to the power of the horse who travels to the otherworld. The horse thus connects the land of the living to the land of the spirits, the dead and the magic of the earth. Rhiannon, as partly equine herself, takes on that role for Pwyll and therefore the people of Dyfed, although she travels in the opposite direction - into the land of the living, carrying the magic with her. The horse is akin to the psychopomp, a being that can cross boundaries on behalf of the people and lend that power to its human companions. As a symbol of power and wealth the sacrifice is an act which commits that power to the earth, marrying the power of the ruler with the land itself. In this kind of sacrifice there is an element of supplication - asking for blessings - and an attempt to gain some control over the power that is sacrificed to. As such, it would seem that the Faerie Queen seated on a mortal throne has much to offer the people she rules.

> *Syne they came to a garden green,*
> *And she pu'd an apple frae a tree:*
> *'Take this for thy wages, true Thomas;*
> *It will give thee the tongue that can never lee.'* [341]

The power of the horse is clearly evident in the tales of the Faerie Queens, in turn their boundary-crossing magic is clear whether a magical horse is present or not. Rhiannon embodies the role of benevolent Queen and the magic of the land through her actions and her connection to horses. She is mother to foals, bringer of wisdom and a compassionate ruler. This is the Faerie Queen in her kindest aspect. She is the magic of the land, the wisdom older than humanity and the blessing of life. The *Border Ballads*, when compared to *Y Mabinogi*, demonstrate how she changes her face as our relationship to the land changes and where her role as the Queen of the Dead leads her to offer the risk of death alongside every action of life. As life and death are impossible for the children of earth to separate it is therefore understandable that the people of Dyfed feared Rhiannon as much as they loved her.

It seems to me that this is why the Fae have been presented in such diminutive forms as the years have passed; as we remove ourselves from the land and assert dominance over it we belittle the powers of life and death held within it. The Faerie Queen becomes Shakespeare's Titania, a fool for love. Later she is merely Tinkerbell, beloved by many but seen as powerless – a bit player in a child's dream of everlasting youth. The Faerie Queen, as

---

[341] Anon, "Thomas the Rhymer", *A Book of Narrative Verse*, 1930:45.

benevolent Rhiannon or the wild female of Tam Lin's tale still resides in our dreams and stories, showing to us the relationship we have to our land. We would do well to remember Rhiannon and ask her to return to us, before we turn the entire world into a resource for entertainment and lose the understanding required to pass between the worlds.

The magic of faerie and the power of the Dead can be reached through the hoofbeats of the Faerie Queen's horse, that wild delight and beauty seen in horses cantering across the moor is not lost to us. In recent years there has been a growing interest in *'equine therapy'*, a therapy involving horses in the healing process,[342] evidence that since horses moved from beasts of burden and vehicles of war they have become more associated with leisure and healing. It is interesting that young girls are now the target audience for most horse related toys and books, with the *'My Little Pony'* range being a notable example. Perhaps the perceived connection between horses and the *'feminine'* reflects a move towards applying those qualities associated in our culture with *'the female'* to an image of power and our connection to the land which we have attempted to dominate for many generations now. This shift from their use in executing power over the world to healing and finding happiness is an important move for horses, showing that Rhiannon is definitely present in our world and is still capable of offering compassionate guidance to her people despite the humiliation she suffered through fear and the abuse which horses are often subjected to throughout the world. The growing *'equine therapy'* industry, with its emphasis on relating to the horses in a partnership is perhaps a good indication of the potential for humanity to move back into a healthy relationship with the non-human natural world.

In this discussion we have seen how Rhiannon is a Faerie Queen, though that does not preclude her from being a goddess - a discussion for another time perhaps? We have also discovered how the tales of horse-riding Faerie Queens from different parts of Britain can show us that the nature of Faerie is intimately connected to the wildness of the land and the places outside of human control and yet these two realms can be united and work together in harmony. Rhiannon gave herself to our world; the land's magic embodied in an equine queen bestowing wisdom and compassion upon the people of Dyfed. Let us remember her fondly and welcome her back into our lives. Listen for the sound of her hoofbeats and let the magic touch your heart.

## Bibliography & Further Reading

Andrews, Elizabeth (2006) *Faeries and Folklore of the British Isles*. Gloucestershire: Arris Books

Collins, Vere H. (ed.) (1930) *"Thomas the Rhymer"*, in *A Book of Narrative Verse*. Oxford: Oxford University Press

---

[342] Kohanov, *The Tao of Equus*, 2007.

Fairport Convention, *"Tam Lin"*, *Liege and Lief* (Island, 1969)

Green, Miranda (2004) *The Gods of the Celts*. Stroud: Sutton Publishing Ltd

Guest, Lady Charlotte (trans.) (1877) *Y Mabinogi*. London: Bernard Quaritch

Heidegger, Martin, & J. MacQuarrie & E. Robinson (trans.) (2004) *Being and Time*. Oxford: Blackwell Publishing

Jones, Gwyn & Thomas (trans.) (1949) *The Mabinogian*. Georgia: Camelot Press Ltd

Kohanov, Linda (2007) *The Tao of Equus*. California: New World Library

Purkiss, Diane (2007) *Fairies and Fairy Stories A History*. Stroud: Tempus Publishing Limited

Stewart, R.J. (1995) "Young Tam Lin", in *The Living World of Faery*. North Carolina: Mercury Publishing

Wedderburn, Robert (1979) *The Complaynt of Scotland*. Edinburgh: Scottish Text Society

# ÁINE

## Celtic Faerie Queen of the Summer Solstice

# JOANNA ROWAN MULLANE

In the Isle of Mists, where the trees speak in ancient tongues, the stones breathe life into Solstice circles and megaliths, and the twilight hour summons the Sidhe of the between times; there waits a Faerie Goddess of the Earth and Sun. Her name is many throughout the sacred land of Eire and she has many guises in which her tales and folklore have been weaved into a rich tapestry much like the landscape in which she dwells. In Ireland she is known as Áine of Knockaine; Faerie Queen of the Hill of Cnoc Áine and the revered lake of Lough Gur with many a hill, mound and sacred site scattered throughout the land that bears her name and honours her to this day.

In Celtic myth and folklore she is of the Tuatha de Danann, the Sidhe, or Faery race of ancient Ireland who became known as the People of the Sidhe Mounds. In this aspect she rules the between time of twilight and the Summer Solstice also known as Midsummer where she becomes a Goddess of the Sun. Though there are many a Faerie Queen within the tales of Celtic myth, there is little known about Áine when compared to the other Celtic Faerie Queens such as Queen Maeve or Fuamnach. This is not to imply that she is somehow lesser in presence of the land, quite the contrary actually, only that fewer tales have been found in written form. In centuries past she has been celebrated, honoured and respected as Faerie Queen and Mountain Goddess of the Land, bestowing the gifts of love, fertility, sovereignty and agriculture, to include that of the animals and crops, to all who call upon her. Let us now explore what legends and folklore have been preserved as well as how we, in this present time, may show reverence for this ancient Faerie Goddess of Eire.

Within the great tellings of Irish mythology, the name Áine is given to multiple fairy women. Her stories, although small in number, are wide and varied across county to county. In the Irish language a Faerie Queen is often called *'bean righan na brugh'* (queen of the fairy palace), or simply *'bean sidhe'* (fairy woman). These queens are most often noble and skilful women that can be either ruthless, or quite helpful, to the mortals of their choosing. They often embody the goddess of a local tribe or the ancestral deity or guardian of a specific clan or region. The following section of the ballad by F.J. Child entitled *Alison Gross* is but one example of a scorned Faerie Queen turned benevolent:

> *But as it feel out on last Hallow-even,*
> *When the seely court was ridin by,*
> *The Queen lighted down on a gowany bank,*
> *Nae far frae the tree where I wont to lye.*
> *She took me up in her milk-white han,*
> *An she's stroakd me three times oer her knee;*
> *She chang'd me again to my ain proper shape,*
> *An nae mair I toddle about the tree.*

Áine, whose name means *'delight'*, *'radiant'* or *'glowing'*, is tied to the landscape of the province of Munster to the South West, as well as the province of Ulster to the North. In these regions her presence watches over many sacred sites that may still be visited today. I have had the privilege of being able to travel to Ireland once a year to study their mythic stories and folklore and have been able to see firsthand the sheer beauty and rich tales that make up her realms. Within Limerick her presence is strongly felt and remembered by the people in the place names and customs that are still honoured today. At the Lake of Lough Gur she is said to have appeared there in her triple aspect in the form of a mermaid (the Maiden), a young woman (Mother), and the hag (Crone). In her mermaid form she rises like the Phoenix from beneath her home within the lake. In the form of Mother she inspires and nurtures her people. In her Crone or hag aspect, she guards and defends her realm.

One of the most cherished tales about Áine and her connection to Lough Gur is a story of the Swan Maiden and Gerold, the 1st Earl of Desmond who was a local landowner. In ancient Ireland it was customary that at the inauguration of a new tribal chief or leader, that he seek union or the blessing of the goddess of the land. This ritual ceremony was known as a *feis* which translates as *'to spend the evening'*. One night the Earl of Desmond came upon Áine by the lake combing her hair. The Earl, being so struck by her beauty, fell instantly in love with her and decided he would take her for himself. He snuck upon her and stole her cloak relinquishing her power and taking her as his bride. In this union they produced a child that was gifted with great magical abilities. The *geasa* or taboo, which was placed upon Gerold, was that he may never express any form of surprise or awe at what their son might do and with that she transformed into a swan and swam away upon Lough Gur. One day the father witnessed his son showing off to some young maidens by jumping into a bottle and back out again. The Earl failed to hold in his gasp of surprise and their son quickly left him turning into the form of a wild goose or phantom that every seven years must ride upon the lake until his silver shoes have but worn away. In other legends it is said that once in every seven years, the lake dries up to reveal a sacred Yew tree (representing the Tree of Life) at the bottom of the lake covered with a gilded green cloth. Áine in her Crone, or hag form, keeps watch while knitting, ensuring the creation and recreation, of the great weave of life. From my own experience, this lake is one of the most peaceful places within all of Ireland where one can truly connect to the presence of Áine. Filled now with trees of old, forts and cairns gradually becoming reclaimed by the Earth, it is also a place that demands respect, for one quickly realizes one is walking upon fairy grounds; in essence one is a mortal guest of the Sidhe or Fair Folk and that should tread with care in this ancient place.

Cnoc Áine, (Knockainy), is considered to be the sacred mound of Áine, an inauguration site of kings and her seat of power within the land. There are three ringed barrows, or mounds, upon Cnoc Áine, similar in nature to those upon the Hill of Tara in County Meath, that to some represent the Hills of the Three Ancestors. There are many variations of this story but the following version from the twelfth-century *Book of Leinster* further shows the consequences of mortals interfering with the Sidhe or a Faerie Queen. King Ailill of Munster it seemed was having a problem with his grass disappearing in the middle of the night when he fell asleep. When this act happened three times, he believed it to be due to magic. Ailill then consulted his Druid who advised him to visit Knockainy upon the next Samhain Eve. Ailill and his Druid went to Cnoc Áine at Samhain but the King fell asleep while waiting. He awoke to witness the People of the Sidhe coming out of the cairn with their king and his daughter Áine closely behind. Upon seeing this lovely maiden appear, Ailill being filled with his lust for her, killed her father and raped Áine. In her anger at this violence, Áine maimed him by biting off his ear and in so doing, stripped him of his kingly sovereignty for he was no longer *'perfect'* as was the way of Celtic tradition. From then on he was known as Ailill One Ear.

In ancient times Midsummer's Eve was celebrated by lighting sacred fires upon all the hills of Ireland. They were called Baal Fires and incorporated the burning of sacred woods to honour the Sun and its life-giving properties. Until the late 1880's, locals from County Limerick remembered her as the Faerie Queen each year upon what is now called St. Johns' Eve, by forming a procession around the hill of Cnoc Áine. Carrying lit torches through the fields they would walk clockwise around the barrows. This honoured tradition was to ensure the blessing of Áine for a bountiful, fertile harvest of the crops and animals and it was often said that Áine herself was seen leading the procession. Their belief was that in so doing, they were recreating the rite of the faeries that performed this sacred ritual as Áine impregnated the land with her life giving solar energy. Within the Celtic Wheel of the Year, the night before ancient Sun Festivals such as

Beltaine (May 1st), Lughnasadh (August 1st) or Samhain (November 1st), was considered to be the between time, when the veil was thinnest and the entrance to the otherworld was easily accessible with the celebration of Midsummer's Eve being an especially potent time. To the Celts, time was circular not linear, and the structure of the seasonal celebrations revolved around seasonal quarters that divided the solar year and marked the fire festivals, solstices and equinoxes. The celebration of Beltane is sometimes suggested to be named after the sun god Bel. In further study one could also suggest it be named after Áine in her Sun Goddess aspect that would mean the opening or the start of summer. Furthermore, Samhain could also be interpreted as meaning summer or twin; *'Samh'* equalling the end of summer and the twin of Áine representing the twin half of the Great Wheel – Beltaine.

Throughout most of Ireland Áine is known to have been the wife to Manannan mac Lir, the Celtic Sea God and Lord of the Fairy Tribes who dwells in the Land of Promise, though in other tales he is her father. Further legend suggests she may have also been married to Echdae the Horse God. She used her inherent gifts of music and sweet poetry to woo mortal lovers giving her the name of Leanan Sidhe or Sweetheart of the Sidhe. In much darker folklore surrounding her, there is a strong tradition of Áine and Dun Áine, which marks the entrance to Dundalk Bay. Legend states that the people of this region feared her, and that the days following the celebration of Lammas were considered unlucky so much so that the people of the town would not bathe, nor the fishermen go out to sea, in fear of drowning and becoming a sacrifice to the relentless Áine. In another tale she is associated with a stone or stone chair called Cathair Áine. If any man would sit upon it he would risk losing his mind, if he sat upon it three times, he would lose it forever.

To herbalist and folk-healers she is believed to have given the herb Meadowsweet its scent. Meadowsweet is a sacred herb to the Druids and that herb may be used for any special rites or celebrations that involve calling upon her. John Gerard, who in 1633 wrote *The Generall Historie of Plantes*, writes the following about Meadowsweet, which fits well within the qualities and attributes of Áine:

> *"The leaves and floures of Meadowsweet farre excelle all other strowing herbs for to decke up houses, to strawe in chambers, halls and banqueting-houses in the summer-time, for the smell thereof makes the heart merrie and joyful and delighteth the senses."*

Some folklore suggests that with specific herbs, she maintained the power of enchantment over the entire body suggesting her adeptness with the healing arts. Within my own studies in working with Áine, the following chant is a beautiful way in which one can connect and call upon her.

AINE 'HEART OF THE FOREST' BY JOANNA ROWAN MULLANE

*I call upon Áine; Faerie Queen of the twilight veil*
*Deep within the Sidhe mound you dwell*
*Keeper of Cnoc Áine, mistress of the Midsummer Sun*
*Noble, Bright & Shining One*
*I ask your abundance within my life*
*I ask of your fertile wisdom be true*
*May your presence be ever felt within the land*
*As the people forever call out to you.*

In many ways Áine takes her place amongst the great and beloved Faerie Queens of lore and legend treading softly back within her Sidhe mound upon her hill. Though nothing is ever truly lost forever when we choose to keep the Baal fires burning upon the hills. Throughout time, she will forever remain a Celtic Faery Queen and a Goddess of the Sun shining her light upon her people, and her domains, as she awaits our return to her within the shrouded mists of Eire.

## Bibliography

Briggs, Katharine (1976) *A Dictionary of Faeries*. London: Penguin Books Ltd

Briggs, Katherine (1967) *The Faeries in Tradition and Literature*. London: Lowe & Brydone Printers Ltd

Evans-Wentz, W.Y. (2004) *The Fairy Faith in Celtic Countries*. Franklin Lakes: Career Press

Gerard, John (1633) The Generall Historie of Plantes. London: Norton & Whittakers

Gregory, Lady (2000) *Lady Gregory's Complete Irish Mythology*. London: Chancellor Press

Meehan, Cary (2002) *Sacred Ireland*. Glastonbury: Gothic Image Publications

Roberts, Jack (1996) *The Sacred Mythological Centres in Ireland*. Sligo: Bandia Publishing

Logan, Patrick (1981) *The Old Gods; The Facts about Irish Faeries*. Belfast: Appletree Press

Spence, Lewis (1948) *The Minor Traditions of British Mythology*. Essex: The Anchor Press, Ltd.

Wilde, Lady (1902) *Ancient Legends of Ireland*. London: Chatto & Windus

# WHOSE QUEEN?

## THEA FAYE

The Wheel of the Year is widely recognised and celebrated in modern times by neopagans. It is said that Gerald Gardner and Ross Nichols, when piecing it together, decided that it would be good to have an excuse for a party every six weeks or so, and thus melded the Greater Sabbats of Candlemass, Beltane, Lammas and Samhain with the Lesser Sabbats, comprising the solstices and equinoxes. Although it is widely recognised that the Wheel is a late invention and no ancient people celebrated all eight festivals,[343] what is perhaps not so well known is that almost all of the sabbats were important dates in faery lore. Indeed, many periods which are held to be magickally important, such as the witch's apprenticeship of a year and a day or the three days surrounding full moon, or times of the day, e.g. the *'in-between times'* of dusk and dawn, as well as midnight and midday, were also held to be important to the Little Folk and their court. A lot of surviving folk traditions owe a great debt to the Fey.

For example, just as there is a tradition of lighting bonfires at Beltane, Katharine Briggs reports an eyewitness account of the Sluagh Sidhe, or People of the Hills, in Ireland doing the same, allegedly as recently as within the last century:

> *"I was only a chile – I was not much then but many a time I remember hearing about the wee people on Slieve Gullion. Many a night there was light on the top an' the wee people cud be seen as plain as ye like disportin' themselves aroun' the bonfires. There'd be scores of fires an' hundreds of wee people. An' some of them was mounted an' wud ride their horses through the flames. Lots of the oul ones saw them. I saw the fires once but didn't see the horsemen."*[344]

So why are all those dates special in fairy lore when they were not all recognised by any one ancient people? In *The Fairies in Tradition and*

---

[343] Duir, *The Eightfold Wheel of the Year*, http://www.manygods.org.uk/articles/festivals/wheel.shtml
[344] Briggs, *The Fairies in Tradition and Literature*

*Literature*, Katharine Briggs posits that this may possibly be explained by the Fey being worshipped by two distinct groups, one splitting the year by June and December, the other by May and November. Since the Fey show interest in both cattle and crops, one set of people were agriculturalists, the other, shepherds and thus the different types of farmers developed different ways of approaching the Little People.[345] There is another explanation as well – that different Fairy Folk had different responsibilities and superstitions, each court having its own royalty, with different courts celebrating different festivals. To support the notion that there were different tribes within the Little Folk, there are documented cases of the Fey at war with one another, sometimes recruiting human help for the battle. In *The Fairy-Faith in Celtic Countries*, Evans Wentz gave an account by Thady Steed of fairy warfare:

> *"When the fairy tribes under the various kings and queens have a battle, one side manages to have a living man among them, and he by knocking the fairies about turns the battle in case the side he is on is losing. It is always usual for the Munster king to challenge Finvarra, the Connaught fairy king."*[346]

Not only were there multiple courts, a king may have more than one queen. As such, when trying to decipher the Queen and her role within the court, it can be hard to pin down who exactly is under discussion. To take Finvarra as an example, he was apparently married to Oonagh, whose *"golden hair sweeps the ground, and she is robed in silver gossamer all glittering as if with diamonds, but they are dew-drops that sparkle over it. The queen is more beautiful than any woman of earth, yet Finvarra loves the mortal women best, and wiles them down to his fairy palace by the subtle charm of his fairy music."* Not only was he married to Oonagh and had an eye for human women, he was also said to be married to Nuala – and that was merely one king in one court.[347]

However, whilst the king might take human lovers, so too did the Queen and there does not appear to be any sign that polyamory was frowned upon by the Fey, since neither King nor Queen seemed to face the retribution of a jealous spouse in traditional lore. It was believed that young men were often lured away if they were gifted musically, although good looks alone could also be enough to attract Otherworldly admiration.[348] When looking at fairy lore collectively, certain patterns begin to emerge and certain rituals crop up in different places with the same significance, even if the original meaning has been forgotten by modern practitioners.

---

[345] Ibid.
[346] Evans Wentz, *The Fairy-Faith in Celtic Countries*
[347] Briggs, *An Encyclopaedia of Fairies*
[348] Wilde, *Ancient Legends of Ireland*

May Day holds a special place in the heart of many British people. To this day, many towns and villages hold fayres with maypole dancing, Morris dancing and the crowning of the May Queen. But the true Queen was Fey.

Probably the most famous example of the Queen falling for a human is the story of Thomas the Rhymer. Deeds still existing prove that he was a real Scotsman who lived in the thirteenth century, which give this legend a particularly intriguing edge.

Thomas Rhymer de Erceldoune was a talented harpist, which is presumably what drew the attention of the Queen. One May morning, he was sitting under a thorn tree, playing a tune, when he saw a beautiful woman riding towards him. She was the Elf Queen and offered to take him to Fairyland: *"But… one kiss of my rosy, red lips will seal a stiff fate upon you: you will have to serve me in Elfland for seven years – through weal or woe, good times or bad."*[349] Kiss her he did and he was whisked off to the Otherworld, where he was forbidden from talking, otherwise he'd have to stay forever. He kept his side of the bargain, witnessing many wonders, and when the seven years were over, he was sent back home with the double edged gifts of prophecy and truth. He built up a great reputation and fortune with his prophecies, foretelling the death of King Alexander III in 1286. As was so often the case with those who'd visited the faery realm, however, it never truly lost its hold on him and legend has it that one night, a white doe came. Such creatures were believed to be a visitor from the Otherland, and Thomas the Rhymer took his harp and went to meet it, never to be seen in this world again, although there are tales that he was sometimes glimpsed by other visitors to Fairyland, acting as a councillor to the Fey, or sometimes sent out to buy horses for the warriors who sleep under the Scottish hills.

The story contains many widely acknowledged *'truths'* about faery lore. It is worth noting that it was on May morning that Thomas first encountered the Queen, who was driven by love to take him. Many May traditions have a basis in affairs of the heart. Girls would wash their faces in the May dew to make themselves beautiful in the coming year and couples would pair off, driven by the sap rising. As Kipling wrote in *Puck of Pook's Hill*:

> *Oh, do not tell the Priest our plight,*
> *Or he would call it a sin;*
> *But we have been out in the woods all night,*
> *A-conjuring Summer in!*[350]

The Queen was known to assist young girls in their romantic endeavours and Thomas Campion's poem, *The Fairy Lady Proserpine*

---

[349] Jarvie (ed), *Scottish Folk and Fairy Tales*.
[350] Kipling, *Puck of Pook's Hill*.

describes the Fairy Queen as a guardian of lovers, one who would make young girls pretty and help them win the object of their desires:

> *"All you that will hold watch with loue,*
> *The Fairie Queene Proserpina*
> *Will make you fairer then Diones doue ;*
> *Roses red, Lillies white,*
> *And the cleare damaske hue,*
> *Shall on your cheekes alight :*
> *Loue will adorne you.*
>
> *All you that loue, or lou'd before,*
> *The Fairie Queene Proserpina*
> *Bids you encrease that louing humour more :*
> *They that yet haue not fed*
> *On delight amorous,*
> *She vowes that they shall lead*
> *Apes in Auernus."*[351]

However, any romance between Queen and human was entirely at her discretion and there is a story of a fisherman who entered Fairyland through Morecambe Bay. He was given food and gold and fell madly in love with the Queen. However, because he tried to kiss her feet, he was punished for his insolence and dumped back in his boat without any gold. A year later, both he and his boat were lost.[352]

It was also believed that May Day was a date upon which you could enter the realm of the Fey and not only was Thomas a great musician, he was sitting beneath a thorn tree on that day, which was traditionally a way to open a gate to the Otherworld.

Another ancient festival which has survived in one form or another through to modern times is Samhain, or Hallowe'en as it is more commonly called now. Children would dress up in fearful costumes and go trick or treating in order to scare away any evil spirits that might consider threatening the town. It was well known that it was a night when the fairy folk were out and about, causing mischief and the tales surrounding this time of year tend to be much darker.

Just as you could easily fall into Fairyland if you were in the right (or wrong) place on May Day, so too, was the case on All Hallow's Eve, October 31st. There is a legend of a young man who fell asleep under a haystack on this night and awoke in the Otherworld. He watched the preparation for a banquet for the royal court, which involved an old woman being chopped up and boiled to serve at the feast, but when he came to the

---

[351] Campion, *A Booke of Ayres XIX*.
[352] Briggs, *An Encyclopaedia of Fairies*.

banquet, all he could see were fruits, poultry, cakes and red wine. He was invited to join the festivities by the prince, but since the food had not been blessed by a priest, he declined. The prince pressed him to at least try some wine and the young man accepted, being treated to the most delicious draught he'd ever had. As he put down the glass, a clap of thunder sounded, the lights went out and the man was back under the haystack where he'd started. His rudeness proved fatal, for the fairy wine was poisonous and he died.

An encounter with the Fairy Court might not always be fatal at Hallowe'en, but it was bound to be terrifying, as there were many associations of the Fey with the spirits of the dead at this time of year. Another young man foolish enough to be caught out after dark found himself caught up with a band of fairies going to a fair. There he met with Finvarra, the Fairy King, and Oonagh, the Queen. He was well received, wined, dined, given gifts of gold, but when he examined those around him, he recognised some of the revellers as deceased neighbours. Once identified, they danced around him, shrieking, and trying to force him to dance with them. He fought them off and eventually fainted. When he awoke the next morning, he was covered in bruises.[353]

Probably the most famous tale of the Queen at this time of year is that of Tam Lin, a young man who had been stolen away by her and now haunted the Carterhaugh pinewoods. Any girl who encountered him would fall under his spell and pay a high price for so doing.

The Laird of Carterhaugh had a daughter, Janet, who decided to ignore the warnings and go to see if she could find the fairy well rumoured to be in the middle of the woods. She eventually found it – and met Tam Lin. She fell in love with him and he confided in her that he was afraid that he was due to be the human tithe to Hell the fairy folk owed every seven years. (It was this tithe that had made the Fairy Queen set Thomas the Rhymer free for fear that he be demanded by the devil.)

> *"The Queen o Fairies she caught me,*
> *In yon green hill to dwell.*
> *And pleasant is the fairy land*
> *But, an eerie tale to tell,*
> *Ay at the end of seven years*
> *We pay a tiend to Hell;*
> *I am sae fair and fu o flesh*
> *I'm feared it be mysel.'"*[354]

Tam Lin told Janet how to free him. Since it was Hallowe'en, it was the one night of the year when he could be saved. She was to hide in the

---

[353] Wilde, *Ancient Legends of Ireland*, Volume I.
[354] Child, *Tam Lin*, *The English and Scottish Popular Ballads*.

woods and wait for the fairy folk to ride by in procession at midnight, the witching hour. Tam Lin would be riding on the third horse and she had to pull him off the horse and hold fast, no matter what. The Fairy Queen would try all sorts of tricks to make her drop him, but once he was turned into a burning lead weight, then, and only then, could she throw him into the water of the well, whereupon he'd climb out a free, mortal man once more. Janet did as she was instructed and although Tam was turned into all manner of frightening creatures, she held fast until at last he was transformed into a burning lead weight. She threw the weight into the well and Tam was free once more.[355]

> "Up then spake the Queen o Fairies,
> Out o a bush o broom:
> 'She that has borrowd young Tamlane
> Has gotten a stately groom.'
> Up then spake the Queen o Fairies,
> Out o a bush o rye:
> 'She's taen awa the bonniest knight
> In a' my cumpanie.
> 'But had I kennd, Tamlane,' she says,
> 'A lady wad borrowd thee
> I wad taen out thy twa grey een,
> Put in twa een o tree.
> 'Had I but kennd, Tamlane,' she says,
> 'Before ye came frae hame,
> I wad taen out your heart o flesh,
> Put in a heart o stane.
> 'Had I but had the wit yestreen
> That I hae coft the day,
> I'd paid my kane seven times to hell
> Ere you'd been won away.'"[356]

The Queen's cursing at losing such a prize shows a much darker aspect to her, one which is malicious and willing to perform all sorts of wickedness rather than be thwarted. Alexander Montgomery's poem, *The Flyting Betwixt Montgomery and Polwart*, also depicts the Queen riding out in procession on Hallowe'en, and although the rhyme owes more to satire than folklore, aiming to insult Montgomerie's rival, Polwart, nevertheless, the imagery is very interesting:

> "In the hinder end of harvet on alhallow even,
> Quhen our good neighboures doth ryd, if I reid rycht,

---

[355] Jarvie (ed), *Scottish Folk and Fairy Tales*.
[356] Child, *Tam Lin, The English and Scottish Popular Ballads*.

> *Som buckled on a buinvared, and som one a bene,*
> *Ay trottand in trowpes from the twylycht;*
> *Some saidland a sho ape all graithid into greine*
> *With mony elrich Incubus was rydand that nycht.*
> *Some hoblard one ane hempstalk, havand to be heicht,*
> *The King of phairie and his Court with the elph queine.'*[357]

If we dig deeper into the fairy lore surrounding each of the modern sabbats, we find that, with the exception of the equinoxes, there are legends involving the Queen and her court around each festival. For example, there is the tale of the miser who, greedy for fairy gold, set out to find the court feasting at Lammas. Although he finds what he is looking for, he comes away empty handed, the Spriggans, a type of Cornish hobgoblin, capturing him until the morning comes and he was able to break free of the cobwebs binding him down.[358] Doors into the Otherworld could also be opened at midsummer and midwinter and the Wild Hunt could be heard riding through the countryside at these times.

What is, perhaps, most interesting to note is how the Fairy Queen changes with the seasons. Just as those who follow the Wheel of the Year often weave in tales of the Goddess to symbolically follow her development from maiden to mother then crone, so, too, do the stories of the Queen change according to the tides of Nature. She has a soft, loving side – although there is no date mentioned, she was allegedly involved in the creation and birthing of Tom Thumb, an unusual twist on the more usual tale of human midwifery skills being needed to birth fairy children.[359] During Beltane, she is a friend to lovers, someone to help young girls find the man of their dreams. As the tale of Thomas the Rhymer tells us, she genuinely cares for those she loves, warning Thomas not to speak so that he is not trapped in her world and ensuring that he leaves before the tithe to Hell is due. But as the year progresses, her darker side comes out and sightings report her being surrounded by the spirits of the dead. The young man who witnessed an old woman being prepared for the courtly table is not the only one to see humans being mistreated by the Fair Folk – Thomas the Rhymer is warned about a terrible monster, who turns out to be nothing more than a human child, stolen by the fairies, grown old and now constantly tormented by them. Moreover, although Tam Lin had served her faithfully and she describes him as the fairest of her servants, the Queen laments not having given him over to Hell sooner.

The Queen is a powerful figure in British folklore, an equal to her King and she seems to be much more interested in working with humans, sometimes even helping them, than he is. The tales surrounding her

---

[357] Montgomery, *The Flying Betwixt Montgomery and Polwart*.
[358] Briggs, *The Fairies in Tradition and Literature*.
[359] Rackham, *English Fairy Tales*, Ill.

frequently omit to mention her consort and there is seemingly no bar to her being involved with other men, perhaps because her King is not threatened by any mere mortal. Following her development over the course of the year leads one along a fascinating trail – but it is a path to be trodden with caution, for it is a rare person who encounters her and escapes unscathed. Most die within the year and even Thomas the Rhymer, blessed by her as he was, found that her gifts were as much of a curse and ultimately, even he couldn't stay away from her forever, despite his human wife and son. As with so many mystical beings, it was often the case that the price for dealing with her was disproportionately high, and so most people chose to stay inside, safe away from her and her Court at those times of the year when she was known to be abroad. Such was her power that modern traditions surrounding days such as May Day and Hallowe'en have their roots in fairy lore and how to co-exist with such Otherworldly creatures. If you know what you are looking for, it is easy to see that she is still being celebrated and acknowledged, despite a general ignorance of this fact.

# Queen of The Underworld

## and the Fruit of Knowledge

### FELICITY FYR LE FAY

It was a sparkling summer's day. Languishing beneath an Elder Tree, Thomas suddenly found his daydreams broken by a cascade of jingling bells. Hoof-beats joined the music and Thomas sat up to meet the eyes of the most beautiful, ethereal woman he had ever seen. She was clothed in succulent shades of green, with a flowing cloak of the finest velvet. The sound that had broken his reverie came from fifty-nine silver bells tied into the mane of her glittering white palfrey.

*"Hail to thee, Mary Queen of Heaven,"* Thomas stuttered, ripping off his cap and bowing low before her.

*"Oh no, Thomas"* she said. *"That name does not belong to me. I am the Queen of fair Elfland, and have come hither to visit thee. Come and join me on my ride. But beware - if you dare to kiss my lips I will take my pleasure of your body."*

And so Thomas found himself enjoying the lavish embrace of the Faery Queen, and afterwards was so enchanted as to agree to become her servant. Seated behind her amid the pealing bells, he was whisked away on horseback. Swifter than the wind they travelled, past the boundaries of the land of the living. Here, in the deserts at the edge of the Otherworld, the Queen showed him three pathways. That of Righteousness stretched through thorns, that of Wickedness was exquisitely paved, but they departed along the third – the road to Elfland.

The journey was long. As they galloped through the wild landscape no sun, moon or stars shone to light their way. At times the horse was wading through high crimson rivers, for all the blood shed on the earth pours from a spring into that Otherworld country. Finally the tempestuous ride came to a halt in a lush garden, where the Faery Queen plucked an apple from a tree. *"Take this for thy wages, true Thomas;"* she said. *"It will give thee a tongue that can never lie."*

Three days passed at the Faery Castle while Thomas stayed in service, but on his return to the land of the living, he found seven long mortal years had gone by. True to the Faery Queen's word though, when he opened his mouth Thomas had been blessed with the gift of prophecy.

********

The tale of *'Thomas the Rhymer'* or *'True Thomas'* comes to us in a collection of ballads and romances, the earliest versions dating as far back as the thirteenth century. Thomas was a real personality, either Thomas Rymour de Ercildoun or his son Thomas de Ercildoun, and it is possible that he wrote the first of these ballads himself! By the mid fourteenth century Thomas the Rhymer's fame as a soothsayer was established. Attributed to him are many predictions, including the death of Alexander III, the bankruptcy of Ercildourne and an event perhaps of the future to come: *York was, London is, and Edinburgh shall be; The biggest and bonniest o' the three*. Via ballad or word of mouth, Thomas the Rhymer's fame grew so great that he was compared to Merlin. Prophesies of his were even fabricated to give the Scots good cheer while under English invasion! In any case, the blessing of the Faery Queen, be it fiction or fact, has gone a long way towards illuminating this man's name on the pages of history.

The themes of the True Thomas tale are many layered. This is one of many legends where we see the Faery Queen as a Gate Keeper of Space and Time. She takes Thomas outside the land of the living, through the Otherworld realms, and later returns him intact. The Faery Queen is also portrayed as being beyond the dominion of human morality. She shows Thomas both the roads to righteousness (Heaven) and wickedness (Hell); but the path to Faeryland is a third option without the need for designated ethics. Catholic academics have often interpreted Faeryland as being symbolic of Purgatory, wherein souls enter a state of torment for purification. In the romance variation of this tale the Faery Queen reveals five paths including both Purgatory and the Fae Realm. In this instance it is more likely that Faeryland is a remnant of an older Celtic afterlife view – an Otherworld resting place without judgement, as the soul continues in a cycle of reincarnation. So in the story of True Thomas, our Monarch holds keys to the Otherworlds, and also takes on a mantle as one of the Queens of the Dead.

The apple is another key symbol in this tale. Representing knowledge, the apple is born by the Faery Queen in several legends, sometimes as a silver bough of apple blossoms or fruit. One bite may reveal the mysteries - but perhaps impart more awareness than the hungry can handle. In the tale of True Thomas, the Faery Queen joins Eve, Persephone, and Venus; all of whom have altered the cycle of Destiny with this most hallowed of fruits and the gifts it represents.

The popular whimsy of our modern era has the Faery Queen dressed almost as an angel in white, with tiny faeries glittering like stars about her in a halo. She bequeaths gifts to delighted children, kindly watches over the seasons and blesses the new life of spring. So how does this lady of light connect to the darkness of Death and the Underworld? How does our Queen find herself as a Gate Keeper of Space and Time? Where did the Apple of Knowledge come from and why is it in her outstretched hand? Let us begin by looking at the Fair Folk themselves and a little section of their history.

The English word *'Fairy'* or *'Faery'* comes from the Italian *'Fata'* or Latin *'Fatus'* – Fate. If we cast our minds over to Greek and Roman mythology we remember the Fates were three ancient women who spun and cut the thread of mankind's lives. The spinning wheel itself can be seen as the Wheel of Fortune (an image often used in the Tarot) showing the rise and fall of abundance, or as the pagan wheel of the year as cycle after cycle turns on its axis. The shears these women held represent the action of time, a slightly kinder way to envision the reaper's scythe. As personifications of providence, the Fates are ancestors of our fairies today.

The concept of the Fae having control over destiny is a very long held tradition. In Egypt, Hathor was a Goddess of love and fertility who can be equated to Venus and Aphrodite. She was able to split herself into seven Hathors who later became elementals or fairies. These beings were present at births and would make predictions about the unfolding life of the child. In Lithuania, the Goddess Laima had a similar role. She is often confused with the Lithuanian Laumė (fairies) who, fascinatingly, were particularly skilled in weaving and spinning. Like the Hathors, the Laumė would foretell the future of the newborn child. They supposedly gleaned this information from conversing with the spirits of the newly deceased on their journey to the afterlife. A more recent example of these traditions appears in many popular European folk tales. *Sleeping Beauty*, for example, features the faeries offering gifts/predictions to a newborn – the baby Princess. Then a dark faery of malevolent intent appears and curses the baby so that she will one day prick her finger upon something poisonous. And what dangerous object might that be? A spinning wheel or spindle of course! And so the girl's fate is sealed. Through the evolution of folklore, we can see the connection between the Fates of ancient Greece and the faeries of children's tales today.

Like the Goddesses Hathor and Laume, our Faery Queen has been known to make predictions. Indeed, in several versions of the Thomas Rhymer ballads, the Faery Queen returns him to the elder tree after describing coming battles, deaths and Henry IV's invasion of Scotland. It was a common confession during witch trials that Faeries or the Faery Queen had bequeathed the gift of prophecy to those poor folk interrogated.

In this we can see that the oracle Goddesses Hathor and Laima, surrounded by their elementals, are forerunners of our modern Faery Monarch. Each is an eternal deity outside our mortal realms of space and time, and they share the ability to predict Destiny, if not dictate it.

As we continue to clamber along the branches of Faery history, another limb takes us to the Underworld, the Realm of the Dead. When W.Y. Evans Wentz began collecting material in 1908 for his study *The Fairy-Faith in Celtic Countries* he discovered a widely held belief across Cornwall, Wales, Scotland, Ireland and Brittany that the Fae held many spirits of the mortal deceased in their numbers. Several of the villagers he interviewed had tales of having glimpsed friends or relatives among the Fae revels. These Celtic Faeries often haunted barrows, which are ancient burial mounds. There is some conjecture that, in regarding the barrow Fae with awe and respect, the locals were upholding a half remembered ritual honouring their own ancestors. Wentz concluded that there was often no distinguishable difference between faeries and ghosts, and that indeed Faeryland itself might well be one and the same as the Celtic Realm of the Dead.

To make sense of this we must understand a bit about the Celts and their Underworld. The Celts were a hugely successful collection of tribes that, at their height, spanned Europe from the British Isles to Galatia (central Turkey) in the Iron Age. The invading Romans conquered most of these tribes, with Britain as the Celts' last stronghold. What remains of Celtic mythology is a rich lore from Wales, Cornwall, Scotland and particularly Ireland; but we can imagine it would have applied to the peoples of a much larger area.

The Celts were pagans and together worshipped more than four hundred deities; they also believed in reincarnation. Death was the soul returning to the Otherworld, while birth was the soul departing those distant lands to return to the earth. Therefore any sojourn in the other dimensions was temporary, part of a continuing cycle. The Celtic Otherworld included the domains of the Gods, Heroes and Faeries. The *'Underworld'* specifically describes one of these Otherworld domains - the Land of the Dead. This Underworld could be below ground, as the name implies, but also under the sea or on an island of either suffering or paradise. While in some legends the Land of the Dead may be an island of writhing souls (as in the Irish rocky isle of Tech Duinn), in other tales mortal spirits may partake in a delicious realm of plenty, sharing with the Gods and the Fae alike (such as in Tir Na nOg). It's possible the Celtic Otherworld was originally one domain housing all types of Gods, spirits and sprites; and portrayals of the darker Land of the Dead only arrived later, with the Christian influence of hellfire and damnation.

There is much folklore and literature connecting the Underworld with Faeryland. A strong link can be seen in the legends of the Tuatha de Danann. The Tuatha were the original Faery people of Ireland. Tall, shining and god-like, they were much like Tolkien's Elves, and in true Faery tradition gifted in music, magic and war. Sadly, their long reign came to a violent end by human hands. The Tuatha de Danann fell in two bloody battles, cut down by the invading Milesian Celts. The Faeries who remained were forced to flee. From this tragic tale, Tolkien took his sorrowful vision of the Elves leaving Middle Earth for their Otherworld far to the West. In the same manner, many of the Tuatha De Danann left for the far away Isle of Tir Na Og or *'Land of the Ever Young'*. Other Fae remained, and went below ground to build a Faeryland in the hollow hills.

Tir Na nOg was an island paradise without sickness or death. It had many names, including Tír nam Beo *'the Land of the Living'* and Mag Mell *'Delightful Plain'*. This land was once visible in the direction of sunset every seven years. Under the name of Hy Brazil it can be found plotted on many old maps. Tir Na nOg has been cited as a place of mortal afterlife, but, much like the Norse Alfheimr (Elfland), it was really only the chosen few heroes who ever arrived at its lush green vales.

Closer to the Underworld in description are the Faerylands beneath the earth. The Tuatha who remained in Ireland took up residence in a parallel world to ours, beneath the sidhe mounds. In fact all over the Celtic parts of Britain the belief that the faeries lived inside the hollow hills was prevalent. It was also common belief that many of the human dead were cavorting among the Faery catacombs. Much evidence for this comes from witch trials, where several of the accused *'confessed'* to consorting with faeries and seeing deceased neighbours and relatives at the Fae festivities. This motif often appears in folk tales such as that of William Noy, who found his late departed fiancé among the Fair Folk at once of their late night fiestas. Upon the host vanishing with his sweet love, poor William lost his passion for living. Slightly stranger is the tale of Cherry of Zennor. This Cornish lass was taken on as nursemaid in a Faery household and after using forbidden ointment on her eye was able to see her master flirting with Faery maidens. Previously, without the ointment, Cherry had thought these maidens to be preserved dead, or marbled statues. The master's favourite was a tiny beauty that arose from a polished coffin.

The Welsh Otherworld Annwn was again believed to be either an island or situated beneath the earth. Mortals could gain entry to it at various magical portals, including Lundy Island and Glastonbury Tor. Annwn has been at various times described as a fertile land of delights or an Underworld inhabited by tormented souls and demons. Here we have our most definitive link between the Underworld and Faeryland - as the ruler of Annwn, Gwyn ap Nudd is both King of the Faeries and of the Dead. He is one of the leaders of the famed Wild Hunt, and so, with his baying hounds, their red tipped ears the colour of blood, he chases spirits across the skies. When they are captured, Gwyn sweeps them back to the Underworld through the portal of Glastonbury Tor.

Returning to query Wentz's conclusion that Faeryland and the Celtic Underworld are one and the same, perhaps it's more helpful to consider whether all Otherworlds are one realm. Do Faeries, Gods, Demons and the Mortal Dead share one dimension, or occupy several? To answer these questions would require an essay on its own. Even so, it is clear that human souls do find their way to be under the rule of the King and Queen of the Faeries. Our Faery Queen in her realm of the Otherworld is as much a deity of death as she is of nature and life. As the Celts believed in death and reincarnation as part of a natural cycle, we can see that Queen of the Underworld is one of the Fae Queen's many duties as, of course, would befit a royal representative of Mother Nature.

It's not only the Celtic Underworlds that can be connected with the Faery Kingdom. The most famous of them all, the Greek Hades is linked to our Faery Queen's darker realm. The bond between them is the radiant Goddess, Persephone. Indeed comparisons can make Persephone almost appear to be a Queen of Faery. Persephone is the daughter of Demeter, Goddess of fertile abundance and the harvest. Both mother and daughter can be viewed as representing the seasons and cycles of Mother Nature, much like the Faery Queen. Nymphs are the elemental Faeries of Greek mythology, and Persephone spends the days of her maidenhood picking blooms in their company. On one such beautiful day, Persephone was innocently enjoying the sunshine in a field of narcissus when Hades rode out from the Underworld and kidnapped her.

Hades' abduction of Persephone can be paralleled to similar antics by the Faery King Gwyn ap Nudd from Annwn. In the Arthurian tale of *Culhwch and Olwen*, Gwyn ap Nudd was besotted with the maiden Creiddylad. Before she could be married to another man he carried her off by force. King Arthur resolved the dispute by having both suitors duel for her hand every May Day until Doomsday, while Creiddylad resides in the house of her father. Here, Gwyn ap Nudd represents the King of Winter and the forces of Darkness, while his opponent is the Sun King and forces of light. Like Persephone, the Faery Queen–in-waiting Creiddylad has become a symbol of summer versus winter, the changing seasons and the passage of time. But the most potent link between Persephone and the Faery Queen is that dangerous fruit - the pomegranate.

After Persephone suddenly found herself the Queen of the Underworld, she slowly came to love its King, rough round the edges though he might be. Meanwhile, her mother Demeter had let the earth go barren while mourning her daughter's departure, and so Zeus, the King of the Gods sent a messenger out for Persephone's return. Back in the Land of the Living, mother and daughter were reunited, but this was to be temporary. Eating the food of Faeryland, or of the Underworld, is known to be dangerous. While trying to abstain, hungry Persephone had sucked on six seeds of a pomegranate. Because she had tasted the dark land's bounty, it was deemed she must return to that underground kingdom for six months every year. Each time Persephone departed, Demeter was in anguish and allowed the winter seasons to be born.

The story of Persephone and the pomegranate is similar to that of Eve and the apple. While Persephone's forbidden snack brought about winter, Eve's brought about loss of innocence and the concept of sin. The discovery of these mysteries may appear ominous, but there is another way to look at them. Persephone had understood the cyclic nature of life and death, as reflected in the seasons; Eve learned of her own sexuality, morality and mortality. Both of them had devoured the seeds of knowledge.

The word *'pomegranate'* derives from Latin *'pōmum'*, meaning apple, and *'grānātum'*, alluding to its many seeds. This exotic fruit is interchangeable with the apple as a symbol of fruitfulness, learning, wisdom and knowledge. In Jewish lore the pomegranate is said to have 613 seeds, representing the 613 commandments in the *Torah*. The Bible says this fruit was depicted on the two pillars - Joachim and Boaz – in front of the Temple of Solomon. These pillars, surrounded by pomegranates, feature in the Tarot's traditional Rider-Waite rendering of the *'The High Priestess'*. This Tarot card is about subconscious universal knowledge or *'the mysteries'* and has also been illustrated as Persephone entering the Underworld. Interestingly, the traditional Rider-Waite Priestess figure is crowned in the style of the Egyptian Goddess Hathor, linking Persephone again to the Faery Queen. The *'High Priestess'* is also identified with *'Shekinah'*, the Hebrew divine feminine. Personified in the Kabbalah, Shekinah presides over *'the Holy Apple Garden'*, which calls to mind images of the Celtic Avalon, *'the Isle of Apples'*. So we can equate the High Priestess with Persephone of the Underworld, and also with Avalon's Faery Queens: the Lady of the Lake and Morgan Le Fay, again entwining the Queen of the Dead with the Queen of Faeryland.

It is also interesting to look specifically at the mythology behind the apple. We all know of Eve who was enticed to pluck this forbidden fruit. Through devouring its flesh she and Adam became aware of *'good'* and *'evil'* thus losing their innocence and causing themselves to be expelled from the Garden of Eden and into a world that knew mortality. It was also an apple that in effect caused the Trojan War in the Greek myths. When an apple mysteriously appeared with an inscription *'for the fairest'*, the Goddesses all offered Paris bribes to judge them the most beautiful. Aphrodite's bribe was to offer Paris the most gorgeous woman in the world – Helen. When Paris tossed Aphrodite the apple, the events that would result in the war were begun, for Helen duly ran away with Paris; and her husband, King Menaleus, made war on the Trojans to get her back. The apple in this tale came from a sacred apple tree in possession of the Goddess Hera. The fruit of this tree bestowed immortality on anyone who ate it. Norse mythology also reveres the apple, and again it is associated with immortality. The Goddess Idunn was the keeper of the apples and she fed them to the Norse Gods and

Goddesses to maintain their youth.. So the apple is an important symbol in many mythologies. It is also, as we will soon see, the Faery Queen's bounty.

A strong tie between the apple and the Faery Queen can be found in astrology. Both the apple and the Faery Queen can be related to the planet Venus! Cutting an apple in half horizontally reveals a five-pointed star, or pentagram. This is a very ancient magical symbol. One of its origins is the path the planet Venus draws in the night sky, transiting past the face of the sun over an eight year long cycle. This is where we get our *'star'* shape from, as Venus was thought to be two separate stars (one rising in the morning and one rising in the evening) that drew this pentagram pattern. Later, of course, astronomers realised she was a planet! Venus the deity is the Roman version of our apple Goddess Aphrodite, who instigated the Trojan War, so apples are often regarded as the fruit of Venus, and are used traditionally to predict love outcomes. The planet Venus is also related to the Jewish Shekinah. Shekinah is the Hebrew feminine God-energy, but also has been beheld as an event in the night sky – representing God's light. This was said to appear at random times and many scholars now think this would have been the rare conjunction of Venus and Mercury. This conjunction has also been theorised to be the star of Bethlehem, and therefore ties into Mother Mary. In Catholicism, Mary is often depicted as the Queen of Heaven. Artists portray her with a halo of twelve stars; this portrait can also be interpreted as the pentagram of Venus, surrounded by the twelve constellations of the zodiac. We remember Thomas Rhymer first addresses the Faery Queen as *'Hail to thee, Mary, Queen of Heaven'*. So the apple again leads us in a planetary cycle spinning through the greatest of the Goddesses and returning to our Faery Queen.

In Otherworld mythology, the Faery Queen is often in possession of an apple or a silver apple bough. Much as in the tale of True Thomas, this sacred fruit possesses mystical powers. The silver bough could be given to a hero as a passport into Faeryland. Its fruit would maintain his youth, as several years in Tir Na Og sometimes equates to a hundred or more in the mortal realm. In the silver bough, we find another parallel between Faeryland and the Underworld realm of Persephone.

In Virgil's epic poem *The Aeneid*, the Sybil instructed Aeneas to break a golden apple bough from a sacred tree as a gift to Proserpine (Persephone). This turned out to be hugely beneficial when Aeneas was nearly thwarted on his journey by Charon, the boatman upon the River Styx. The river had to be crossed to pass into the Underworld but Charon would only ferry those who have had a proper burial, while Aeneas was still clearly one of the living. The Sybil solved this crisis by revealing the golden bough from beneath the folds of her cloak. They were both then allowed passage on board the creaking vessel.

The golden bough in *The Aeneid* mirrors the silver bough in the Irish legend *The Voyage of Bran*. Bran was out wandering one day when entranced by beautiful music. He was unable to find its source, and in his search he fell blissfully asleep. When he woke, the most exquisite silver branch covered in white blossoms lay next to him. Bran returned to his royal castle with his wondrous find, but later that evening a beautiful maiden appeared. She described the luscious land the silver branch came from in glittering song, and then the branch leapt from Bran's hand to hers. The maiden disappeared leaving Bran full of longing and determined to take on the long sea voyage to find the branch, the maiden and the enchanted island of which she had spoken.

The legend of Connla gives us another vivid illustration of the power of the Faery Queen's sacred harvest. Connla of the Fiery Hair was out one day with his father King Conn of a Hundred Fights when he spied the most stunning maiden. She had a form and grace that could only be Otherworldly and a bearing with the fragrance of royalty. They began a conversation wherein this lush Faery maiden declared her love, but as they spoke it became clear to Connla that none others of his company could see her.

*"To whom art thou talking, my son?"* the King enquired with concern.

All present heard the Faery lass reply like tinkling bells dancing in the air: *'I come from the far away isles that no pain, hunger or death may touch. I love your son Connla and request that he come away with me, that he will sit crowned at my side.'*

The King was disturbed hugely at this, and summoned his druidic priest. Immediately the priest began spells and incantations to banish this elemental being – but not before she could throw Connla a token from her charmed kingdom ... an apple.

For a month Connla pined after the beautiful Faery, and nothing would he eat but fleshy bites from her magical apple. Each time he had almost consumed it; the apple would be whole again in his hand. At the end of the month he was standing on the Plain of Arcomin with his father when he saw the ethereal woman of his fascination coming towards them.

*"Come with me fair Connla, to the Land of the Ever Living, Moy Mell, the Plain of Pleasure,"* she said.

The King still could not see her, but on hearing the Faery maiden's voice he summoned his druid and the attention of his men around him. Even so, he was at a loss. It seemed that Connla was under some sort of enchantment. He took the hand of the Faery maiden (which seemed to the company like nothing but air) and departed across the plains to a glittering crystal canoe. Seated inside, he launched the craft into the ocean... and was never seen on earth again. And so concludes the story of Connla. Or almost....

Now many heroes cast off from Ireland's graceful shores in search of the Faery Isles. They included Bran on his quest for the beautiful bearer of the silver bough; Saint Brendan, determined that the Isle of Paradise was indeed the Isle of Saints; and Teigue, Prince of Westminster. When Teigue made it to the Promised Isles he disembarked his faithful ship and soon discovered three castles. At the first, he was welcomed by a Faery maiden, who told him it was the dwelling of all the Pagan Kings of Ireland. The second was a palace of gold, and he was told it was reserved for all the Christian Kings of Ireland. In the third castle he found Connla, with his beautiful Faery bride, both all clothed in green. There they lived happily, sustained in eternal youth by eating nothing but enchanted apples.

In the tale of Connla we find his Faery Queen connected to Fate, Death and the Underworld, as Connla was never seen on earth again. We also see her bearing the gift of immortality in the form of the sacred apple, once more making her a custodian of Time.

There is a final gem on the Faery Queen's crown in her role as Gate-Keeper to the Otherworld: rebirth. The Celts were pagans and therefore believed that life was cyclic; our Queen of the Underworld also has the powers of healing and reincarnation. We can find evidence for this in the legends of that most sacred Isle: Avalon.

The entrancing Isle of Avalon is especially hallowed, as it was here that King Arthur's sword Excalibur was forged; here where King Arthur's fatally wounded body was borne; and from here he will rise again in Britain's greatest hour of need. Avalon is very likely one and the same as Tir Na nOg, Moy Mell, Hy Brazil and all other famous Faery Islands. Its first written record appeared in Geoffrey of Monmouth's *Historia Regum Britanniae* of 1136. Monmouth's later work *The Vita Merlini* describes Avalon as the 'Fortunate Isle': *'Of its own accord it produces grain and grapes, and apple trees grow in its woods from the close-clipped grass. The ground of its own accord produces everything instead of merely grass, and people live there a hundred years or more.'* Monmouth also writes that the Isle is reached after a long journey across the sea. The name *'Avalon'* itself is another likely tie to Moy Mell and the Faery Kingdom. It comes from the Old Welsh world for apple *'abal'* (later changed to *'aval'* and now *'afal'*); indeed in Welsh manuscripts Avalon is often called *'Ynys Afallach'* the Isle of Apples.

The Faery Queen of Avalon is Morgan Le Fay. Her lineage is revealed in her name: *'Morgan'* most likely coming from the Morrigan, a wild battle Goddess who was one of the great Queens of the Tuatha De Danann; and *'Le Fay'*, meaning either *'the Faery'* or *'the Fate'*. Geoffrey of Monmouth describes her as the most beautiful and skilled in the healing arts of nine sisters, who ruled the Isle by a pleasing set of laws. In an older Welsh poem called *Preiddeu Annfwyn*, dating from somewhere between the sixth and ninth centuries, nine maidens guard the sacred cauldron of the underworld Annwn, which Arthur tries to steal. This poem is one of the earliest written accounts of the Arthurian legends and provides some very special links. We can conclude the nine maidens are the same as those mentioned by Monmouth, and therefore identify Annwn with the Faery Isles and Avalon.

Morgan being chief among these maidens would indicate that the cauldron is the cauldron of the Daghda. The Daghda was the King of the Tuatha Faeries and husband to the Morrigan. This vessel was one of abundance; it would never leave the hungry unsatisfied and also would restore the dead to life. So we can imagine how that same cauldron would become resident in the Welsh Underworld, as the Celts believed in reincarnation. The poem *Preiddeu Annfwyn*, and its early story of the questing King Arthur, also ties together this Faery cauldron of the Tuatha De Danann with Christ's Holy Grail, which Arthur's knights were searching for in the later legends. Like the cauldron, the grail was also a giver of plenty and divine healing, but while the cauldron resurrects the soul in a new life, the grail completes the soul in this one. Both vessels, and perhaps they are one and the same, are rumoured now to be resting in Avalon. It makes sense, then, that the Arthurian legends conclude there. After a battle in which Arthur is fatally wounded, the dying hero was ferried through the mists to that sacred isle. There, Morgan, who has presided over his fate from childhood, tends to his wounds and prepares him for resurrection when the Great Isles of Britain should need their legendary King again.

The Faery Queen is revealed in all her roles in the story of Morgan Le Fay and Ogier le Danios. Morgan appears in versions of this tale from the fifteenth century onwards and plays out the cyclic role of Destiny. First, as one of the Faeries of Fate, Morgan arrives at the cradle of baby Ogier and predicts he will have a long career of battle and glory, then be given immortality at her castle in Avalon. Ogier indeed leads a charmed life of legend, but when he reaches one hundred Morgan has him shipwrecked near to Avalon. On this sacred Faery Isle, Ogier is tempted to partake of an apple. Tasting its flesh he has an experience similar to that of Eve and Persephone, in that he gains an obsessive Knowledge of the Underworld and can think of nothing but death. Then, manifesting as the most pure and blessed of Goddesses, Morgan sweeps him to her castle in the Otherworld. Two hundred years pass, and France finds itself at war and needing its hero Ogier le Danios. And so Morgan restores memory to the great knight and bids him adieu, that he may join the battle for victory.

Bearing the Holy Grail or Cauldron of the Daghda, the Faery Queen, embodied by Morgan Le Fay, becomes a deity of re-birth. Beginning as Fate, who can predict the achievements and lengths of men's lives, the Faery Queen becomes Goddess of Knowledge, granting mankind the apple of wisdom, and then moves in the role of Queen of the Underworld. The cycle concludes as she gives the gift of new life. In this cycle we see the Faery Queen as Mother Nature herself.

# Bibliography

Barber, Chris, & David Pykitt (1993) *Journey to Avalon: the final discovery of King Arthur.* Abergavenny: Blorenge

Briggs, K.M. (1970) The Fairies and the Realms of the Dead, in Folklore 81.2:81-96

Child, Francis James (ed.) (1884) *The English and Scottish popular ballads.* Vol. 1. Boston: Houghton, Mifflin

Evans-Wentz. W. Y. (1911) *The Fairy Faith in Celtic Countries.* London: Henry Frowde

Jacobs, Joseph (1892) *Celtic Fairy Tales.* London: David Nutt

Larrington, Carolyne (2006) King Arthur's enchantresses: Morgan and her sisters in Arthurian Tradition. London: I.B. Tauris

Mackenzie, Donald Alexander (1917) *Wonder Tales from Scottish Myth and Legend.* London: Blackie

Mann, Nicholas R. (1996) *The Isle of Avalon: Sacred Mysteries of Arthur and Glastonbury Tor.* St. Paul: Llewellyn

Paton, Lucy Allen (1960) Studies in the fairy mythology of Arthurian romance. New York: Burt Franklin

Suckling, Nigel (2007) *Faeries of the Celtic Lands.* London: AAPPL

Thomas of Erceldoune, called the Rhymer & Murray, J.A.H. (ed) (1875) *The romance and prophecies of Thomas of Erceldoune: printed from five manuscripts.* London: Trubner

MERLIN & NIMUE BY EMILY CARDING

# Fairy Poetry

## THE PASTIME AND RECREATION OF THE QUEEN OF THE FAIRIES IN FAIRYLAND, THE CENTRE OF THE EARTH

## MARGARET CAVENDISH
### The Duchess of Newcastle (1623-73)

*Queen Mab, and all her company*
*Dance on a pleasant mole-hill high.*
*To small straw-pipes, wherein great pleasure*
*They take, and keep just time, and measure;*
*All hand in hand, around, around,*
*They dance upon this fairy ground;*
*And when she leaves her dancing ball,*
*She doth for her attendants call.*
*To wait upon her to a bower,*
*Where she doth sit beneath a flower;*
*To shade her from the moonshine bright,*
*Where gnats do sing for her delight;*
*A dewy waving leaf's made fit*
*For the Queen's bath, where she doth sit,*
*And her white limbs in beauty shew,*
*Like a new fallen flake of snow;*
*Her maids do put her garments on,*
*Made of the pure light from the sun,*
*Which do so many colours take,*
*As various objects shadows make:*
*Then to her dinner she goes straight,*
*Where Fairies all in order wait;*
*A cover of a cobweb made,*
*Is there upon a mushroom laid;*
*Her stool is of a thistledown,*
*And for her cup an acorn's crown,*
*Which of strong nectar full is fill'd,*
*That from sweet flowers is distill'd;*

*The Faerie Queens*

*When din'd she goes to take the air*
*In coach, which is a nutshell fair;*
*The lining soft and rich within,*
*Made of a glistering adder's skin,*
*And there six crickets drae her fast,*
*Whe she a journey takes in haste;*
*Or else to serve to pace a round,*
*And trample on the fairy ground -*
*In hawks sometimes she takes delight,*
*Which hornets are most swift in flight;*
*Whose horns instead of talons will*
*A fly, as hawks a partridge, kill.*
*But if she will a hunting go,*
*Then she the lizard makes the doe,*
*Which is so swift and fleet in chase,*
*As he slow coach cannot keep pace:*
*Then on a grasshopper she'll ride,*
*And gallop in the forest wide;*
*Her bow is of a willow branch,*
*To shoot the lizard on the haunch;*
*Her arrow sharp, much like a blade,*
*Of a rosemary leaf is made:*
*Then home she's called by the cock,*
*Who gives her warning what's o'clock;*
*And when the moon doth hide her head,*
*Their day is done, she goes to bed;*
*Meteors do serve, when they are bright,*
*As torches do, to give her light;*
*Glow-worms for candles lighted up,*
*Stand on her table, while she sup.*
*But women, that inconstant kind,*
*Can ne're fix in one place their mind;*
*For she impatient of long stay,*
*Drives to the upper-earth away.*

# The Pastime of the Queen of Fairies When She Comes Upon the Earth Out of the Centre

## Margaret Cavendish
### The Duchess of Newcastle (1623-73)

This lovely, sweet, and beauteous Fairy Queen,
Begins to rise, when Hesperus is seen;
For she is kin unto the God of night,
Unto Diana, and the stars so bright;
And so to all the rest in some degrees,
Yet not so near relation as to these:
As for Apollo, she disclaims him quite,
And swears, she ne'er will come within his light;
This makes the cock give notice, as they say,
That when he rises, she may go her way;
And makes the owl her favourite to be,
Because Apollo's face she hates to see:
For owls do sleep all day, and in the night
They shout and hollow, that th'are out of sight;
and so the glow-worm all day hides his head,
But lights his taper-tail, when he's abed,
To wait upon the fairest Fairy Queen,
Whilst she is sporting on the meady-green:
Her pastime only is, when she's on earth,
To pinch the sluts, which make Hobgoblin mirth;
Or changes children, while the nurses sleep,
Making the father rich, whose child they keep:
This hobgoblin's the Queen of Fairies fool,

*The Faerie Queens*

*Turning himself to horse, cown, tree, or stool,*
*Or any thing to cross by harmless play,*
*As to lead travellers out of their way;*
*To kick down milk-pails, cause curds not to turn*
*To cheese, or hinder butter in the churn,*
*Which makes the farmers wife to scold and fret,*
*That she can neither cheese nor butter get;*
*The good-wife sad, squats down upon a stool,*
*Not at all thinking it was Hob the fool,*
*And frowning sits, then Hob gives her a flip,*
*And down she falls, whereby she hurts her hip:*
*Thus many pranks doth Hob play on our stage,*
*With Tom Thumb, his companion, the Queen's page*
*In this the Queen of Fairies takes delight,*
*In summers even, and in winters night;*
*And when as she is weary of these plays,*
*She takes her coach and doth go her ways,*
*Unto her paradise the centre deep,*
*Where she the store-house doth of nature keep.*

Colman, George & Barber, Mary (1775) *Poems by the Most Eminent Ladies of Great Britain and Ireland Vol 1*. London: W. Stafford

## Entertainment of the Queen and Prince at Althorpe

### Ben Jonson
**1603**

This is Mab, the mistress fairy,
That doth nightly rob the dairy,
And can hurt or help the churning,
(As she please) without discerning.
She that pinches country-wenches
If they rub not clean their benches,
And with sharper nails remembers
When they rake no up their embers;
But, if so they chance to feast her,
In a shoe she drops a tester.
This is she that empties cradles,
Takes out children, puts in ladles;
Trains forth midwives in their slumber,
With a sieve the holes to number;
And thus leads them from her boroughs,
Home through ponds and water-furrows.
She can start our franklin's daughters,
In their sleep, with shrieks and laughters,
And on sweet St. Agens' night
Feed them with a promised sight,
Some of husbands, some of lovers,
Which an empty dream discovers.

# Queen Mab

## Percy Bysshe Shelley
### 1813

Behold the chariot of the Fairy Queen!
Celestial coursers paw the unyielding air;
Their filmy pennons at her word they furl,
And stop obedient to the reins of light;
These the Queen of Spells drew in;
She spread a charm around the spot,
And, leaning graceful from the ethereal car,
Long did she gaze, and silently,
Upon the slumbering maid.

## Song of the Twilight Fairies

## Thomas Lake Harris

*Vestal moon, vestal moon,*
*Star of Love's delight,*
*Rise, and gild our'festal noon—*
*Noon of Fairy-night.*
*Vestal moon, vestal moon,*
*Up the golden height.*
*Thou art rising to thy noon—*
*We to Love's delight.*
*Fairies hide in cowslip bells*
*Through the garish light ;*
*Naiads rest in purple shells,*
*By the sea-marge bright.*
*Fairy-Queen, appear, appear,*
*From thy citron nest ;*
*Wake, O wake ! come, Sweet, for here*
*Shines the moonlight blest.*
*Golden Fairies in the sun*
*Wind their elfin horn.*
*Where the dancing streamlets run,*
*And the Day is born.*
*Silver Fairies haunt the night*
*When the Sun's asleep ;*
*Azure Fays the heavenly height,*
*'Mid the starry sheep.*
*Fays of Silver, Gold, and Blue*
*Wake to Love's delight ;*

*Drink your fill of sweet May-dew,*
*Chase the star-flakes bright.*
*Lo ! we come, we come, we come,*
*From the foxglove bells,*
*Some from golden brake, and some*
*From the asphodels.*
*Vestal moon, vestal moon,*
*From your golden height,*
*Gaze through all the fairy noon*
*On our Love's delight.*

# Fairy Revels

## Anonymous

The fairies are dancing by brake and bower,
For this in their land is the merriest hour.
Their steps are soft, and their robes are light,
And they trip it at ease in the clear moonlight.
Their queen is in youth and in beauty there,
And the daughters of earth are not half so fair.
Her glance is quick, and her eyes are bright,
And they glitter with wild and unearthly light.
Her brow is all calm, and her looks are kind.
But the look that she gives leaves but pain behind.
Her voice is soft and her smiles are sweet,
But woe to thee who such smiles shall meet.
She will meet thee at dusk like a lady fair,
But go not, for danger awaits thee there.
She will take thee to ramble by grove and by glen.
And the friends of thy youth shall not know thee again.

# Fairy Song

## Felicia Hemans

*Have ye left the greenwood lone?*
*Are your steps for ever gone?*
*Fairy King and Elfin Queen,*
*Come ye to the sylvan scene,*
*From your dim and distant shore.*
*Never more?*
*Shall the pilgrim never hear*
*With a thrill of joy and fear,*
*In the hush of moonlight hours,*
*Voices from the folded flowers,*
*Faint sweet flute-notes as of yore,*
*Never more?*
*"Mortal! ne'er shall bowers of earth*
*Hear again our midnight mirth:*
*By our brooks and dingles green*
*Since unhallow'd steps have been,*
*Ours shall thread the forests hoar*
*Never more.*
*Ne'er on earthborn lily's stem*
*Will we hang the dewdrop's gem;*
*Ne'er shall reed or cowslip's head*
*Quiver to our dancing tread.*
*By sweet fount or murmuring shore,*
*Never more!"*

SIDHE KNOWS THE WAY BY EMILY CARDING

# An A-Z of European Faerie Queens

## Áine (Irish)

Áine is the faerie queen of the Hill of Cnoc Áine, the wife of the sea god Manannan mac Lir, who was also viewed as a solar goddess and bestower of blessings on crops and livestock. Áine is an example of the connection between faerie queens and noble families, as she is said to be the mother of Earl Fitzgerald by the Earl of Desmond. Áine is mentioned in the 12th century texts *The Battle of Magh Mucrama* (*Cath Magh Mucrama*) and *The Book of Invasions* (*Lebor Gabála Érenn*).

## Aoibheal/Aeval (Irish)

Aoibheal was the faerie queen of Craig Liath, who wreaked her revenge for being rejected by men by providing a golden harp upon hearing which men died soon after. Her death foretelling nature (in the manner of the banshee) was also seen in the death of the Irish high king Brian Boru, and she predicted which son should succeed him, recorded in the 12th century tale *The War of the Gaedhil with the Gaill* (*Cogadh Gaedhel re Gallaibh*).

## Argante (English)

Argante is a faerie queen mentioned in the twelfth century Middle English poem *Brut* (also known as *The Chronicle of Britain*) by the poet Layamon. Here she is the queen of Avalon, who heals King Arthur and enjoys his company while he waits for his return to the mortal realm. Argante is also mentioned briefly later in Spenser's *Faerie Queene* as a malicious faerie.

## Aureola (English)

Aureola is a Persephone-like faerie queen found in the entertainments put on for Queen Elizabeth I at Elvetham in the sixteenth century (1591). Aureola describes herself as married to Auberon (Oberon) and presented Queen Elizabeth with a *"chaplet, given me by Auberon, the Fairy King ... made in the form of an imperial crowne"*.

## Bebo (Irish)

Bebo was the wife of Iubdan in the 13th century tale *The Adventure of Fergus mac Léti* (Echtra Fergusa maic Léti), which also includes the first currently known historical appearance of leprechauns. Bebo and Iubdan went to visit the court of king Fergus, but being tiny fell in a bowl of porridge and would have drowned if Fergus didn't rescue them. Fergus then took Bebo as his lover for a year (!) until Iubdan made and gave him a pair of flying shoes. It has been suggested that this tale provided the inspiration for the diminutive land of Lilliput in Swift's tale *Gulliver's Travels*.

## Caelia/Celia (English)

Caelia is a faerie queen in several fictional works, first in Spenser's *The Faerie Queene* (1590-1596) as the Heavenly Spirit who is the mother of Faith, Hope & Charity, and subsequently in the heroic romance *Tom a Lincoln* by Richard Johnson (c.1599-1607). In *Tom a Lincoln*, Caelia and the other women have slain all the warmongering men on their island, called Fiery Land, and Caelia sleeps with Tom and bears him a son called the Faerie Knight. The name Celia also turns up later in Gilbert and Sullivan's comic opera *Iolanthe* (1882) as an attendant of the faerie queen, who takes a mortal lover.

## Cailleach (Scottish/Irish/Manx)

The Cailleach is an earth-shaping crone sometimes depicted as a giantess, and said to be one of the oldest beings in existence. Known as a winter goddess, shapeshifter and protector of wild animals (especially deer), the Cailleach is found in numerous folk tales throughout Scotland, Ireland and the Isle of Man. A number of megalithic sites found on the island of Jersey are attributed to the Cailleach as fairy queen, and in Ireland the Cailleach Béarra lived on the summit of Cnoc na Sidhe (Hill of the Fairy Mound), where the wind always blew. Like a number of other faery queens, the Cailleach was known to assume bird form, particularly that of the barn owl and the heron, the latter when she was married to the sea god Manannan (who seems to have had a penchant for fairy queens!).

## Cliodhna/Cliodna/Clidna (Irish)

Cliodhna was described as queen of the banshees, a love goddess or a faerie queen, who drowned when she slept in Glandore harbour, giving her name to the tide there (Cliodhna's wave). She was famed for her three magical birds, a quality that she shared with the Welsh figure of Rhiannon. Like other Irish fairy queens, Cliodhna was particularly associated with some of the noble families, including the O'Keeffes and FitzGeralds. It has been suggested that Cliodhna is derived from the Gallic goddess Clutonda.

## Diana (Roman)

Diana is the Roman virgin goddess of the hunt and new moon, who became viewed as the faerie queen across Europe, especially in Italy, France, England and Scotland, as seen in religious, alchemical and literary writings. By the tenth century CE she was already linked with the faeries as their queen in Christian writings. Diana and her nymphs may have been an early version of the faery court, a position she was noted for from the ninth-tenth century onwards, and as the huntress she is the leader of the Wild Hunt.

## Doamna Zinelor (Roumanian)

Doamna Zinelor means '*queen of the faeries*', and she is seen as a Roumanian version of the goddess Diana, who leads a troupe of (usually seven or nine) dancers, whose dance heals.

## Eambia (English)

Eambia is a name given to a faerie queen in the sixteenth century (in 1575) in the faerie masque held in honour of Queen Elizabeth I at Woodstock in Oxfordshire. Significantly, the character of Sibyllia also turns up in the faerie masque as a prophetess.

## Fand (Irish)

Fand is a faerie queen who appears with her sister Li Ban in the tale *The Wasting Sickness of Cú Chulainn* (*Serglige Con Culainn*). The hero Cú Chulainn throws stones at the sisters, who are in bird form connected by a golden chain. In return he is made sick for a year, and in his fever visits their realm where he becomes the lover of Fand and fights for her as her champion. Fand's beauty was so great that it was likened to a tear as the only thing which could compare to it. Fand provided inspiration for the Irish composer Arnold Bax, who wrote a tone poem for orchestra called *The Garden of Fand* (1916).

## Fuamnach (Irish)

Fuamnach is a faerie queen who was the first wife of the faerie king Midir, whose jealousy of his love for the maiden Etain resulted in her death at the hands of Angus MacOg. She was said to be a powerful druid and sorceress, who used a rowan wand (a noted fairy wood) to cause Etain to change into different forms including a pool of blood and a fly.

## Glaistig (Scottish)

The Glaistigs are a class of Scottish fairy, containing both malicious and benevolent members. Some are described as green-clad beautiful women who are guardians of animals, children and the sick, and who may be regarded as faerie queens. The Glaistigs are sometimes equated to the Cailleachs, and in contrast some are regarded as blood-suckers who lure men to their deaths.

## Gloriana (Spenser)

Gloriana (also called Tanaquill) is a faerie queen in Spenser's epic poem *The Faerie Queene* (1590/96). Drawing on classical myth, medieval and Arthurian romance, Gloriana is derived from figures including the Roman goddess Diana (hence the use of some of her titles including Cynthia and Phoebe) and is an allegorical figure for Queen Elizabeth I of England.

## Gwenhidw (Wales)

The Welsh Faerie Queen and wife of the faerie king Gwydion ab Don, after whom small fleece-like clouds are named, being called 'Sheep of Gwenhidw'. She is particularly noteworthy for her beauty, ability to fly, and her benevolent nature.

## Gyre Carling (Scotland)

The faerie queen went by this name in Fife (Scotland), whom Walter Scott called the Gyre Carling (Gay Old Wife), the *"mother witch of the Scottish peasantry"* in private correspondence. Gyre Carling is perceived as being a malevolent fairy queen, the Bannatyne MS describes her as a flesh-eating hag who could shape-shift and who carried an iron club. She was often described as a giantess, and has been equated with the Cailleach Bheur, and was equated by Walter Scott in *Minstrelsy of the Scottish Border* (1821) with the figure of Nicneven

## Habundia (French)

Dame Habonde appears in the thirteenth century epic poem *Roman de la Rose*, and may be the same figure as the Domina (Mistress) Abundia mentioned around the same time by Bishop William of Auvergne. This being the case her roots can be seen in the Roman goddess of abundance and prosperity, Abundantia. Nineteenth century folklorists claimed she was a Celtic fairy, a view which has gained much popularity in recent decades. William Morris included the figure of Habundia as a fairy godmother in his classic novel *The Water of the Wondrous Isles* (1897).

## Hekate (Greek)

The Greek crossroads goddess Hekate was named as a faerie queen in literature in Renaissance England and Scotland, such as William Warner's *Albion's England* (1586). In *The Flyting Betwixt Montgomery and Polwart* (1585) she is equated with Nicneven, a theme repeated centuries later by Walter Scott in Letter V of his *Letters on Demonology and Witchcraft* (1830) where her name is also used as a title for the head of Scottish covens. The famous witch scene in *Macbeth* also focuses on Hekate, and it is likely that Shakespeare (or whoever wrote that scene) was aware of the connection between Hekate, faeries and witches.

## Herodias (Jewish)

Originally the wife of the Biblical King Herod, Herodias became transformed into a witch and faerie queen equated to the goddess Diana, as seen by medieval Church writings from the twelfth century onwards, e.g. MSS Cotton. Faust. A. viii, fol. 32. The American anthropologist Charles Leland equated Herodias with the messianic Italian witch figure of Aradia in his work *The Gospel of the Witches* (1899). Interestingly, Herodias is a beautiful queen abducted by the faeries in the fourteenth century Scottish tale *Orfeo and Heruodis*.

## Kalé (Greek)

Kalé was originally derived from a name of Artemis which was subsequently famously used for one of the huntresses who accompanied her (Kallisto). She was viewed both as a saint and an ambivalent wandering faerie queen of capricious whim who could heal or harm depending on her mood. Her origins are described in the *Alexander Romance* (C5th-8th CE) as the immortal daughter of Alexander the Great. A depiction of her with the title of Lady of the mountains in the 15th century manuscript Bononiensis 3632 shows her having a serpentine lower body, recalling images of both the lamia and Melusine.

## Li Ban (Irish)

Li Ban is the sister of the faerie queen Fand, who appears with her in *The Wasting Sickness of Cú Chulainn (Serglige Con Culainn)*. She appears as a bird and is the mediator in the story. There is also an Irish tale of a woman of the same name who was turned into a mermaid and centuries later restored to her human form on being blessed by monks.

## Mab/Mabb (English/Irish)

The diminutive Faerie queen found in Shakespeare's *Romeo and Juliet*, who may be derived from the Irish Queen Madb or Maeve. Other writers continued this tradition, such as Drayton in his classic poem *Nymphidia*, Ben Jonson in *The Entertainment at Althorp* (1603), Poole's *The English Parnassus* (1657) as the wife of Oberion, and the English Romantic poet, Percy Bysshe Shelley's *Queen Mab: A Philosophical Poem* (1813). The name Mabb is also given in the 17th century Sloane MS 1727 as one of the spirits. Keightley suggested in *The Fairy Mythology* (1833) that Mab might be a contraction of Habundia and equated the two queens.

## Melior (French)

Melior was one of Melusine's two sisters, who was cursed by her mother to guard the Castle of l'Espervier (Sparrowhawk) in Armenia and grant gifts (apart from herself) to any who could remain awake there for three nights around the eve of 25th June. One of her sister's descendants succeeds in this quest, but insists on Melior's hand in marriage, leading her to curse the kings of Armenia to suffer great misfortune and lose their kingdom after nine generations

## Melusine (French)

Melusine is the tragic heroine of the tales of the same name, a beautiful and powerful faerie queen who bestows sovereignty through her magic and wealth. Cursed to have a serpentine lower body every Saturday by her mother for imprisoning their runaway father, Melusine has a long happy life with her husband, producing ten sons who are the source of many noble and royal lines in Europe, until her secret is revealed and she flees in despair. Melusine is unusual in that she operated within the Church, having new buildings built, and having a doomed aim of gaining a human soul and a Christian burial.

## Micob/Mycob/Mycal/Mical (English Grimoire)

Faerie queen conjured in various grimoires in the 16th-18th century CE for her assistance, sometimes paired with Oberion as her husband. She is mentioned in the seventeenth century manuscript Sloane 1727. A spirit called *'Micol'* the *'queen of the pygmies'* is mentioned by the noted seventeenth century English astrologer, William Lilly, used to call Micol into a crystal by *"Ellen Evans, daughter of my tutor Evans"*. In Sloane MS 3824 reference is made to the faeries, *"these spirits there are too who are Set over the Hierarchy, as the Supream head thereof, whose names are Mycob and Oberion"*. Finally, another variant of the name Mycob, appears alongside Oberion, in Folger MS. V.b.26 (c. 1580).

## Morgan Le Fay/Le Fee (Celtic/Arthurian/French)

Morgan Le Fay is the sorceress half-sister of King Arthur, whose faerie nature is indicated by her name, and who is one of the three queens of Avalon. In the French Arthurian tales her faerie queen nature is emphasised more emphatically. The perceptions of Morgan have changed greatly from the earliest references, which did not have the negativity later attributed to and her actions, rather she is the most beautiful and talented healer of nine sisters, with the ability to shapeshift, mentioned in Geoffrey of Monmouth's *Vita Merlini* (*The Life of Merlin*) in c.1150 CE. It has been suggested that she is derived from the Irish war and sorcery goddess, the Morrigan.

## Morrigan (Irish)

Irish goddess of battle who name means *'Great Queen'* (or *'Phantom/Faerie Queen'*), and who also became viewed as a faerie queen, leading her host across the land on the night of Samhain, the feast of the dead. The whole of the conflict of the *Táin* is linked to the Morrígan's role as Faery Queen of the folk and beings of the otherworld. The two great bulls whose conflict sparks the human conflict are reincarnations of two swineherds to the fairy kings of Connacht and Munster. These two were originally friends but their masters were enemies, and they ended up becoming enemies as well. As Faery Queen, by creating the situation where the two could fight again (as the bulls), the Morrígan brings an unresolved fairy feud into the mortal realm, which also has the added benefit of a huge amount of slaughter to keep her more bloodthirsty side happy.

## Morveren (Cornish)

Morveren is a sea faerie queen with an exquisite voice and a love of beautiful men. Morveren could provide help or hindrance depending on her mood. As with other faerie queens of the sea, she has a mermaid form, and this has been recorded in the local Cornish church of St Senara in Zennor.

## Nicneven (Scottish)

Nicneven, or Nic-Nevis (*'daughter of Nevis'*, this being Ben Nevis, the highest mountain in Scotland) is a Scottish faerie queen equated with Hekate in *The Flyting Betwixt Montgomery and Polwart* (1585). Walter Scott in Letter V of his *Letters on Demonology and Witchcraft* (1830) used both the names Nicneven and Hekate to describe the head of a Scottish covine (coven) of witches practising necromancy. She is described as a giantess, and has also been equated with Gyre Carling and the Cailleach, partaking of the bloodthirsty nature of the former.

### Nimue/Niniane/Viviane (Arthurian)

Nimue is the enchanting faerie queen who occupied different roles in the Arthurian cycle including as lady of the lake (who raised Lancelot) and as the nymph-like beguiler of Merlin who traps him. She is also mentioned in the late 12th or early 13th century Swiss tale *Lanzelet* by Ulrich von Zatzikhoven, and became conflated with the goddess Diana. Through all these roles, she is always associated with water, emphasizing her liminal nature.

### Oonagh/Una/Nuala/Donagh (Irish)

Oonagh was the most beautiful faerie queen of the west of Ireland, whose husband Finvarra had a penchant for mortal women less beautiful than his wife. Their faerie host is also described in tales as being comprised of the dead. She was the high queen of the faery folk, with Finvarra having been the high king who negotiated the truce with the Milesians which allowed the Tuatha de Danann to remain in Ireland under the ground.

### Ounaheencha (Irish)

Ounaheencha is an oceanic faerie queen who sailed the coasts of Clare and Kerry searching for handsome young men to abduct and keep in her cave for her pleasure.

### Palatine (French)

Palatine (or Palestine) was one of Melusine's two sisters, cursed by her mother to guard her father's treasure in the mountain of Conigo in Aragon until a knight of their lineage came to take the treasure to use it in conquering the Holy Land.

### Pressine (French)

Pressine is the faerie queen who is mother of Melusine and her sister Melior and Palatine by king Elinas of Scotland in the Melusine romances. She rears her daughters on the island of Avalon, and curses them with their respective curses when they magically imprison their absentee father (her husband) under a mountain.

## Proserpina (Roman)

Proserpina is the Roman goddess, derived from the Greek goddess Persephone, who became viewed as a faerie queen in literature in England, as seen in writings such as Chaucer's *Merchants Tale* (late 14th century), and Campion's *Hark, All You Ladies* (1601). Proserpine is also mentioned in Spenser's *The Faerie Queene* as the mother of Lucifera. With her twin roles as spring maiden associated with flowers and plants, and queen of the dead, it is easy to see why Proserpina should have been viewed as a faerie queen.

## Queen of the Hidden Isle (French)

Unnamed faerie queen of the Hidden Isle in the 13th century French epic *Huon de Bordeaux*. Her lovers included Julius Caeser and Oberon was one of her sons. The island was identified as the Greek Ionian island of Cephalonia (Avalon in the west).

## Rhiannon (Welsh)

Rhiannon is the Welsh horse-riding faerie queen famed for her beauty, wisdom and generosity, who married the mortal Pwyll, and later the magic god Manawyddan. Her story is told in the fourteenth century works, the *Red Book of Hergest* and *White Book of Rhydderch*. The name Rhiannon is usually considered as being derived from that of the Celtic sovereignty goddess Rigatona, meaning *"Great Queen"* (also one of the translations of Morrígan). It has been suggested however that her name may be derived from the Welsh words *"rhian"* and *"annwn"*, which would translate as "Maiden of the Otherworld". Rhiannon's symbols include her white horse and her magical birds, both classic faerie motifs, as is the mound Pwyll was standing on when he first saw her.

## Sibyllia/Sympilia (English/Greek Grimoire)

Sibyllia is a faerie queen conjured in the grimoires, mentioned in Folger V.b.26 (c. 1580), by Scot in his *Discoverie of Witchcraft* (1584) and also in the 15th century Greek *Hygromanteia* by the name of Sympilia. Sibyllia was mentioned in the earlier 13th century *Huon de Bordeaux*, suggesting there was a substantial tradition associated with this faerie queen. It is possible her name is derived from the ancient Sibyls, who acted as oracles of the gods.

## Titania/Tytan (Shakespeare/Grimoire)

Titania is a faerie queen made famous in Shakespeare's play *A Midsummer Night's Dream*, the popularity of which resulted in her name being used in much other fiction since. Shakespeare may have decided to use Titania as it was an epithet of the goddess Diana, who was already associated with the role of faerie queen, or he may have derived it from the 12th century Old French *Lanval* by Marie de France which gives Olyroun (cf Oberon) and Titania as faerie king and queen, or Thomas Chestre's derivative 14th century English *Romance of Sir Launfal*. The similar name Tytan appears in a 17th century grimoire text (Sloane MS 1727), and is probably derived from the ancient Greek Titans.

## Tryamour (French epic)

The faerie queen beloved of Sir Launfal in the *Romance of Sir Launfal*, the Arthurian knight who chooses to leave the human realm to dwell with Tryamour in the faerie realm of Avalon. This romance is also noteworthy for having Queen Guinevere as the villain who tries to seduce the loyal knight.

# CONJURATIONS

## From the Grimoires

## DAVID RANKINE

When the medium Edward Kelley was introduced to Dr John Dee in 1582, one of the first things he told Dee was *"I can show you faeries"*. This was not an uncommon phenomenon, with faeries being popular at the time in literature and art, and with plays and balls being put on by late sixteenth century aristocrats. A good example of this is how Queen Elizabeth I was greeted at a ball in Kenilworth in 1575 by a woman dressed as the faerie queen Sibylia (9 years before Scot wrote about her) who made prophecies for the reigning monarch. This trend continued, and seventeenth century magicians like Goodwin Wharton, the Lord Admiral of the Fleet, were keen angel and faerie magicians. Wharton was even said to have found a gate to a faerie kingdom, a fact which was hidden in a manuscript for centuries.

This style of magic is very different to the poetic and fluid form of working used by many modern pagans, and the contrast shows how much social perceptions have changed as well as methods of practising magic. One of the most obvious changes is that the magicians practising these rituals were also practicing Christians, and saw no dichotomy between their religious worship and their magical work. This is why the names of God are used to control the faeries and ensure their co-operation, as well as for protection from their wiles.

Despite this rich history, it is only in recent times that attention has fallen on the prevalence of faeries in some of the grimoire texts. Dan Harms' essay *Spirits at the Table: Faerie Queens in the Grimoires* goes far in addressing this oversight, and his translation with Joseph Peterson and Phil Legard of the Folger V.b.26 manuscript (c. 1580) when published will provide a major work in this field, as it is an entire grimoire text focused on faeries (especially the faery king Oberion). Scot's *Discoverie of Witchcraft* (1584) includes conjurations of the faerie queen Sibyllia, and there are also references in some of the seventeenth century Sloane manuscripts (in the British Library) to working with faeries, and discussion of their classification into different categories.

The manuscript Sloane 3825 dates to 1641, and comprises three parts: *Janua Magica Reserata* (The Keys to the Gateway of Magic), Dr Rudd's *Nine Great Celestial Keys* and *Conjurations of the Demon Princes*. The first part includes a discussion of faeries, and shows how to the Renaissance magician, the distinctions between different categories of spiritual creatures, be they faeries, angels or demons, were blurred, as they all fitted into the category of non-human entities to conjure and communicate with. The detail found in this discussion makes it clear that to the seventeenth century magician, it was not a case of whether you believed in faeries, but rather which ones you were trying to contact.

*****

## Sloane MS 3825 - Some further Considerations, Distinctions, & Dignifications, of this Subject touching Spirits

There are also a Certain Kind of spirits, not so noxious, offensive, hurtful, noisome, or Displeasing, but most near to Men, & are affected with human passions, Delighting much in Man's Society & do willingly dwell with him.

Some also there are, which often meet poor men, Women & Children, but they are afraid of & fly from men of constant, credulous & undaunted minds and Resolutions; And to good & pure men they are no way offensive, but to men that are wicked & impure they are very noxious & hurtful.

Some likewise, there are who dote upon Women, some upon Children, some there be that are Delighted in the Company of Diverse domestic & evil Animals, some inhabit Woods, & parks, some dwell about fountains & Meadows (Cummultis alis) but for brevity sake, we have inserted a necessary table following, describing briefly the names of most of these Kinds of Terrestrial Spirits, Fairies, Elfs, Goblins, or whatsoever else they may be called: together with what places and things they do inhabit, Delight, & Dwell in.

| | |
|---|---|
| *Fairies, Hobgoblins, Elfs in* | *Champion fields* |
| *Naiads* | *Fountains* |
| *Potamides* | *Rivers* |
| *Nymphs* | *Marshes & ponds* |
| *Oreads* | *Mountains* |
| *Hamedes* | *Meadows* |
| *Dryads & Hamadryads* | *Woods* |
| *Satyrs & Sylvani* | *Trees Breaks & Bushes* |

| | |
|---|---|
| Napta & Agapta | *Flowers* |
| Dodona | *Acorns, fruits* |
| Palea & Fenilia | *Fodder & the Country* |

The nature of those spirits, or Elves is, they are affected with and Love all those that Love them, & hate all those that hate them; yea they Know both our minds & thoughts in a great measure, whereby it comes to pass, that we may Easily Move them to come to us, if we Rightly understand the Rules thereof.

Of this terrestrial order are likewise those, which are commonly called Fairies, of which they are so even Sisters thus nominated.

Lillia, Raffilia, Foca, Tolla, Affrica, Julia, Venulla

It is Credibly Asserted, that in ancient times that many of those aforesaid Gnomes, Fairies Elves & other terrestrial wandering spirits, have been seen & heard amongst Men, but now it is said & believed that they are not so frequent: yet it is certainly averred & Creditably Reported, that some of them have been Discovered & seen, but here we shall Acquiesce touching the Differences of their not appearing, or being not so conversant with and amongst Men, so frequently in Latter times, as they are said usually to do in Ancient times; by Reason the cause thereof may be very easily Conjectured, by the Meanest Capacity.

*****

The material from Sloane 3824 (1649) goes into detail as to the offerings that should be made to the faeries, and also again refers to their hierarchy. The conjuration is unusual in that it does not seek to constrain the faeries in a triangle (used for demons) or a circle (used for angels), but rather has a pentagram as the gateway for the faeries to manifest through. This perhaps emphasises the view that faeries were seen as already existing in the physical world, or at least much closer to it than beings like angels.

Unlike the conjuration of angels and demons, where the beings are ordered to obey, this is much more a negotiation between equals, with offerings being made to the faeries (for more on this see Dan Harms' essay), although the same formula of appealing to God as the highest power to encourage the agreement of the faeries is found that is also seen in conjurations of angels and demons.

The invocation to be performed is written with practical advice on how to best achieve the result. Thus we see suggestions such as having your demands written down, so you do not forget anything. It is also interesting to note the occurrence of the words from the classic Sator magic square used in the invocation.

## Sloane 3824 The Method of Calling Faeries

These spirits may be also called upon as the other, in such places where Either they haunt or foremost frequent in, and the place which is appointed or set apart for action must be Suffumigated with good Aromatic Odours, and a Clean Cloth spread on the Ground or a table nine foot Distant from the Circle, upon which there must be Either a Chicken or any Kind of small joint, or piece of meat handsomely Roasted, and a white mantle, a Basin or little Dish like a Coffee Dish of fair Running water, half a pint of Salt in a bottle, a bottle of Ale Containing a Quart, Some food and a pint of Cream in a Dish provided Ceremonies they are much pleased & delighted with; and doth allure them to friendly familiarity willingly & Readily fulfilling your desires &c: without much Difficulty, and some have used no Circle at all, to the Calling of these spirits, but only being Clean was heard and apparelled, sit at another table or place only Covered with Clean Linen Cloth, nine foot Distant & so invocate.

Those Kind of Terrestrial spirits are vulgarly Called of all people generally Fairies or Elves, and the natures and Quality of them are well Known to many, those spirits there are too who are Set over the Hierarchy as the Supreme head thereof, whose names are Mycob and Oberion, under whom again are Seven Sisters, placed as the next principal, whose names, Are, Lilia, Rostilia, Foca, Folla, Africa, Julia, Venulla, under whom again are many Legions as Subjects and Subservient &c: who (as aforesaid) wander to & fro upon the Earth, and have the Keeping also of many Treasures that are hidden or Buried, especially such as are hidden in those places that they frequent, inhabit, or Delight in, and that Are innocently hidden by good honest people; Either for Security, or future preservation, who many times Die, & leave it so unrevealed, then are Such treasures Seized on and Kept by these terrestrial Elves; if ever they happen to come where it is &c: then the Magical Philosopher understanding, that any treasures are Kept by the terrestrial spirits of this order, And would obtain the same, and would have converse with them, let him observe the foregoing Directions, and at the appointed time repair to the place designated for action, and invocate as followeth,

*I Exorcise, adjure, call upon, urge and Earnestly Require you terrestrial spirits, that are the supreme head of the Hierarchy, of those that Are called Fairies, and who are Called by the names of Mycob and Oberyon, In the name of the Almighty, Everliving and heavenly God Jehova, and of his only Begotten & well beloved son Jesus Christ our Lord, Messias, Sother, Emanuel, the high King & Lord of all the world, I do hereby call upon and importunately Desiring Spirits Mycob and Oberyon, to command the Seven Sisters Lilia, Rostilia, Foca, Folla, Africa, Julia, Venulla, or some one of them, to appear visibly to us, or in Your friendly Benevolence, to send some one or other spirit or spirits, of your Hierarchy or orders, to accommodate instruct and assist us, in such of our Requests* wherein they may: the which I confidently & Earnestly importune of you as are our friends, & we are your friends, and all of us servants to the Highest in whose name I vow Call upon you and humbly urge, and most Earnestly Desire you, to Send one of the Seven Sisters next subservient under you, to Appear visibly to us, & to assist us in the obtaining and recovering of their Treasures, that are hidden or Buried in the House or place, or Elsewhere adjacent hereabouts, or to send some one Subject Subservient of your Hierarchy, to Assist and help us herein, and also in all Such matters And things as we shall Desire their Instructions and accommodations in,

Wherein, they may Continue this invocation for seven nights from the Hour of Eleven till two, and invocate nine times an hour but withal observing that if Any Apparition or Vision should appear, in form and manner, willing to Continue Commune with us, in the Interim, you may then cease, and desire to Know the name & seal of Such Spirit, and when you have taken a note thereof you may proceed to your Demands, which you ought to have fairly written Down, because then they are In A greater Readiness, and Chargeth not the memory to recollect It Self, for being So stumbled & hobbled in your conceptions, you may Chance to lose that opportunity and peradventure your Design too, but If nothing happens in the interim, then after the first seven nights, always beginning the next night after the Change of the moon, you shall invocate or call upon the Seven Sisters as followeth,

*Sator Arepo Tenet Opera Rotas*

*Kyrie. Eloyson. Christe Eloyson. Kyrie Eloyson. Adonay Cui Pater Cui Filius Cui Spiritus Sanctus Allelujah.*

*I exorcise, adjure command constrain & most Earnestly urge and request you Akerayes, the Sisters of those terrestrial spirits, who are Called Fairies or Elves by & in the name of the incomprehensible God of heaven & Earth, & all Creatures whatsoever are there In Contained and Comprehended, Jehovah, Elohim, Agla, El, Tetragrammaton, & in the name of Jesus Christ, begotten of a Virgin by the Holy Ghost, and born in the flesh at Nazareth, the second person In trinity, And the Saviour of the World. Especially of all believers, & those who lay hold upon him by faith, Thereby Confidently and firmly laying hold on the promises, that whatsoever we Ask our Heavenly Father, or shall any ways act, or do in his name, nothing shall be Denied us, nor be impossible to us, in whose name & through whose authority*[360] *we as true believers do Call upon, constrain and very Confidently Urgently and Earnestly Importune you, in the name also, and by the power of the Head and Supreme of your orders, or Hierarchy, and to whom you are the next In Order, governing over many Legions of other your Subjects & Subservients or some one of you Lilia, Rostilia, Foca, Folla, Africa, Julia, Venulla, to appear visibly to us, or to send someone other of your Subjected Subservients to help and Assist us in the obtaining of the treasures that are hidden or Buried in this house or place, or Elsewhere adjacent hereabouts, And more Especially the spirit or spirits that hath the Keeping thereof, Leave, Be Discharged & quit therefrom, & so avoid the*

---

[360] Word unclear in the original.

*same, and forthwith to Donate, Yield up & Surrender the Same, into our possession, so that we may bear the same away, and convert it to our necessary uses, without fraud or any other Crafts or Subtleties, that may in any wise deprive us thereof,*

*I do once again Exorcise, adjure and command thee Lilia & all thy Sisters & subjects By the imperial throne, and by the majesty & Deity of the Everliving God, that some or other spirit of your orders, and more Especially Such spirit or spirits, that have the Keeping of the treasures that are Hidden or Buried In this house or place, or near adjacent hereabouts Do appear visibly before us, to Resolve us friendly, and verily in all such Matters & things, as we shall rationally Desire, and Demand of you, that Amongst the Rest in particular as concerning our recovering and obtaining the treasures, that Lyeth hidden or Buried here or Elsewhere, let the spirit or spirits that hath the Keeping thereof, be Discharged and quitted of It, & immediately in all peace & quietness avoid & Depart therefrom, and Permit & yield up the Same to us as aforesaid: And the Peace of God always Remain Between you & us, in the name of the Father & of the Son and of the holy Ghost, And do for us herein as for the servants of the highest,*

Let the first of these four invocations be observed to be practiced, the first seven nights of the moon's increase, beginning the next night after She Change, as is before taught, and then the Eighth night, beginneth the Latter, & invocate nine times an hour, in the right season, from Eleven of the Clock till two, for that they being most frequently then visible, and stirring about, therefore Most convenient, and opportune, to Call upon them: for God hath So decreed, that they Shall not be visible and frequent in the Day as in the night, Except they are privately Called upon in the Day, because they shall not be frightful nor offensive, to harmless & innocent people, for he hath bounded all things, and they Cannot pass their Limits without permission.

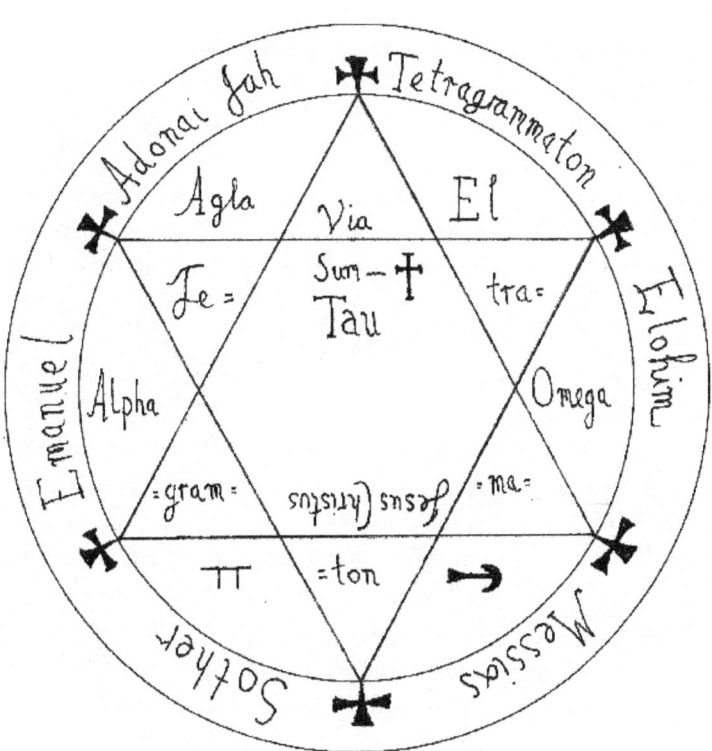

*Magic Circle for Fairy Conjuration*

## Reginald Scot - To call Sibylia and her Sisters

In 1584 the English Member of Parliament Reginald Scot wrote a hugely significant work called *The Discoverie of Witchcraft*. Scot's aim in writing this book was to counter the witch-hunt craze, and he sought to show that witchcraft and magic were delusions and that people accused of witchcraft were not evil and should not be killed, because witchcraft did not really exist. However, to do this Scot put together a huge amount of folklore and practical material, with the result that his work became known as a handbook for aspiring magicians and conjurors. For this reason, the rabidly anti-witchcraft King James I of England ordered all copies of the book to be burned, though some survived and later editions were reprinted after his death with many extra chapters containing more conjurations added by the editors.

Amongst the practical material in *The Discoverie of Witchcraft*, Scot goes into great detail in several chapters of Book XV about the calling of certain beings of the faery hierarchy. What is particularly noteworthy is the way that the faery queen Sibylia is called in connection with the dead. The magician conjures a dead spirit and asks it to fetch Sibylia to him, emphasising the common notion that the faery queens had dominion over the land of the dead. Another significant point is that Sibylia is also connected with the location of treasure, another common belief as the faeries were believed to know where all the hidden treasure in the earth was.

## Chapter VIII. An experiment of the dead.

First fast and pray three days, and abstain thee from all filthiness; go to one that is new buried, such a one as killed himself or destroyed himself wilfully: or else get thee promise of one that shall be hanged, and let him swear an oath to thee, after his body is dead, that his spirit shall come to thee, and do thee true service, at thy commandments, in all days, hours, and minutes. And let no persons see thy doings, but thy fellow. And about eleven a clock in the night, go to the place where he was buried, and say with a bold faith & hearty desire, to have the spirit come that thou dost call for, thy fellow having a candle in his left hand, and in his right hand a crystal stone, and say these words following, the master having a hazel wand in his right hand, and these names of God written thereupon, Tetragrammaton + Adonay + Agla + Craton + Then strike three strokes on the ground, and say;

*Arise N. Arise N. Arise N. I conjure thee spirit N. by the resurrection of our Lord Jesus Christ, that thou do obey to my words, and come unto me this night verily and truly, as thou believe to be saved at the day of judgement. And I will swear to thee on oath, by the peril of my soul, that if thou will come to me, and appear to me this night, and show me true visions in this crystal stone, and fetch me the fairie Sibylia, that I may talk with her visibly, and she may come before me, as the conjuration leadeth: and in so doing, I will give thee an alms deed, and pray for thee N. to my Lord God, whereby thou may be restored to thy salvation at the resurrection day, to be received as one of the elect of God, to the everlasting glory, Amen.*

The master standing at the head of the grave, his fellow having in his hands the candle and the stone, must begin the conjuration as followeth, and the spirit will appear to you in the crystal stone, in a faire form of a child of twelve years of age. And when he is in, feel the stone, and it will be hot; and fear nothing, for he or she will show many delusions, to drive you from your work. Fear God, but fear him not. This is to constrain him, as followeth.

*I conjure thee spirit N. by the living God, the true God, and by the holy God, and by their virtues and powers which have created both thee and me, and all the world. I conjure thee N. by these holy names of God, Tetragrammaton + Adonay + Algramay + Saday + Sabaoth + Planaboth + Panthon + Craton + Neupmaton + Deus + Homo + Omnipotens + Sempiturnus + Ysus + Terra + Unigenitus + Salvator + Via + Vita + Manus + Fons + Origo + Filius + And by their virtues and powers, and by all their names, by the which God gave power to man, both to speak or think; so by their virtues and powers I conjure thee spirit N. that now immediately thou do appear in this crystal stone, visibly to me and to my fellow, without any tarrying or deceit. I conjure thee N. by the excellent name of Jesus Christ A and Omega, the first and the last. For this holy name of Jesus is above all names: for in this name of Jesus every knee doth bow and obey, both of heavenly things, earthly things, and infernal. And every tongue doth confess, that our Lord Jesus Christ is in the glory of the father: neither is there any other name given to man, whereby he must be saved. Therefore in the name of Jesus of Nazareth, and by his nativity, resurrection, and ascension, and by all that appertains unto his passion, and by their virtues and powers I conjure thee spirit N. that thou do appear visibly in this crystal stone to me, and to my fellow, without any dissimulation. I conjure thee N. by the blood of the innocent lamb Jesus Christ, which was shed for us upon the cross: for all those that do believe in the virtue of his blood, shall be saved. I conjure thee N. by the virtues and powers of all the real names and words of the living God of me pronounced, that thou be obedient unto me and to my words rehearsed. If thou refuse this to do, I by the holy trinity, and their virtues and powers do condemn thee thou spirit N. into the place where there is no hope of remedy or rest, but everlasting horror and pain there dwelling, and a place where is pain upon pain, daily, horribly, and lamentably, thy pain to be there augmented as the stars in the heaven, as the gravel or sand in the sea: except thou spirit N. do appear to me and to my fellow visibly, immediately in this crystal stone, and in a faire form and shape of a child of twelve years of age, and that thou alter not thy shape, I charge thee upon pain of everlasting condemnation. I conjure thee spirit N. by the golden girdle, which girded the loins of our Lord Jesus Christ: so thou spirit N. be thou bound into the perpetual pains of hell fire, for thy disobedience and unreverent regard, that thou hast to the holy names and words, and his precepts. I conjure thee N. by the two edged sword, which John saw proceed out of the mouth of the almighty; and so thou spirit N. be torn and cut in pieces with that sword, and to be condemned into everlasting pain, where the fire goeth not out, and where the worm dies not. I conjure thee N. by the heavens, and by the celestial city of Jerusalem, and by the earth and the sea, and by all things contained in them, and by their virtues & powers. I conjure thee spirit N. by the obedience that thou dost owe unto the principal prince. And except thou spirit N. do come and appear in this crystal stone visibly in my presence, here immediately as it is aforesaid. Let the great curse of God, the anger of God, the shadow and darkness of death, and of eternal condemnation be upon thee spirit N. for ever and ever; because thou hast denied thy faith, thy health, & salvation. For thy great disobedience, thou art worthy to be condemned. Therefore let the divine trinity, thrones, dominions, principates, potestates, virtues, cherubim and seraphim, and all the souls of saints, both of men and women, condemn thee for ever, and be a witness against thee at the day of judgement, because of thy disobedience. And let all creatures of our Lord Jesus Christ, say thereunto; Fiat, fiat, fiat: Amen.*

And when he is appeared in the crystal stone, as is said before, bind him with this bond as followeth; to wit,

*I conjure thee spirit N. that art appeared to me in this crystal stone, to me and to my fellow; I conjure thee by all the real words aforesaid, the which did constrain thee to appear therein, and their virtues; I charge thee spirit by them all, that thou shalt not depart out of this crystal stone, until my will being fulfilled, thou be licensed to depart. I conjure and bind thee spirit N. by that omnipotent God, which commanded the angel Michael to drive Lucifer out of the heavens with a sword of vengeance, and to fall from joy to pain; and for dread of such pain as he is in, I charge thee spirit N. that thou shalt not go out of the crystal stone; nor yet to alter thy shape at this time, except I command thee otherwise; but to come unto me at all places, and in all hours and minutes, when and wheresoever I shall call thee, by the virtue of our Lord Jesus Christ, or by any conjuration of words that is written in this book, and to show me and my friends true visions in this crystal stone, of any thing or things that we would see, at any time or times: and also to go and to fetch me the fairy Sibylia, that I may talk with her in all kind of talk, as I shall call her by any conjuration of words contained in this book. I conjure thee spirit N. by the great wisdom and divinity of his godhead, my will to fulfill, as is aforesaid: I charge thee upon pain of condemnation, both in this world, and in the world to come, Fiat, fiat, fiat: Amen.*

This done, go to a place fast by, and in a faire parlour or chamber, make a circle with chalk, as hereafter followeth: and make another circle for the fairy Sibylia to appear in, four foot from the circle thou art in, & make no names therein, nor cast any holy thing therein, but make a circle round with chalk; & let the master and his fellow sit down in the first circle, the master having the book in his hand, his fellow having the crystal stone in his right hand, looking in the stone when the fairy doth appear. The master also must have upon his breast this figure here written in parchment, and begin to work in the new of the ☽ and in the hour of ♃ the ☉ and the ☽ to be in one of inhabiter's signs, as ♋ ♐ ♓. This bond as followeth, is to cause the spirit in the crystal stone, to fetch unto thee the fairy Sibylia. All things fulfilled, begin this bond as followeth, and be bold, for doubles they will come before thee, before the conjuration be read seven times.

*I conjure thee spirit N. in this crystal stone, by God the father, by God the son Jesus Christ, and by God the Holy-ghost, three persons and one God, and by their virtues. I conjure thee spirit, that thou do go in peace, and also to come again to me quickly, and to bring with thee into that circle appointed, Sibylia fairy, that I may talk with her in those matters that shall be to her honour and glory; and sol charge thee declare unto her. I conjure thee spirit N. by the blood of the innocent lamb, the which redeemed all the world; by the virtue thereof I charge thee thou spirit in the crystal stone, that thou do declare unto her this message. Also I conjure thee spirit N. by all angels and archangels, thrones, dominations, principates, potestates, virtues, cherubim and seraphim, and by their virtues and powers. I conjure the N. that thou do depart with speed, and also to come again with speed, and to bring with thee the fairy Sibylia, to appear in that circle, before I do read the conjuration in this book seven times. Thus I charge thee my will to be fulfilled, upon pain of everlasting condemnation: Fiat, fiat, fiat; Amen.*

Then the figure aforesaid pinned on thy breast, rehearse the words therein, and say,

+ *Sorthie* + *Sorthia* + *Sorthios* +

then begin your conjuration as followeth here, and say;

*I conjure thee Sibylia, O gentle virgin of fairies, by the mercy of the Holy-ghost, and by the dreadful dale of doom, and by their virtues and powers; I conjure thee Sibylia, O gentle virgin of fairies, and by all the angels of* ♃ *and their characters and virtues, and by all the spirits of* ♃ *and* ♀ *and their characters and virtues, and by all the characters that be in the firmament, and by the king and queen of fairies, and their virtues, and by the faith and obedience that thou bearest unto them. I conjure thee Sibylia by the blood that ran out of the side of our Lord Jesus Christ crucified, and by the opening of heaven, and by the renting of the temple, and by the darkness of the sun in the time of his death, and by the rising up of the dead in the time of his resurrection, and by the virgin Marie mother of our Lord Jesus Christ, and by the unspeakable name of God, Tetragrammaton. I conjure thee O Sibylia, O blessed and beautiful virgin, by all the real words aforesaid; I conjure thee Sibylia by all their virtues to appear in that circle before me visible, in the form and shape of a beautiful woman in a bright and vesture white, adorned and garnished most faire, and to appear to me quickly without deceit or tarrying, and that thou fail not to fulfil my will & desire effectually. For I will choose thee to be my blessed virgin, & will have common copulation with thee. Therefore make hast & speed to come unto me, and to appear as I said before: to whom be honour and glory for ever and ever, Amen.*

The which done and ended, if she come not, repeat the conjuration till they do come: for doubtless they will come. And when she is appeared, take your censers, and incense her with frankincense, then bind her with the bond as followeth.

*I do conjure thee Sibylia, by God the Father, God the son, and God the Holy-ghost, three persons and one God, and by the blessed virgin Marie mother of our Lord Jesus Christ, and by all the whole and holy company of heaven, and by the dreadful day of doom, and by all angels and archangels, thrones, dominations, principates, potestates, virtues, cherubim and seraphim, and their virtues and powers. I conjure thee, and bind thee Sibylia, that thou shalt not depart out of the circle wherein thou art appeared, nor yet to alter thy shape, except I give thee licence to depart. I conjure thee Sibylia by the blood that ran out of the side of our Lord Jesus Christ crucified, and by the virtue hereof I conjure thee Sibylia to come to me, and to appear to me at all times visibly, as the conjuration of words leadeth, written in this book, I conjure thee Sibylia, O blessed virgin of fairies, by the opening of heaven, and by the renting of the temple, and by the darkness of the sun at the time of his death, and by the rising of the dead in the time of his glorious resurrection, and by the unspeakable name of God + Tetragrammaton + and by the king and queen of fairies, & by their virtues I conjure thee Sibylia to appear, before the conjuration be read over four times, and that visibly to appear, as the conjuration leadeth written in this book, and to give me good counsel at all times, and to come by treasures hidden in the earth, and all other things that is to do me pleasure, and to fulfill my will, without any deceit or tarrying; nor yet that thou shalt have any power of my body or soul, earthly or ghostly, nor yet to perish so much of my body as one hair of my head. I conjure thee Sibylia by all the real words aforesaid, and by their virtues and powers, I charge and bind thee by the virtue thereof, to be obedient unto me, and to all the words aforesaid, and this bond to stand between thee and me, upon pain of everlasting condemnation, Fiat, fiat, fiat, Amen.*

## CHAPTER IX. A license for Sibylia to go and come by at all times.

*I CONJURE thee Sibylia, which art come hither before me, by the commandment of thy Lord and mine, that thou shalt have no powers, in thy going or coming unto me, imagining any evil in any manner of ways, in the earth or under the earth, of evil doings, to any person or persons. I conjure and command thee Sibylia by all the reall words and virtues that be written in this book, that thou shalt not go to the place from whence thou came, but shalt remain peaceably invisibly, and look thou be ready to come unto me, when thou art called by any conjuration of words that be written in this book, to come (I say) at my commandment, and to answer unto me truly and duly of all things, my will quickly to be fulfilled. Vade in pace, in nomine patris, & filii, & spiritus sancti. And the holy + cross + be between thee and me, or between us and you, and the lion of Judah, the root of*

*Jesse, the kindred of David, be between thee & me + Christ cometh + Christ commandeth + Christ giveth power + Christ defend me + and his innocent blood + from all perils of body and soul, sleeping or waking: Fiat, fiat, Amen.*

## CHAPTER X. To know of treasure hidden in the earth.

Write in paper these characters following, on the Saturday, in the hour of ☽, and lay it where thou thinkest treasure to be: if there be any, the paper will burn, else not. And these be the characters.

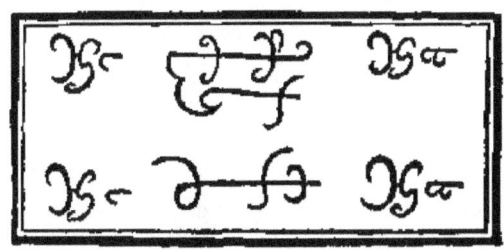

This is the way to go invisible by these three sisters of fairies.

In the name of the Father, and of the Son, and of the Holy-ghost.

First go to a faire parlour or chamber, & an even ground, and in no loft, and from people nine days; for it is the better: and let all thy clothing be clean and sweet. Then make a candle of virgin wax, and light it, and make a fair fire of charcoals, in a fair place, in the middle of the parlour or chamber. Then take faire clean water, that runs against the east, and set it upon the fire: and ere thou wash thy self, say these words, going about the fire, three times, holding the candle in the right hand

*+ Panthon + Graton + Muriton + Bisecognaton + Siston + Diaton + Maton + Tetragrammaton + Agla + Agarion + Tegra + Pentessaron + Tendicata +*

Then rehearse these names

*+ Sorthie + Sorthia + Sorthios + Milia + Achilia + Sibylia + in nomine patris, & filii, & spiritus sancti, Amen. I conjure you three sisters of fairies, Milia, Achilia, Sibylia, by the father, by the son, and by the Holy-ghost, and by their virtues and powers, and by the most merciful and living God, that will command his angel to blow the trumpet at the day of judgement; and he shall say, Come, come, come to judgement; and by all angels, archangels, thrones, dominations, principates, potestates, virtues, cherubim and seraphim, and by their virtues and powers. I conjure you three sisters, by the virtue of all the real words aforesaid: I charge you that you do appear before me visibly, in form and shape of faire women, in white vestures, and to bring with you to me, the ring of*

*invisibility, by the which I may go invisible at mine own will and pleasure, and that in all hours, and minutes: in nomine patris, & filii, & spiritus sancti, Amen.*

Being appeared, say this bond following.

*O blessed virgins + Milia + Achilia + I conjure you in the name of the father, in the name of the son, and in the name of the Holy-ghost, and by their virtues I charge you to depart from me in peace, for a time. And Sibylia, I conjure thee, by the virtue of our Lord Jesus Christ, and by the virtue of his flesh and precious blood, that he took of our blessed lady the virgin, and by all the holy company in heaven: I charge thee Sibylia, by all the virtues aforesaid, that thou be obedient unto me, in the name of God; that when, and at what time and place I shall call thee by this foresaid conjuration written in this book, look thou be ready to come unto me, at all hours and minutes, and to bring unto me the ring of invisibility, whereby I may go invisible at my will and pleasure, and that at all hours and minutes; Fiat, fiat, Amen.*

And if they come not the first night, then do the same the second night, and so the third night, until they do come: for doubtless they will come, and lie thou in thy bed, in the same parlour or chamber. And lay thy right hand out of the bed, and look thou have a fair silken handkerchief bound about thy head, and be not afraid, they will do thee no harm. For there will come before thee three faire women, and all in white clothing; and one of them will put a ring upon thy finger, wherewith thou shalt go invisible. Then with speed bind them with the bond aforesaid. When thou hast this ring on thy finger, look in a glass, and thou shalt not see thy self. And when thou wilt go invisible, put it on thy finger, the same finger that they did put it on, and every new ☽ renew it again. For after the first time thou shalt ever have it, and ever begin this work in the new of the ☽ and in the hour of ♃ and the ☽ in ♋ ♐ ♓.

## Bibliography

Rankine, David (2009) *The Book of Treasure Spirits.* (Contains partial transcription of Sloane MS 3824) London: Avalonia

Rankine, David (2007) *Faeries in the Grimoires.* Unpublished notes from private lecture

Rankine, David & Skinner, Stephen (2005) *The Keys to the Gateway of Magic.* (Contains transcription of Sloane MS 3825). Singapore: Golden Hoard Press

Scot, Reginald (1990) *The Discoverie of Witchcraft.* (Originally 1584) London: Dover Publications

*The Faerie Queens*

# INDEX

## A

*A Midsummer Night's Dream* .. 31, 34, 237
Abundantia .................................. 233
Abundia ............................... 53, 233
Accolon, Sir 152, 153, 159, 160, 161
Achilia .......................... 48, 251, 252
Adam, Helen ..................... 75, 83, 86
Aefsati ............................................ 115
*Aeneid* ................. 21, 23, 47, 58, 211
Afallach ................................ 158, 213
Africa ................... 45, 241, 242, 243
Agrippa, Henry Cornelius ..... 51, 55
Ailill, King ................................... 192
Aimery, Count ............................... 88
Áine ... 9, 20, 24, 175, 177, 178, 190, 191, 192, 193, 195, 229
*Albion's England* .......................... 233
*Alexander Romance* .... 43, 44, 56, 233
Alexander the Great ........ 43, 94, 233
All Hallow's Eve ............................ 28
Allecto .......................................... 130
Anderson, Isobel ................. 137, 143
Angus MacOg ............................. 232
Annwn ........ 167, 181, 208, 209, 213
Aoibheal ...................................... 229
Aoibhinn ............................. 175, 178
Aphrodite ........... 156, 206, 210, 211
Apollo ................................. 162, 220
Apple. 187, 205, 210, 211, 212, 213, 214
Arawn ................................. 181, 183
Argante ........................................ 229
Aricia ................................... 122, 129
Ariosto, Ludivico ........................... 21
Arnold, Matthew .......... 60, 138, 139
Artemis ...... 16, 23, 35, 42, 119, 126, 129, 233, 264
Arthur, King . 21, 24, 31, 34, 45, 49, 56, 60, 71, 140, 141, 149, 150, 151, 152, 153, 154, 155, 156, 157, 158, 159, 160, 161, 162, 163, 164, 166, 167, 168, 170, 171, 172, 173, 202, 209, 213, 214, 215, 229, 235
Astaroth ......................................... 46
Asteria ............................................ 35
Atlantis ........................................... 81
Auberon ................. 230, *See* Oberon
Aureola .......................................... 230
Avalon ..... 10, 13, 23, 24, 27, 34, 61, 88, 92, 150, 151, 155, 156, 157, 158, 160, 161, 162, 163, 164, 165, 166, 171, 172, 210, 213, 214, 215, 229, 235, 236, 237, 238
Avernus ........................................... 23

## B

Balin ............................................... 61
Bannatyne MS ............................. 232
Banshee ............................... 92, 174
*Battlefield* ..................................... 130
Bean Nighe .................................... 93
Bean-Sidhe .................................... 33
Bear ..... 42, 50, 70, 98, 116, 190, 244
Bebo ............................................. 230
Bel ................................................ 193
Bellhouse, William Dawson ......... 49
Bellona ........................................ 130
*bells* ............................................... 19
Belphoebe ..................................... 21
Beltane ................ 108, 193, 196, 202
Beltane Eve ................................. 108
Ben Nevis ...................... 23, 36, 235
Bersuire, Pierre ............................. 89
bird ............. 103, 131, 230, 231, 234
Birto ............................................... 99
Bishop of Exeter ................ 125, 126
Black Dog ..................................... 33
Blake, William ........................ 76, 78
Bononiensis 3632 ............ 44, 45, 233
*Border Ballads* ......... 79, 180, 182, 187
Bradley, Marion Zimmer ... 61, 150, 155, 160, 166
Bran ..................................... 211, 212
Briggs, Katharine 196, 197, 199, 202
Brighde ........................................... 70

*Britannia's Pastorals* .......................... 26
Browne, William ............................ 26
*Brut* ................................................. 229
Brynhildr ................................ 130, 134
Burfex ............................................... 46

## C

Caeilte ............................................... 66
Caelia ............................................... 230
Cailleach ..11, 16, 20, 24, 29, 68, 69, 70, 71, 72, 73, 74, 230, 232, 236
Cailleach Bhéarra...69, *See* Cailleach
Callisto .............................................. 42
Camelot ........61, 150, 153, 154, 156, 160, 189
Camlann ................................. 155, 156
Campbell, John ....................... 66, 71
Campion, Thomas ........198, 199, 237
Candlemass .................................. 196
*Canon Episcopi* ................... 25, 53, 104
Capercaillie ................................... 109
*Carduino* ............................................ 90
*Cath Magh Mucrama* ..................... 229
Catholic .....21, 47, 61, 125, 129, 205
Cauldron ........................................ 214
Cavendish, Margaret .......... 218, 220
*Chaldean Oracles* ............................. 40
Charon ........................................... 211
Chaucer, Geoffrey ....................... 237
*Cherry of Zennor* ...................... 38, 208
Choosers of the Slain ................. 130
*Clavicula Salomonis* ...... 44, *See* Key of Solomon
Cliodhna ....9, 20, 24, 174, 175, 176, 177, 231
Clutonda ....................................... 231
Cnoc Áine ..................................... 192
*Cogadh Gaedhel re Gallaibh* ............ 229
Cokars, John .................................. 47
*Colloquy of the Ancients* ..................... 66
*Confessor* ........................................... 53
Connla .................................. 212, 213
Cooper, Susan ............................. 146
*Cornish Folk Tales* .........137, 140, 149
Coudrette ............................... 94, 98
Creiddylad .................................... 209
Crow ................................................ 34
Crowley, Aleister ........................... 46

crystal...45, 46, 48, 64, 80, 177, 212, 235, 246, 247, 248, 249
Cú Chulainn .................. 34, 231, 234
*Culhwch and Olwen* .................. 92, 209
Cumaean Sibyl ........................ 23, 47

## D

d'Arras, Jean .............21, 91, 94, 100
Daghda ......................................... 214
Dali ................................................ 116
Dame Habonde. 233, *See* Habundia
d'Arras, Jean ............................ 87, 89
*Das Märchen von der Schönen Melusine* .................................................. 99
Davidson, Ellis .. 102, 103, 105, 131
de la Motte Fouque, Friedrich...142
de Leon, Hervé ................. 23, 91, 92
*De Nugis Curialum* .......................... 90
de Troyes, Chrétien ... 157, 161, 167
*De Vita Longa* .................................. 96
de Voragine, Jacobus .................... 53
dead....22, 25, 33, 34, 35, 48, 50, 79, 110, 111, 121, 125, 126, 154, 172, 184, 185, 187, 200, 202, 208, 214, 235, 236, 237, 246, 249, 250
Dee, Dr John ............................... 239
Deer ...66, 68, 70, 71, 72, 73, 74, 81, 104, 230
Delforia ........................................... 49
Delphi ............................................. 47
Demeter .................................. 95, 209
Demophon ..................................... 95
Diana .19, 20, 23, 24, 25, 26, 28, 34, 35, 53, 82, 119, 120, 121, 122, 123, 124, 125, 126, 127, 128, 129, 167, 168, 169, 170, 172, 220, 231, 232, 233, 236, 237
*Die Schöne Melusine* .................. 94, 95
*Discoverie of Witchcraft* .22, 47, 49, 56, 237, 239, 246, 252
Doamna Zinelor ......................... 231
*Donald Son of Patrick* ...................... 73
Drayton, Michael .......................... 22
dryads ...................................... 20, 21
Dryden ......................................... 124
Duncan, Robert ............... 78, 83, 85
Dylan ............................................ 138

## E

e. Mus. 173 .......................................51
Eambia..........................................231
Echdae .......................................... 193
Echidna...........................................91
Edem................................................91
Edward IV, King............98, 99, 151
Egyptian...................................... 264
Elinas, King..................87, 94, 236
Elizabeth I, Queen.......21, 230, 231, 232, 239
Elk..................70, 71, 108, 109, 111
Elphame .........................5, 25, 27, 80
Endymion............................168, 169
Epiphany ..............................53, 104
*Erec et Enide* .................................. 157
Erinyes...........................................130
*Estoire de Merlin*.....................158, 168
Etain.........................................177, 232
Evans, Ellen...........................45, 235
Evans-Wentz, W.Y. ....73, 141, 148, 156, 157, 174, 195, 215
Eve 93, 94, 105, 192, 199, 205, 210, 214
Excalibur ...150, 152, 153, 155, 163, 213

## F

Fand ...............................141, 231, 234
Fate.. 6, 33, 34, 36, 39, 40, 206, 213, 214
Fates............39, 53, 54, 55, 168, 206
fauns..........................................20, 21
Faust, Johann.................................52
Finvarra 22, 174, 175, 197, 200, 236
Florella.............................................45
Flyting................. 127, 201, 233, 235
Foca....................... 45, 241, 242, 243
Folger V.b.26 ..45, 46, 49, 235, 237, 239
Folla ................................45, 242, 243
Fountain of the Fairies .......... 88, 89
*Fourth Book of Occult Philosophy*51, 55
Fox .........................................73, 110
Foxwood, Orion 139, 140, 141, 142
Frau Holle ... 101, 102, 103, 104, *See* Holda
Freya..... 34, 109, 111, 114, 116, 118

Frigga............................101, 102, 104
Fromont............................. 92, 93, 97
Fuamnach .......................... 190, 232

## G

Galadriel..........................................31
Ganieda ................................ 169, 170
Gardner, Gerald........................196
Gauntlet, Arthur .............. 45, 49, 56
*Gawain and the Green Knight*.........157
Gawaine, Sir..................................155
Geoffrey of Monmouth... 155, 156, 157, 158, 159, 161, 162, 167, 170, 171, 213, 235
Geoffroy....................88, 92, 93, 97
Gerard, John...............................193
Gervaise of Tilbury.......................90
Gimbutas, Marija .........74, 101, 106
Ginsberg, Allen ..............................78
Glaistig ...65, 66, 71, 72, 73, 74, 232
Glaistig Uaine .......... 71, *See* Glaistig
Glaistigs..........................................24
Gloriana...................21, 24, 27, 232
goddesses 19, 20, 23, 24, 25, 26, 29, 53, 116, 119, 123, 126, 127, 128, 134, 168
*Goetia*.......................................46, 58
*Golden Legend* ...............................53
Gollveir ........................................132
Gorlois................................. 158, 160
Gowdie, Isobell.............................25
Granberg, Gunnar ....107, 108, 109, 110, 111, 112, 113, 114, 115, 116, 117, 118
*Grand Grimoire*...........................52, 57
*Greenwitch* ............................... 146, 148
Grimm, Jacob...............54, 101, 103
*Grimorium Verum*..............................52
Grouse...........................................109
Gudr ............................................131
Guinevere.............33, 150, 158, 238
*Gulliver's Travels*...........................230
Guyon..............................................24
Gwenhidw.....................................232
Gwrach-y-Rhybin...........................92
Gwydion ab Don ........................232
Gwyn ap Nudd.................. 208, 209
Gyre Carling ...................... 232, 236

256

## H

Habundia ..................... 24, 233, 234
Hades ................................... 22, 209
Halloween .................. 22, 103, 105
Hare................................... 104, 109
*Hark, All You Ladies*.................. 237
Harris, Thomas Lake ................. 224
Hathor ............................... 206, 210
hawthorn .............................. 19, 146
Hekate 12, 15, 16, 20, 22, 23, 26, 35, 36, 38, 40, 119, 126, 127, 129, 170, 233, 235
*Henno cum Dentibus* ........................ 90
Hera...................................... 210
Herodias ..20, 24, 53, 125, 126, 128, 172, 233
Hertha ................................... 102
Hesiod................................. 42, 56
Hippolyta ................................. 34
*Histoire du Merlin* ........................ 59
*Historia Regum Britanniae* .... 158, 161, 167, 173, 213
Hockley, Frederick ........... 45, 46, 56
Holda .... 8, 22, 23, 24, 29, 101, 102, 103, 104, 105, 106
Holy Grail .................................. 214
Holy Spirit .................................. 40
horse......................... 11, 19, 29, 169
Horse 45, 49, 79, 80, 110, 142, 153, 169, 179, 180, 181, 182, 183, 186, 187, 188, 201, 204, 221, 237
Huldbrand ............................... 142
*Huon de Bordeaux* .......................... 237
Hy Brazil ............................. 208, 213
*Hygromanteia* ... 44, 47, 48, 50, 51, 57, 237

## I

Idunn ...................................... 210
*Idylls of the King* ....... 60, 140, 149, 173
Igraine ......... 152, 155, 158, 161, 163
Inuqun .................................... 68
*Iolanthe* .................................. 230
Iscanus .................................. 125
Isis-Hermouthis ........................... 91
Italy ... 119, 120, 122, 128, 167, 172, 231
Iubdan ................................... 230

## J

James I, King ............................. 246
*Janua Magica Reserata* ................. 240
*Jerusalem Delivered* ......................... 21
Johnson, Richard ....................... 230
Jonson, Ben .................. 22, 222, 234
Jörð ....................................... 102
Julia ................. 45, 241, 242, 243
Jung, Carl ............................. 99, 100
Juno Lucina ............................... 168
Jupiter ................................. 46, 53

## K

Kalé ....20, 23, 42, 43, 44, 45, 47, 51, 233
Kami ..................................... 68, 74
Kelley, Edward ........................... 239
*Key of Solomon* ........................ 44, 45
King Arthur .................. 23, 124, 164
Kipling, Rudyard ........................ 198
Kirk, Robert ............................ 38, 67
Kuhleborn ................................. 142
Kybele .................................... 23

## L

La Belle Dame sans Merci ......... 173
*Lacnunga* ................................. 131
Lady of the Lake ....... 31, 60, 61, 62, 150, 153, 154, 160, 161, 163, 166, 167, 169, 170, 171, 173, 210
Laima .............................. 206, 207
Lake Nemi ................................ 168
Lamia ...................................... 47
Lammas ................ 193, 196, 202, *See* Lughnasadh
Lancelot ..... 150, 158, 159, 160, 161, 167, 168, 172, 236
*Lancelot Propre* .............................. 158
*Lanzelet* .......................... 90, 167, 236
Latis ...................................... 171
Launcelot ...... 154, 160, *See* Lancelot
Launfal, Sir .............................. 238
Layamon ................................. 229
*Le Morte d'Arthur* .60, 150, 152, 154, 155, 158, 159, 161, 162, 163
*Le Roman de Parthenay* .............. 94, 98
*Lebor Gabála Érenn* ............... 23, 229
Leland .120, 121, 122, 128, 129, 233

*Letters on Demonology and Witchcraft* ............... 26, 171, 173, 233, 236
Lewis, C.S. .................................... 101
Li Ban .................................... 231, 234
*Liber de Nymphis, Sylphis, Pygmaeis et Salamandris* .................................. 96
Lilia ............... 45, 241, 242, 243, 244
Lilith ......................................... 77, 94
Lilly, William . 41, 42, 45, 46, 47, 57, 235
Llyr ............................... 138, 139, 141
Lost Island .................................... 88
Lucifer ............ 25, 46, 114, 121, 248
Lucifera .................................. 21, 237
Lug .............................................. 91
Lughnasadh ............................... 193
Lutey ........... 137, 138, 139, 141, 143
*Lutey and the Mermaid* .......... 137, 139
*Lybeaus Desconus* ............................ 90
Lyonesse .................................... 140

## M

Mab . 22, 42, 46, 163, 172, 218, 222, 223, 234
Mabb ................... 45, 234, *See* Mab
*Mabinogi* .. 71, 74, 179, 184, 187, 189
*Mac Ian Year* .................................. 73
*Macbeth* .................................. 35, 233
Macha ......................................... 179
MacKenzie, Donald ............... 68, 70
*Magia Naturalis et Innaturalis* ... 52, 53
magician ... 11, 24, 45, 46, 47, 48, 49, 50, 51, 52, 60, 63, 64, 240, 246
Malory, Thomas ... 60, 62, 150, 151, 152, 153, 154, 155, 156, 158, 159, 161, 162, 163, 169, 172, 173
Manannan .. 138, 141, 145, 146, 176, 178, 193, 229, 230
Map, Walter .................................. 90
Mary, Queen .................................. 21
Mathers, MacGregor ..................... 46
May Day ....... 28, 198, 199, 203, 209
Medb, Queen .................................. 46
Megumoowesoo ........................... 68
Melior ..................... 87, 99, 234, 236
Melusine .. 23, 24, 27, 33, 36, 39, 40, 87, 88, 89, 90, 91, 92, 93, 94, 95, 96, 97, 98, 99, 100, 233, 234, 236

Melusine de Lusignan ..... 21, 24, 89, 99
*Merchants Tale* ............................... 237
Merlin ...... 40, 59, 60, 61, 62, 63, 64, 150, 152, 155, 156, 158, 159, 162, 163, 167, 168, 169, 170, 171, 172, 173, 205, 235, 236
Mermaid 95, 96, 117, 137, 138, 139, 140, 141, 142, 146, 167, 191, 234, 235
*Mermaid of Zennor* ......................... 139
Merseburg Charm ....................... 132
Metsänhaltia ............................... 116
Mical ................... 45, 234, *See* Micob
Micob ................... 42, 45, 49, 234
Micol ............ 45, 46, 235, *See* Micob
Midir ......................................... 232
Midsummer Eve ......................... 192
Milia ............................... 48, 251, 252
*Minstrelsy of the Scottish Border* . 79, 86, 232
Mistele, Williams ................ 142, 145
Mithraism ..................................... 17
Modron ............................... 158, 163
Moirai ............................................ 34
Montgomery. Alexander ... 201, 202
Moon .............. 6, 33, 34, 39, 77, 141
Mordred ................. 61, 140, 155, 160
Morgan leFay 23, 24, 40, 59, 60, 62, 92, 150, 151, 152, 153, 154, 155, 156, 159, 161, 163, 164, 166, 167, 171, 172, 210, 213, 214, 235
Morgana Le Fay 33, 34, *See* Morgan leFay
Morrigan .. 11, 20, 23, 24, 28, 34, 40, 93, 100, 134, 213, 235
Mortzē ........................................... 51
Morveren ..... 24, 137, 139, 140, 141, 142, 143, 144, 145, 146, 147, 148, 235
*Morveren's Lullaby* ................ 137, 143
Morverna ............ 137, 138, 139, *See* Morveren
MSS Cotton. Faust. A ................ 233
Mycob 45, 46, 52, 234, 235, 242, *See* Micob
Myrddin Wyllt ........................... 169

## N

Nagas .......................................... 91, 100
Naimh ............................................... 141
Nemain ............................. 169, 170, 171
Nemi ................................................. 122
Nemoralia ....................................... 122
Nemorensis .......................... 122, 123
Nephesh ............................................. 36
Nereida .............................................. 43
Nerthus ........................................... 102
Neshamah ......................................... 36
Neyve ................... 59, 60, *See* Viviane
Níamh .............................................. 169
Nichols, Ross .................................. 196
Nicneven ... 20, 23, 26, 36, 127, 172, 232, 233, 235
Nicnevin ..... 169, 171, *See* Nicneven
Nimue 9, 12, 23, 31, 40, 59, 61, 153, 155, 161, 163, 166, 167, 168, 169, 170, 171, 172, 216, 236
*Nine Great Celestial Keys* ................ 240
Niniane 61, 166, 167, 169, 170, 236, *See* Viviane
Ninianne ........................................... 59
Norns ............................... 34, 104, 131
Norse ............................................... 130
Nyfain ..................................... 169, 171
*Nymphidia* ............................... 22, 234
nymphs .... 12, 20, 21, 25, 28, 43, 82, 96, 126, 127, 231

## O

Oberion ......... 45, 234, 239, 242, *See* Oberon
Oberon ........... 33, 46, 230, 237, 238
Odin .. 101, 102, 114, 130, 131, 134, 187
Officium Spirituum ........................ 45
Ogier le Danios .......................... 214
Oisín ............................................... 169
Onoskelis .......................................... 44
Oonagh ......... 22, 174, 197, 200, 236
*Orfeo* ...................................... 22, 233
*Orlando Furioso* ................................ 21
*Otia Imperialia* ................................ 90
Ounaheencha ....................... 24, 236

## P

Palatine ............................ 87, 99, 236
Palmer, John ................................. 46
Paracelsus ................. 24, 96, 97, 100
Paris Arsenal 3353 ...................... 99
Pausanias ........................ 42, 47, 57
Pegasus ........................................ 187
Perchta ............... 53, 102, 103, 104
Persephone . 22, 205, 209, 210, 211, 214, 230, 237
Phaer, Thomas ............................. 21
Piperno ........................................ 122
Plato ............................................... 39
Poseidon ........................................ 47
*Preiddeu Annfwyn* ....................... 213
Pressine ... 23, 24, 27, 87, 88, 89, 91, 92, 236
Prevallet, Kristin ..................... 75, 86
*Prose Edda* ........................... 131, 136
Proserpina .............. 19, 22, 199, 237
*Puck of Pook's Hill* ...................... 198
Pwyll .. 169, 170, 179, 181, 182, 183, 185, 186, 187, 237

## Q

*Queen Mab A Philosophical Poem* .... 22
Queen of Elfhame ........... 38, 81, 82
Queen of the Hidden Isle ... 24, 237
Quiller-Couch, Arthur ...... 139, 141, 149

## R

Raffilia ..................... 241, *See* Rostilia
Ragnarok ............................. 25, 130
Raven ............................................. 34
Raymondin .... 23, 88, 89, 90, 92, 94, 97, 98
*Red Book of Hergest* ...................... 237
*Reductorium Morale* ........................ 89
*Rex Nemorensis* ............................ 122
Rhiannon ..... 9, 13, 20, 24, 169, 170, 176, 178, 179, 180, 181, 182, 183, 184, 185, 186, 187, 188, 231, 237
Rhine-Maiden .............................. 94
Richard III, King ........................ 98
Rigatona ...................................... 237
*Roman de la Rose* ........................ 233

*Romance of Sir Launfal*................... 238
Rome............................................... 119
*Romeo and Juliet* ................22, 46, 234
Rostilia ...........................45, 242, 243
Róta......................................131, 135
Ruach ................................................36

## S

saints .........20, 42, 53, 114, 141, 248
Samhain ......192, 193, 196, 199, 235
Satan....................................25, 46, 77
Satia...................................................53
Scot, Reginald ........................ 47, 246
Scotland ...15, 20, 25, 66, 68, 71, 76, 77, 78, 79, 80, 87, 88, 105, 119, 123, 124, 126, 127, 128, 129, 160, 171, 180, 183, 184, 206, 207, 230, 231, 232, 233, 235, 236
Scott, Walter..26, 79, 143, 171, 232, 233, 235
*Scottish Folk Lore and Folk Life* ......68
*Second Report of Doctor Faust*...........49
*Serglige Con Culainn*............... 231, 234
Serpent 23, 45, 88, 90, 91, 94, 96, 99
Shahmeran........................................91
Shakespeare, William 21, 22, 31, 33, 34, 35, 36, 40, 41, 49, 187, 233, 234, 237
Sheep..................43, 44, 68, 109, 224
Shekinah ........................40, 210, 211
Shelley, Percy Bysshe ...22, 223, 234
Sibilia............................ 49, *See* Sibylia
Sibylia.......19, 22, 42, 47, 48, 49, 55, 239, 246, 248, 249, 250, 251, 252
Sibyllia 47, 231, 237, 239, *See* Sibylia
Sibyls ...............................19, 47, 237
Sidhe 14, 33, 34, 177, 178, 190, 192, 193, 195, 196, 230
Sigurd........................................... 130
silver 6, 19, 39, 80, 82, 97, 117, 176, 192, 197, 204, 205, 211, 212
Sjörå ................................114, 117, 118
Skeny XI C 42..................................96
Skogsrå......8, 24, 103, 107, 108, 109, 110, 111, 112, 113, 114, 115, 116, 117
Skuld ....................................131, 136
*Sleeping Beauty*................................ 206
Sleipnir.......................................... 187
Sloane 1727 ..................... 45, 46, 234
Sloane 3824....... 45, 46, 52, 99, 235, 241, 242, 252
Sloane 3825........................ 240, 252
Sloane 3851 .....................................49
Solomon, King ...............................47
*Song of Solomon* .................................39
Spencer.......................................... 124
Spenser, Edmund.....21, 24, 27, 229, 230, 232, 237
Spina .............................................. 122
St Guenole .................................... 157
St. Brendan .................................. 212
St. Germain of Auxerre................53
St. Johns' Eve .............................. 192
St. Kalé .............................................43
St. Patrick .......................................66
St. Senara............................. 139, 141
*Suda*..............................................47, 58
*Suite du Merlin* ................................59
sun..................................................264
*Superstitions of the Highlands & Islands of Scotland*.....66, 67, 71, 74
*Svebilius Katekes*............................. 114
swan maidens............................... 131
Symphilia.....................50, *See* Sibylia
Sympilia .............. 47, 237, *See* Sibylia

## T

Taliesin ......................................... 171
Tam Lin...... 38, 79, 81, 85, 180, 182, 183, 186, 188, 189, 200, 201, 202
Tanaquill............... 232, *See* Gloriana
Tarot .......................63, 85, 206, 210
Tartarotti ...................................... 122
Tasso, Torquato ............................21
Tennyson, Sir Alfred ...... 60, 61, 62, 140, 149, 173
*Testament of Solomon*........................ 44
Tethys............................................ 146
*Teutonic Mythology*.................. 103, 106
*The Adventure of Fergus mac Léti*...230
*The Battle of Magh Mucrama* ..........229
*The Book of Leinster*................. 66, 192
*The Book of the Dun Cow* .................66
*The Complaynt of Scotland*..... 180, 189
*The Dream of Rhonabwy*.......... 71, 158

The Entertainment at Althorp.. 22, 234
The Faerie Queene ...... 21, 22, 24, 229, 230, 232, 237
The Faery Teachings ...... 139, 140, 141, 142, 148
The Fairies in Tradition and Literature ............................ 30, 196, 197, 202
The Fairy Lady Proserpine .............. 198
The Fairy-Faith in Celtic Countries 141, 148, 156, 197, 207
The Flyting Betwixt Montgomery and Polwart .............. 201, 202, 233, 235
The Forsaken Merman ............ 138, 139
The Generall Historie of Plantes .... 193, 195
The Mermaid of Zennor.. 137, 139, 148
The Mists of Avalon ......... 61, 161, 166
The Prince and the Fairy-Queen of the Fairies ............................................ 95
The Secret Commonwealth of Elves, Fauns and Faeries ................. 67, 74
The Snow Queen ............ 101, 106, 108
The Tale of Taliesin ........................ 173
The Voyage of Bran ....................... 211
The Wife of Ben-Y-Ghloe ................... 73
The Wizard of Oz ............................... 83
Thomas 9, 19, 21, 25, 27, 38, 39, 54, 57, 60, 80, 85, 100, 123, 150, 164, 168, 169, 172, 173, 180, 182, 183, 184, 186, 187, 188, 189, 198, 199, 200, 202, 203, 204, 205, 206, 211, 215, 224, 238
Thomas the Rhymer .38, 39, 80, 85, 168, 180, 182, 183, 187, 188, 198, 200, 202, 203, 205
Tir Na nOg ........ 169, 207, 208, 213
Tisiphone .................................... 130
Titania 31, 33, 34, 35, 40, 45, 46, 62, 172, 187, 237
Tolkien, J.R.R ........................ 31, 208
Tolla ............................................. 241
Tom a Lincoln ............................. 230
Tonn Cleena ................................ 177
tree. 19, 28, 38, 40, 94, 99, 103, 105, 111, 115, 116, 182, 186, 187, 191, 192, 198, 199, 201, 205, 206, 210, 211, 221
Tristram ........................ 60, 154, 159

Tristram and Iseult ............................ 60
True Thomas ......... 38, 205, 211, *See* Thomas the Rhymer
Tryamour ...................................... 238
Tuatha De Danann ... 34, 66, 77, 80, 166, 174, 190, 207, 208, 213, 236
Tuatha de Danann, ........................ 20
Tytan .......... 45, 237, 238, *See* Titania

**U**

Under Sea, Under Stone .................. 146
Undine .................... 95, 142, 149
Uriens, King ...... 152, 153, 158, 160
Ursa Major ...................................... 42
Uther Pendragon ................ 152, 158

**V**

Valhalla ........................................... 24
Valkyries 8, 16, 22, 24, 34, 130, 131, 132, 133, 134, 136
Venulla ................. 45, 241, 242, 243
Venus ........ 22, 46, 69, 205, 206, 211
Virgil ........... 21, 23, 47, 58, 122, 211
virgin .. 43, 48, 60, 82, 115, 126, 156, 168, 231, 249, 250, 251, 252
Virgin Mary ............................. 19, 44
Vita Merlini 155, 156, 157, 162, 167, 170, 173, 213, 235
Viviane ... 59, 60, 61, 62, 63, 64, 160, 161, 163, 166, 167, 236
Volsungakvida ........................ 130, 132
Volundr .......................................... 131
Voluspa ............................................ 133
Völuspá ........ 102, 105, 134, 135, 136
von Ringoltingen, Thüring ... 29, 94, 95
von Zatzikhoven, Ulrich .... 90, 167, 236
Vulgate Cycle ......... 158, 162, 163, 167

**W**

West, Alice & John .......... 26, 54, 57
Wharton, Goodwin ..................... 239
White Book of Rhydderch ................. 237
wicca .............................................. 121
Wicca .............................. 15, 121, 129
Wild Hunt ... 35, 103, 104, 134, 182, 202, 208, 231

Wilde, Lady .......................... 22, 197
William of Auvergne ....... 53, 58, 233
*Witchcraft & Second Sight in the
    Highlands & Islands of Scotland* .. 66
Wolf ....... 33, 71, 108, 109, 116, 118
Woodville, Elizabeth ..................... 98
World Soul .............................. 39, 40

**Y**

Yeats, W.B. ................. 60, 77, 85, 142
*Ynglinga Saga* ................................. 104
Yvain ............................................... 158
*Yvain, the Knight of the Lion* .......... 158

**Z**

Zeus ................................ 42, 47, 209

*The Faerie Queens*

 *If you enjoyed this book, you may also enjoy some of the other titles published by Avalonia...*

*A Collection of Magical Secrets by David Rankine (editor)*

*Artemis: Virgin Goddess of the Sun & Moon by Sorita d'Este*

*Defences Against the Witches' Craft by John Canard*

*From a Drop of Water (anthology, various contributors) edited by Kim Huggens*

*Heka: Egyptian Magic by David Rankine*

*Hekate Her Sacred Fires (anthology) edited by Sorita d'Este*

*Hekate Liminal Rites (history) by Sorita d'Este & David Rankine*

*Odin's Gateways by Katie Gerrard*

*The Priory of Sion by Jean-luc Chaumeil*

*Seidr: The Gate is Open by Katie Gerrard*

*Stellar Magic by Payam Nabarz*

*The Book of Gold by David Rankine (editor) & Paul Harry Barron (translator)*

*The Cosmic Shekinah by Sorita d'Este & David Rankine*

*The Gods of the Vikings by Marion Pearce*

*The Grimoire of Arthur Gauntlet by David Rankine (editor)*

*The Guises of the Morrigan by David Rankine & Sorita d'Este*

*The Faerie Queens (anthology, various contributors), edited by Sorita d'Este and David Rankine*

*The Isles of the Many Gods by David Rankine & Sorita d'Este*

*The Temple of Hekate by Tara Sanchez*

*Thracian Magic by Georgi Mishev*

*Thoth: The Ancient Egyptian God of Wisdom by Lesley Jackson*

*Visions of the Cailleach by Sorita d'Este & David Rankine*

*Vs. (anthology, various contributors) edited by Kim Huggens*

*Wicca Magickal Beginnings by Sorita d'Este & David Rankine*

*Memento Mori (anthology) by Kim Huggens (editor)*

These and many more unique and interesting esoteric titles are available from our website, **www.avaloniabooks.co.uk**

You can also write to us,
**Avalonia, BM Avalonia, London, WC1N 3XX, United Kimgdom**

www.ingramcontent.com/pod-product-compliance
Lightning Source LLC
Chambersburg PA
CBHW031310150426
**43191CB00005B/167**